pfSense 2.x Cookbook
Second Edition

Manage and maintain your network using pfSense

David Zientara

BIRMINGHAM - MUMBAI

pfSense 2.x Cookbook
Second Edition

Commissioning Editor: Vijin Boricha
Acquisition Editor: Prachi Bisht
Content Development Editor: Sharon Raj
Technical Editor: Mohit Hassija
Copy Editor: Safis Editing
Project Coordinator: Drashti Panchal
Proofreader: Safis Editing
Indexer: Pratik Shirodkar
Graphics: Tom Scaria
Production Coordinator: Jisha Chirayil

First published: March 2011
Second edition: December 2018

Production reference: 1121218

Published by Packt Publishing Ltd.
Livery Place
35 Livery Street
Birmingham
B3 2PB, UK.

ISBN 978-1-78980-642-7

www.packtpub.com

`mapt.io`

Mapt is an online digital library that gives you full access to over 5,000 books and videos, as well as industry leading tools to help you plan your personal development and advance your career. For more information, please visit our website.

Why subscribe?

- Spend less time learning and more time coding with practical eBooks and Videos from over 4,000 industry professionals

- Improve your learning with Skill Plans built especially for you

- Get a free eBook or video every month

- Mapt is fully searchable

- Copy and paste, print, and bookmark content

PacktPub.com

Did you know that Packt offers eBook versions of every book published, with PDF and ePub files available? You can upgrade to the eBook version at `www.Packt.com` and as a print book customer, you are entitled to a discount on the eBook copy. Get in touch with us at `customercare@packtpub.com` for more details.

At `www.Packt.com`, you can also read a collection of free technical articles, sign up for a range of free newsletters, and receive exclusive discounts and offers on Packt books and eBooks.

Contributors

About the author

David Zientara is a software engineer living in northern New Jersey. He has over 20 years of experience in IT. In the mid-1990s, David became the lead software engineer for Oxberry LLC, a digital imaging company headquartered in New Jersey. In this capacity, he played a major role in developing a new software package for the company's equipment. In the mid-2000s, David took an interest in computer networking, an interest that led him to learn about m0n0wall and, eventually, pfSense.

David currently is employed with the Prasad Corporation in a consulting position and is also the author of *Learn pfSense 2.4* and *Mastering pfSense 2.4*, also available from Packt Publishing.

> *I want to thank my parents, especially my father, for fueling my initial interest in computers and technology, and my mother, for providing constant encouragement.*

About the reviewer

Shiva V. N. Parasram is the director of the Computer Forensics and Security Institute and is a cyber security trainer, pentester, and forensic investigator with 14 years of experience in the field. His qualifications include an MSc in network security (distinction), CCISO, CEH, CHFI, and CCNA. As a **Certified EC-Council Instructor (CEI)**, he has also trained several-hundred people in ethical hacking and forensics, and has recently been selected as the sole trainer for cyber security courses for staff at Fujitsu Trinidad. He is also the author of *Digital Forensics with Kali Linux*, published by Packt Publishing.

Packt is searching for authors like you

If you're interested in becoming an author for Packt, please visit `authors.packtpub.com` and apply today. We have worked with thousands of developers and tech professionals, just like you, to help them share their insight with the global tech community. You can make a general application, apply for a specific hot topic that we are recruiting an author for, or submit your own idea.

Table of Contents

Preface   1

Chapter 1: Initial Configuration   7
  Introduction   7
  Applying basic settings to General Setup   8
    Getting ready   8
    How to do it...   9
    See also   11
  Identifying and assigning interfaces   11
    Getting ready   11
    How to do it...   11
    See also   12
  Configuring a WAN interface   12
    Getting ready   12
    How to do it...   13
    How it works...   15
    There's more...   15
    See also   15
  Configuring a LAN interface   15
    Getting ready   15
    How to do it...   16
    How it works...   17
    There's more...   17
    See also   17
  Configuring optional interfaces from the console   18
    Getting ready   18
    How to do it...   19
    How it works...   20
    There's more...   20
    See also   21
  Enabling SSH access   21
    How to do it...   21
    How it works...   22
    There's more...   22
    See also   22
  Generating authorized RSA keys   22
    Getting ready   22
    How to do it...   22
    How it works...   24
    See also   24

Configuring SSH RSA key authentication   24
  Getting ready   24
  How to do it...   24
  How it works...   25
  There's more...   25
  See also   26
Accessing the SSH   26
  Getting ready   26
  How to do it...   26
  How it works...   28
  See also   29
Configuring VLANs   29
  Getting ready   29
  How to do it...   29
  How it works...   31
  There's more...   32
  See also   32
Assigning interfaces from the console   32
  Getting ready   32
  How to do it...   32
  How it works...   34
  See also   34
Configuring a WAN interface from the console   34
  Getting ready   34
  How to do it...   34
  How it works...   36
  See also   36
Configuring a LAN interface from the console   36
  Getting ready   36
  How to do it...   37
  How it works...   38
  See also   38
Configuring optional interfaces from the console   39
  Getting ready   39
  How to do it...   39
  How it works...   40
  See also   40
Configuring VLANs from the console   40
  Getting ready   41
  How to do it...   41
  How it works...   43
  See also   43
Chapter 2: Essential Services   45
  Introduction   45

Configuring the DHCP server   46
  Getting ready   46
  How to do it...   46
  How it works...   47
  There's more...   48
    Deny unknown clients   48
    DNS servers   48
    Gateway   49
    Domain name   49
    Default lease time   49
    Maximum lease time   49
    Failover peer IP   49
    Static ARP   50
    Dynamic DNS   50
    Additional BOOTP/DHCP options   50
  See also   50
Configuring the DHCP6 server   50
  Getting ready   51
  How to do it...   51
  How it works...   52
  There's more...   52
    Prefix delegation   52
  See also   53
Configuring static DHCP mappings   53
  Getting ready   53
  How to do it...   53
  How it works...   55
  There's more...   55
  See also   55
Configuring the DHCP relay   55
  Getting ready   55
  How to do it...   56
  How it works...   57
  There's more...   57
  See also   57
Specifying alternate DNS servers   57
  Getting ready   58
  How to do it...   58
  How it works...   58
    Using the DNS resolver   58
    Using your WAN DNS servers   59
  See also   59
Configuring the DNS resolver   59
  Getting ready   59
  How to do it...   60
  How it works...   62

See also...   62
Configuring a stand-alone DHCP/DNS server   62
How to do it...   62
How it works...   64
Register DHCP leases in DNS resolver   64
See also   64
Configuring dynamic DNS   64
Getting ready   65
How to do it...   65
How it works...   66
Specifying an alternative service using RFC 2136   66
Adding a wireless access point   67
Getting ready   67
How to do it...   67
How it works...   70
See also   70

Chapter 3: Firewall and NAT   71
Introduction   71
Creating and using aliases   72
How to do it...   72
How it works...   73
There's more...   73
Using an alias   74
Editing an alias   74
Deleting an alias   74
Bulk importing aliases   75
See also   76
Creating a firewall rule   76
How to do it...   76
How it works...   78
There's more...   78
The source port   79
Ordering firewall rules   80
Duplicating firewall rules   80
Advanced features   80
See also   81
Setting a firewall rule schedule   81
How to do it...   82
How it works...   83
There's more...   84
Selecting dates or days of the week   84
See also   84
Creating a floating rule   84
How to do it...   85
How it works...   88

There's more...   88
See also   88
Creating a NAT port forwarding entry   88
Getting ready   89
How to do it...   89
How it works...   91
There's more...   92
Port redirection   94
Port redirection example   94
See also   95
Creating an outbound NAT entry   95
How to do it...   96
How it works...   98
There's more...   98
See also   98
Creating a 1:1 NAT entry   98
How to do it...   98
There's more...   100
See also   100
Creating an NPt entry   100
How to do it...   100
How it works...   101
Enabling UPnP and NAT-PnP   102
How to do it...   102
How it works...   102
There's more...   103
Security warning   103
See also   103
Chapter 4: Additional Services   105
Introduction   105
Creating a captive portal without authentication   106
Getting ready   106
How to do it...   107
How it works...   108
There's more...   109
See also   109
Creating a captive portal with voucher authentication   109
How to do it...   110
How it works...   113
There's more...   113
See also   114
Creating a captive portal with User Manager authentication   114
How to do it...   114
How it works...   119
See also   119

Creating a captive portal with RADIUS authentication   119
  Getting ready   120
  How to do it...   120
  How it works...   126
  See also   126
Configuring NTP   126
  How to do it...   127
  There's more...   128
Configuring SNMP   128
  Getting ready   128
  How to do it...   128
  There's more...   130
  See also   130
Chapter 5: Virtual Private Networking   131
  Introduction   131
    Choosing the right VPN server   132
    How to do it...   134
    How it works...   138
    There's more...   139
  Configuring the IPsec VPN service – client/server   141
    How to do it...   141
    How it works...   146
    There's more...   146
  Connecting to the IPsec VPN service   147
    Getting ready   147
    How to do it...   147
  Configuring the OpenVPN service   151
    How to do it...   151
    There's more...   159
  Connecting to the OpenVPN service   160
    Getting ready   160
    How to do it...   160
    There's more...   166
  Configuring the L2TP VPN service   166
    How to do it...   166
Chapter 6: Traffic Shaping   169
  Introduction   169
  Configuring traffic shaping using the traffic-shaping wizard   171
    How to do it...   171
    How it works...   176
    There's more...   176
    See also   178
  Configuring traffic shaping using floating rules   178

Getting ready	178
How to do it...	179
How it works...	181
There's more...	181
See also	181
Configuring traffic shaping using Snort	**182**
How to do it...	182
How it works...	186
There's more...	186
See also	187
Chapter 7: Redundancy, Load Balancing, and Failover	**189**
Introduction	**189**
Adding multiple WAN interfaces	**190**
Getting ready	190
How to do it...	191
How it works...	195
There's more...	197
Configuring server load balancing	**199**
Getting ready	199
How to do it...	200
How it works...	206
There's more...	206
See also	207
Configuring a CARP failover group	**207**
Getting ready	207
How to do it...	208
How it works...	217
There's more...	218
See also	218
Chapter 8: Routing and Bridging	**219**
Introduction	**219**
Routing	219
Dynamic routing	220
Bridging	220
Bridging interfaces	**221**
How to do it...	221
How it works...	222
There's more...	222
Adding a static route	**223**
How to do it...	224
How it works...	225
There's more...	225
Configuring RIP using routed	**227**
How to do it...	227

How it works...   228
Configuring BGP using FRR   228
How to do it...   228
How it works...   230
Configuring OSPF using FRR   230
Getting ready   230
How to do it...   230
How it works...   231
Chapter 9: Services and Maintenance   233
Introduction   233
A structured approach to problem solving   234
Enabling Wake-on-LAN   235
How to do it...   235
How it works...   235
There's more...   236
See also   237
Configuring PPPoE   237
How to do it...   237
How it works...   239
There's more...   240
See also   240
Configuring external logging with a syslog server   240
Getting ready   240
How to do it...   240
Using ping   241
How to do it...   242
How it works...   243
See also   243
Using traceroute   243
How to do it...   243
How it works...   245
See also   245
Using netstat   245
How to do it...   246
Using pfTop   246
How to do it...   247
See also   248
Using tcpdump   249
How to do it...   249
Using tcpflow   249
How to do it...   250

Appendix A: Backing Up and Restoring pfSense   251
Introduction   251

Backing up pfSense   252
How to do it...   252
How it works...   253
There's more...   253
See also   256
Restoring pfSense   256
How to do it...   256
How it works...   257
There's more...   257
Updating pfSense   257
How to do it...   258
How it works...   260
There's more...   260
See also   260
Appendix B: Determining Hardware Requirements   261
Determining our deployment scenario   261
Determining our throughput requirements   264
Determining our interface requirements   266
Choosing a standard or embedded image   268
Choosing a form factor   269
Installing the embedded platform on a desktop/server/laptop   271
Installing the standard platform on an appliance   271
Summary   271
Other Books You May Enjoy   273
Index   277

Preface

pfSense is open source router/firewall software based on the FreeBSD operating system. It provides a frontend to **Packet Filter** (**PF**), FreeBSD's built-in firewall. Originally introduced in 2006, it has achieved a level of scalability, flexibility, and cost-effectiveness that has made it one of the most popular router/firewall distributions. The flexibility of pfSense means that in most cases there are several options available when configuring options and services. In such cases, determining your specific requirements is critical to optimizing results.

This book tries to make this process of obtaining optimal results as easy as possible. It follows a cookbook-style approach to teach you how to use pfSense's many features after determining your security requirements. This book covers everything from configuring network interfaces and basic services such as DHCP and DNS, to more complex capabilities such as load balancing and failover.

Who this book is for

This book is targeted at those with a beginner- or intermediate-level understanding of computer networking. Basic knowledge of the fundamentals of networking is helpful, although basic networking concepts and terms are explained to the greatest extent possible within the scope of the book. No prior knowledge of pfSense or FreeBSD is assumed.

What this book covers

Chapter 1, *Initial Configuration*, covers pfSense firewall configuration from the point of initial installation, and covers much of what most users will need to configure, such as setting up WAN, LAN, and optional interfaces; enabling SSH access and generating RSA keys; and adding VLANs.

Chapter 2, *Essential Services*, includes the services that crucial to virtually every pfSense deployment – namely, DHCP, DHCP6, DNS, and dynamic DNS. This chapter also covers how to configure pfSense for use as a wireless access point.

Chapter 3, *Firewall and NAT*, covers the basics of creating firewall rules (standard and floating), as well as how to leverage aliases and scheduling to impose rules on a flexible basis. Different forms of **Network Address Translation** (**NAT**) are covered, along with two specialized forms of NAT designed to make online gaming easier: UPnP and NAT-PnP.

Chapter 4, *Additional Services*, is a new chapter covering services that are less commonly enabled but still useful for many home and SOHO deployments. Captive portals are covered, including all forms of authentication currently supported by pfSense, including RADIUS authentication. The chapter also covers the **Network Time Protocol (NTP)** and the **Simple Network Management Protocol (SNMP)**.

Chapter 5, *Virtual Private Networking*, shows how to set up pfSense to act as the endpoint of a VPN tunnel, both as a peer-to-peer entity with another firewall at the opposite end of the connection, and as a client-server entity with a mobile client at the other end. Recipes are provided covering the three protocols supported by the current version of pfSense: IPsec, OpenVPN, and L2TP.

Chapter 6, *Traffic Shaping*, is another new chapter. This chapter demonstrates how to leverage the capabilities of pfSense to achieve a certain **Quality of Service (QoS)**, using both the traffic shaper wizard and floating rules for policy-based routing. Deep packet inspection, however, is not possible using the built-in traffic shaper. To make this possible, we need the third-party package known as Snort, and this chapter covers the installation and configuration of Snort.

Chapter 7, *Redundancy, Load Balancing, and Failover*, covers the essential ways in which pfSense provides for load balancing and failover. Namely, it covers multiple WAN setups (which enable us to aggregate bandwidth and/or provide failover capabilities when we have multiple internet connections), load balancing using pfSense's built-in server load balancing capabilities, and the **Common Address Redundancy Protocol (CARP)**, which allows us to have a completely redundant firewall on standby.

Chapter 8, *Routing and Bridging*, covers cases that many pfSense deployments may rarely encounter, if ever. This chapter demonstrates how to bridge interfaces, how to add a static route, and the dynamic routing protocols of the **Routing Information Protocol (RIP)**, **Border Gateway Protocol (BGP)**, and **Open Shortest Path First (OSPF)**.

Chapter 9, *Services and Maintenance*, covers a number of services and utilities, most of which are useful for diagnostics and troubleshooting. **Wake-on LAN (WOL)**, **Point-to-Point over Ethernet (PPPoE)**, and enabling Syslog are covered, as well as command-line utilities such as ping and traceroute.

Appendix A, *Backing Up and Restoring pfSense*, provides a brief guide to backing up pfSense, restoring pfSense from either the web GUI or SSH/command line interface, and the various options for updating pfSense.

Appendix B, *Determining Hardware Requirements*, is a brief primer showing how to choose the best pfSense configuration after you determine your firewall requirements. You will even learn how and where to deploy pfSense to fit your environment's security needs.

To get the most out of this book

Following along with the recipes in this book should not require anything more than a basic knowledge of computer networking and some familiarity with computers and software.

You will get the most out of this book if you follow along with a functioning pfSense system. Thus, it will be helpful you have either spare hardware onto which you can install the current version of pfSense, or virtualization software so that you can run pfSense inside a **virtual machine** (**VM**). I cannot do full justice to all the variants of VMs available, but I can say that Oracle VM Virtual Box has proven quite useful in preparing the material for this book.

This book does not provide a step-by-step guide on how to install pfSense, but if you need such a guide, you can find one here: `https://www.netgate.com/docs/pfsense/install/installing-pfsense.html`.

Download the color images

We also provide a PDF file that has color images of the screenshots/diagrams used in this book. You can download it here: `http://www.packtpub.com/sites/default/files/downloads/9781789806427_ColorImages.pdf`.

Conventions used

There are a number of text conventions used throughout this book.

`CodeInText`: Indicates code words in text, database table names, folder names, filenames, file extensions, pathnames, dummy URLs, user input, and Twitter handles. Here is an example: "In the Name edit box, enter an appropriate name (for example, `WEB_SERVER_IPS`)."

Bold: Indicates a new term, an important word, or words that you see onscreen. For example, words in menus or dialog boxes appear in the text like this. Here is an example: "Click on the **LAN** tab, if it isn't selected already."

Warnings or important notes appear like this.

 Tips and tricks appear like this.

Sections

In this book, you will find several headings that appear frequently (*Getting ready, How to do it..., How it works..., There's more...,* and *See also*).

To give clear instructions on how to complete a recipe, use these sections as follows:

Getting ready

This section tells you what to expect in the recipe and describes how to set up any software or any preliminary settings required for the recipe.

How to do it...

This section contains the steps required to follow the recipe.

How it works...

This section usually consists of a detailed explanation of what happened in the previous section.

There's more...

This section consists of additional information about the recipe in order to make you more knowledgeable about the recipe.

See also

This section provides helpful links to other useful information for the recipe.

Get in touch

Feedback from our readers is always welcome.

General feedback: If you have questions about any aspect of this book, mention the book title in the subject of your message and email us at customercare@packtpub.com.

Errata: Although we have taken every care to ensure the accuracy of our content, mistakes do happen. If you have found a mistake in this book, we would be grateful if you would report this to us. Please visit www.packt.com/submit-errata, selecting your book, clicking on the Errata Submission Form link, and entering the details.

Piracy: If you come across any illegal copies of our works in any form on the Internet, we would be grateful if you would provide us with the location address or website name. Please contact us at copyright@packt.com with a link to the material.

If you are interested in becoming an author: If there is a topic that you have expertise in and you are interested in either writing or contributing to a book, please visit authors.packtpub.com.

Reviews

Please leave a review. Once you have read and used this book, why not leave a review on the site that you purchased it from? Potential readers can then see and use your unbiased opinion to make purchase decisions, we at Packt can understand what you think about our products, and our authors can see your feedback on their book. Thank you!

For more information about Packt, please visit packt.com.

Initial Configuration 1

In this chapter, we will cover the following recipes:

- Applying basic settings to General Setup
- Identifying and assigning interfaces
- Configuring a WAN interface
- Configuring a LAN interface
- Configuring optional interfaces
- Enabling SSH access
- Generating authorized RSA keys
- Configuring SSH RSA authentication
- Accessing the SSH
- Configuring VLANs
- Assigning interfaces from the console
- Configuring a WAN interface from the console
- Configuring a LAN interface from the console
- Configuring optional interfaces from the console
- Configuring VLANs from the console

Introduction

pfSense is open source software that can be used to turn a computer into a firewall/router. Its origins can be traced to the FreeBSD packet-filtering program known as PF, which has been part of FreeBSD since 2001. As PF is a command-line utility, work soon began on developing software that would provide a graphical frontend to PF. The m0n0wall project, which provides an easy-to-use, web-based interface for PF, was thus started. The first release of m0n0wall took place in 2003. pfSense began as a fork of the m0n0wall project.

Version 1.0 of pfSense was released on October 4, 2006, and version 2.0 was released on September 17, 2011. A key point in the development of pfSense took place with the release of Version 2.3 on April 12, 2016. This version phased out support for legacy technologies such as **Point to Point Tunneling Protocol** (**PPTP**), **Wireless Encryption Protocol** (**WEP**), and Single DES, and also provided a face-lift for the web GUI. Version 2.4, released on October 12, 2017, continues this trend of phasing out support for legacy technologies while also adding features. Support for 32 bit x86 architectures has been deprecated, while support for Netgate **Advanced RISC Machines** (**ARM**) devices has been added. A new pfSense installer (based on FreeBSD's bsdinstall) has been incorporated into pfSense, and there is support for the ZFS filesystem, as well as the **Unified Extensible Firmware Interface** (**UEFI**). pfSense now supports multiple languages; the web GUI has been translated into 13 different languages.

This chapter will cover the basic configuration steps common to virtually all deployments. Once you have completed the recipes in this chapter, you will have a fully functional router/firewall. By following the recipes in subsequent chapters, you can enhance that functionality by adding specific firewall rules, enabling traffic shaping, adding load balancing and multi-WAN capabilities, and much more.

Applying basic settings to General Setup

This recipe describes how to configure core pfSense settings from the web GUI.

Getting ready

All that is required for this recipe is a fresh install of pfSense and access to the web GUI.

 On a new install, the default login credentials are **Username**: admin and **Password**: pfsense

How to do it...

1. In the web GUI, navigate to **System | General Setup**.
2. In the first section of the page (**System**), enter a **Hostname**. This name can be used to access the firewall instead of the IP address:

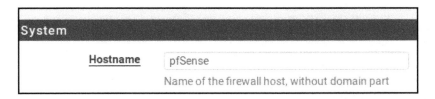

3. In the next field, enter the **Domain**:

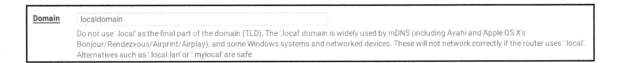

4. The next field is **DNS Servers**. By default, pfSense will act as the primary DNS server; however, you can specify alternate DNS servers here. The **Add DNS Server** button causes an additional edit box to appear, into which you can enter another DNS server; you can add as many alternate DNS servers as is necessary:

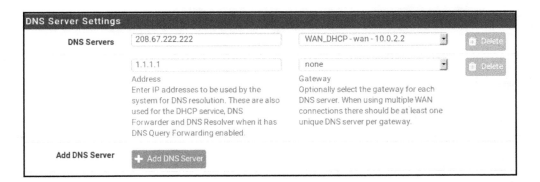

5. Check the **Allow DNS server list to be overridden by DHCP/PPP on WAN** checkbox (it should be checked by default). This ensures that any DNS requests that cannot be processed internally will be passed on to the external DNS servers, as specified by your ISP:

6. In the **Localization** section, specify a **Timezone** and leave **Timeservers** at the default value of **0.pfsense.pool.ntp.org**. Specify the appropriate **Language** (the default is **English**):

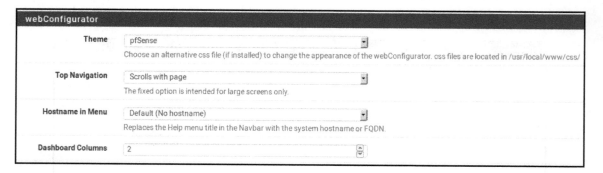

7. In the **webConfigurator** section, I'd recommend the default **Theme** of pfSense. You can set **Top Navigation** to either **Scrolls with page** (appropriate for all screen sizes) or **Fixed** (designed for large screens only). You may also set the number of **Dashboard Columns** (the default is **2**):

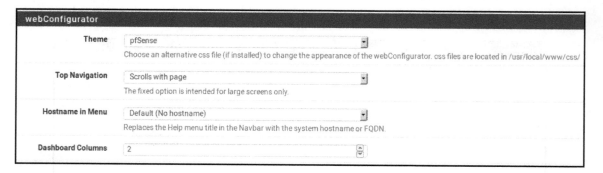

8. When done, click on the **Save** button.

See also

- The *Configuring the DNS Forwarder* recipe in Chapter 2, *Essential Services*.

Identifying and assigning interfaces

This recipe describes how to identify interfaces on a network configuration and how to assign them in pfSense.

Getting ready

You need to identify the MAC addresses for each Ethernet port on your pfSense system before attempting to assign them.

How to do it...

1. Navigate to **Interfaces | Interface Assignments**.
2. Assign a **WAN** interface, first by selecting the correct MAC address from the drop-down list for the **WAN** interface:

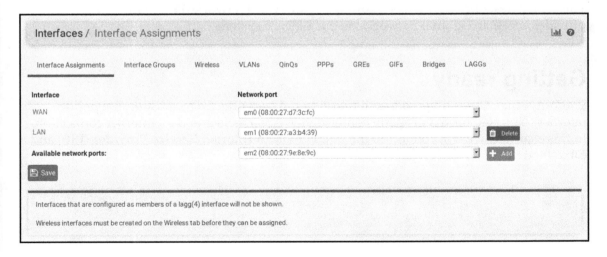

3. Repeat this process for the **LAN** interface, selecting the correct MAC address from the drop-down list for the **LAN** interface. If necessary, add the LAN interface to the list by following this process:

    1. Click on the **Add** button in the **Available network ports** column.
    2. Click on the name of the newly created interface in the **Interfaces** column (it should be OPT1).
    3. When the configuration page for the interface loads, change **Description** to **LAN**.
    4. Click on the **Save** button at the bottom of the page.
    5. Navigate back to **Interfaces | Interface Assignments**.

4. If you want to add optional interfaces, you can do so by repeating step 3 and substituting the name of the optional interface (for example, DMZ) for **LAN**.

5. When you are done assigning interfaces, click on the **Save** button.

See also

- The *Assigning interfaces at the console* recipe

Configuring a WAN interface

This recipe describes how to configure the **Wide Area Network** (**WAN**) interface, which provides access to external networks on our pfSense system.

Getting ready

The WAN interface is your connection to external networks (in most cases, the public internet). You will need a properly configured WAN interface and an internet connection. In this example, we will connect to the internet via an **Internet Service Provider** (**ISP**) and a cable modem.

How to do it...

1. Navigate to **Interfaces** ᛁ **WAN**.
2. Check the **Enable Interface** checkbox (it should be checked by default):

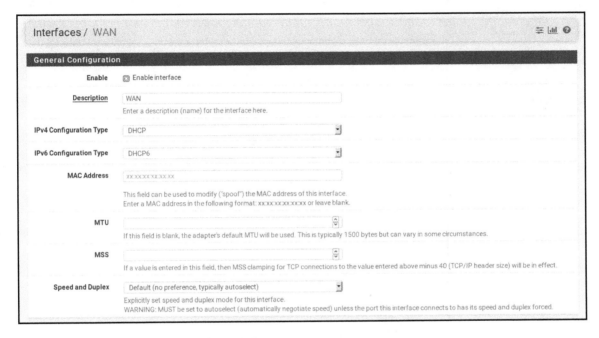

3. Choose an **IPv4 Configuration Type** (usually DHCP).
4. Choose an **IPv6 Configuration Type**, or leave it set to **None**.
5. Leave **MAC Address** blank. Manually entering a MAC address here is known as MAC address spoofing. You can enter a MAC address here if you want to force your ISP to hand you a different IP address, or a different set of DNS servers. Be warned, however, that the MAC address entered must have a valid manufacturer's prefix or it won't work.
6. Leave **MTU**, **MSS**, **Hostname**, and **Alias IP address** blank.

7. Check the **Block private networks and loopback addresses** checkbox (it should be checked by default). This will block RFC 1918 private addresses from being sent out over the public internet.

8. Check the **Block bogon networks** checkbox (it should be checked by default). This will block packets from IP addresses not yet assigned by IANA from being sent or received:

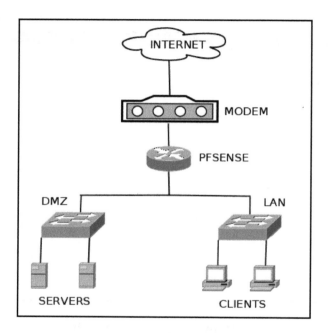

9. Click on the **Save** button when done.

How it works...

We must first establish a connection to the internet before we can configure pfSense to allow other networks to access it. The example we provided is a typical WAN configuration for a **Small Office/Home Office** (**SOHO**) environment. By setting up the WAN interface as the only interface with direct access to the internet, we are securing the network behind the firewall and establishing complete control over our networks. All networks behind the firewall must now abide by the rules we create.

There's more...

Now that we have configured the WAN interface, we can connect the cable modem to the WAN port on pfSense and check the status of the WAN port by navigating to **Status** | **Interfaces**.

See also

- The *Identifying and assigning interfaces* recipe in this chapter
- The *Configuring a LAN interface* recipe in this chapter
- The *Configuring optional interfaces from the console* recipe in this chapter

Configuring a LAN interface

This recipe describes how to configure the **Local Area Network** (**LAN**) internal interface of our pfSense firewall.

Getting ready

The LAN interface is the interface to the internal network through which our nodes will be able to securely connect to other internal nodes and to the internet. An assigned LAN interface is required.

How to do it...

1. Navigate to **Interfaces | LAN**.
2. Check the **Enable Interface** checkbox:

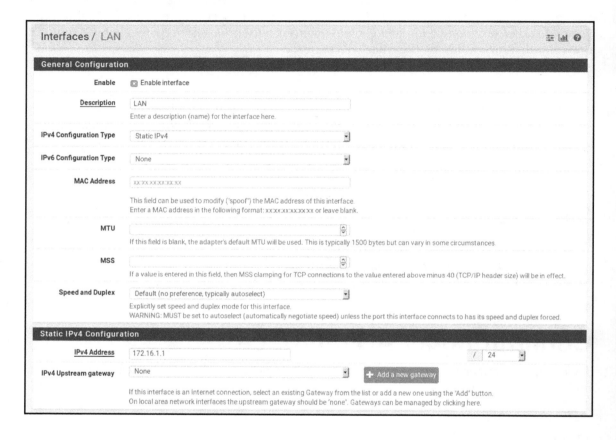

3. Choose an **IPv4 Configuration Type** (usually **Static IPv4**).
4. Choose an **IPv6 Configuration Type** (or leave it set to **None**).
5. Enter an **IPv4 Address** in the appropriate field, and the correct CIDR in the adjacent drop-down box. Leave **IPv4 Upstream gateway** set to **None**.
6. If you enabled IPv6 by setting the **IPv6 Configuration Type**, enter an **IPv4 Address** in the appropriate field and the correct CIDR in the adjacent drop-down box.
7. Leave **Block private networks** and **Block bogon network**s unchecked (they should be unchecked by default).
8. When you are done making changes, click on the **Save** button. When the page reloads, click on the **Apply Changes** button.

How it works...

You have just defined your first internal network. If you have been following these recipes in order, you now have met the minimal requirements for a fully functional network. You can now either continue adding networks, or start configuring the rules to regulate traffic between the networks.

There's more...

You can now connect a switch to the LAN port of your pfSense system, and connect nodes to the LAN network.

See also

- The *Identifying and assigning interfaces* recipe in this chapter
- The *Configuring a WAN interface* recipe in this chapter
- The *Configuring optional interfaces from the console* recipe in this chapter

Configuring optional interfaces from the console

This recipe describes how to configure optional interfaces (for example, a DMZ network) to pfSense.

Getting ready

The optional network you will create in this network will be a **DMZ**, which is short for the **DeMilitarized Zone**. The idea of a DMZ is to have a network where some traffic is allowed to pass and some traffic is not. Typically, traffic in the DMZ is allowed to pass to and from the internet but not to other internal networks. Traffic is allowed to pass from internal networks to the DMZ. Thus, the flow of traffic looks like this:

```
Internet <<>> DMZ << Internal networks
```

Unsafe internet traffic, for example, is allowed to enter a web server in the DMZ. LAN traffic is allowed to enter the DMZ as well, for example, if someone on the LAN wants to access the web server as well. However, the key lies in the fact that no DMZ traffic is allowed to access the internal networks.

To configure a DMZ, you will need at least one spare interface, and you will have to have added it using the procedure outlined in the *Identifying and assigning interfaces* recipe. We will assume that you have added at least one such interface (named OPT1).

How to do it...

1. Navigate to **Interfaces** | **OPT1**.
2. Check the **Enable Interface** checkbox:

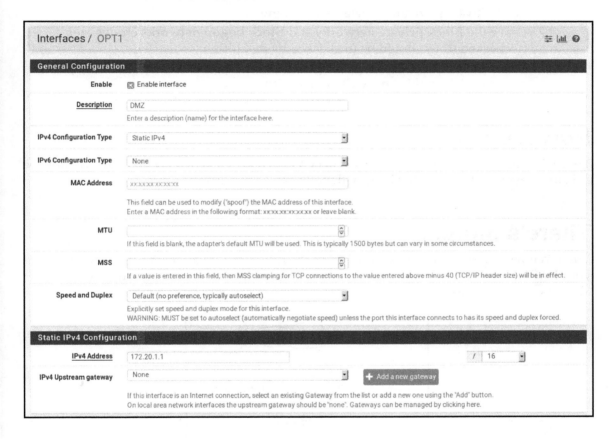

3. Set **Description** to DMZ.

4. Set **IPv4 Configuration Type** to **Static IPv4**.

5. Enter an **IPv4 Address** and the CIDR. In our case, we will use 192.168.2.1 and select **24** from the CIDR dropdown list.

6. Leave **IPv4 Upstream gateway** set to **None**.

7. Leave the **Block private networks** and **Block bogon networks** checkboxes unchecked (they should be unchecked by default).

8. When you are done making changes, click on the **Save** button. When the page reloads, click on the **Apply Changes** button.

How it works...

Your DMZ network will now allow external (WAN) access. Your LAN network will now be able to access the DMZ, but the DMZ will not be able to access the LAN.

There's more...

You can now attach a switch to your DMZ port to allow you to attach multiple nodes to your DMZ network. If you have been following the recipes in this chapter in order, your network will now look like this:

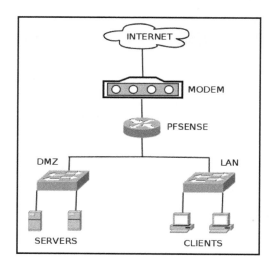

See also

- The *Identifying and assigning interfaces* recipe
- The *Configuring a WAN interface* recipe
- The *Configuring a LAN interface* recipe

Enabling SSH access

This recipe describes how to enable the Secure Shell service in pfSense, thus making remote console login possible.

SSH is a networking protocol that allows encrypted communication between two nodes. Enabling SSH will allow you to gain access to the pfSense console remotely, as if you were at the console.

How to do it...

1. Navigate to **System | Advanced**.
2. In the **Secure Shell** section of the page, check the **Enable Secure Shell** checkbox:

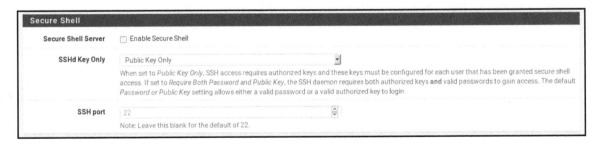

3. With the current settings, you will be prompted for a username and password when logging into the console remotely. But by changing the **SSHd Key Only** setting to **Public Key Only**, you can set it so that only logins with a public key will be allowed. See the next recipe for details on how to generate an RSA public key.
4. Leave **SSH port** set to the default, port **22**.
5. When you are done, click on the **Save** button.

How it works...

Enabling Secure Shell in pfSense turns on pfSense's internal SSH server, which causes pfSense to listen for login attempts on the SSH port (in this case, port 22).

There's more...

Using RSA keys for SSH login is an effective way of securing your system. You can also change the SSH port; this should result in fewer unauthorized login attempts, though you will have to remember the new SSH port.

See also

- The *Generating authorized RSA keys* recipe in this chapter
- The *Enabling RSA key authentication* recipe in this chapter

Generating authorized RSA keys

This recipe describes how to create an authorized RSA key so the user can log in to the pfSense console without using a password.

Getting ready

Linux and macOS users will need the ssh-keygen utility (installed by default in most cases). Windows users will need the puttygen utility.

How to do it...

For Linux/macOS users:

1. In a Terminal window, type ssh-keygen and press *Enter*
2. Enter the name of the file in which to save the public key (or just accept the default value)
3. Enter a passphrase for the new key (not necessary, but recommended)

4. Enter the passphrase a second time for confirmation

5. The program will now generate an RSA public key and save it to the file

For Windows users:

1. Start the `puttygen` utility.

2. In the **Actions** section, click on the **Generate** button to generate a public/private key pair:

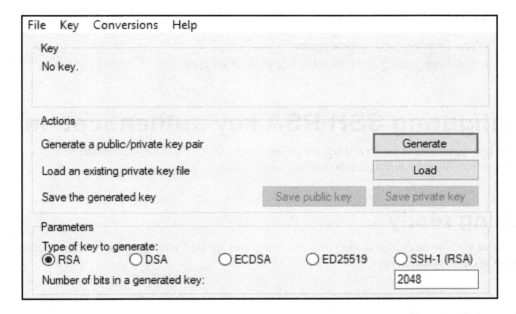

3. Move your mouse over the top section of the puttygen dialog box to generate random activity, as per puttygen's instructions.

4. Enter a passphrase (not necessary, but recommended).

5. Click on the **Save private key** button and specify a filename for the private key (for example, `MyPrivateKey.ppk`).

6. Highlight the public key that was created in the textbox and save it to a file (for example, `MyPublicKey.txt`). Do not use the **Save public key** button because it adds potentially incompatible text to the file.

How it works...

RSA has become a standard for securing client/server connections. A client generates a public/private key pair—a private key file and a public key file, and a possible passphrase for additional security. Any server can then request the client's public key and add it to their system; that client can then authenticate without typing in a password.

See also

- The *Enabling SSH access* recipe
- The *Configuring SSH RSA key authentication* recipe

Configuring SSH RSA key authentication

This recipe describes how to configure pfSense to use an RSA key rather than a username/password combination for authentication.

Getting ready

Make sure you have enabled SSH access and generated an RSA key (if you completed the last two recipes, you have).

How to do it...

1. Navigate to **System** | **Advanced**.
2. Make sure **SSHd Key Only** is set to **Public Key Only:**

3. Navigate to **System | User Manager**. Click on the **Users** tab (it should be selected by default).
4. Click on the **Edit** icon (the pencil) for the admin account.
5. In the **Keys** section, paste the client's public RSA key (that can be the RSA key you created in the previous recipe). When pasted, the key should appear as a single line. Make sure your text editor does not insert any line feeds, or authentication may fail:

6. When done, click on the **Save** button.

How it works...

When you connect using an SSH client, instead of asking for a username and password, the SSH server will now use your public RSA key to send a challenge to you. The challenge can only be read if you have the matching private RSA key.

There's more...

RSA private keys can also be stored encrypted to the client's computer. The SSH client will prompt you for the decryption password. Once entered, it will be able to use the private key for authentication.

See also

- The *Enabling SSH access* recipe
- The *Generating authorized RSA keys* recipe
- The *Accessing the SSH* recipe

Accessing the SSH

This recipe describes how to access the console from any Linux, macOS, or Windows computer.

Getting ready

The SSH server must be enabled and configured on your pfSense box. You must have an SSH client on your computer. An SSH client is installed by default on Linux and macOS. If you are using Windows, you need to install an SSH client such as PuTTY.

How to do it...

In Linux or macOS, follow these steps:

1. Launch a Terminal window and type the following: `ssh admin@192.168.1.1`.
2. If you are using the default configuration, you will be prompted for a password.
3. If you are using RSA key authentication, the client will directly connect to the server, or you may be asked for a passphrase. If asked for a passphrase, use the one you created when creating the RSA key.
4. If you configured SSH to use a different port, you can specify it using the `-p` option; for example, `ssh -p 12345 admin@192.168.1.1`.

In Windows, follow these steps:

1. Launch PuTTY and, on the initial screen, enter the hostname or IP address of pfSense:

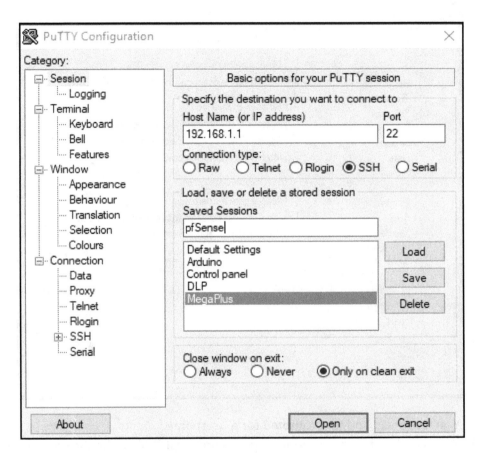

2. Specify an alternate port if necessary.

3. If you are using RSA key authentication, navigate to **Connection** | **SSH** | **Auth** | **Private key file for authentication:**

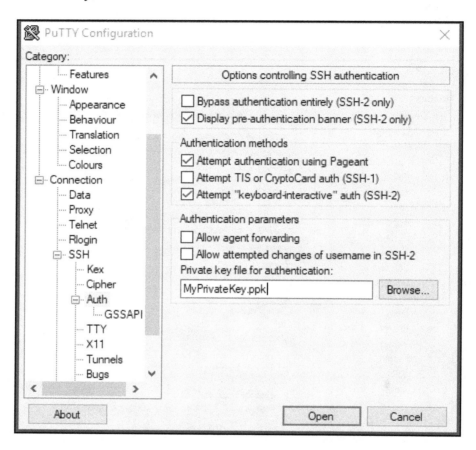

4. You'll connect and be prompted for a username.
5. You will then be prompted for a password, or if RSA authentication is used, you will connect directly, or be prompted for a passphrase.

How it works...

SSH allows access to the pfSense console from any computer or device that has an SSH client installed on it.

See also

- The *Enabling SSH access* recipe
- The *Generating authorized RSA keys* recipe
- The *Configuring SSH RSA auhentication* recipe

Configuring VLANs

This recipe describes how to set up a **Virtual LAN** (**VLAN**) from the pfSense web GUI. For example, we could set up a VLAN for developers.

Getting ready

In order to complete this recipe, you must have at least one unassigned interface to use as the parent interface.

How to do it...

1. Navigate to **Interfaces | Assignments**, and click on the **VLANs** tab.
2. Click on the **Add** button.
3. Choose a **Parent Interface** from the drop-down menu; this should be a currently unassigned interface:

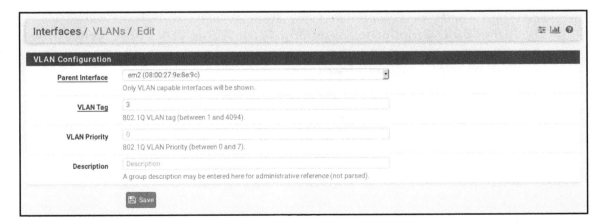

4. Enter a **VLAN Tag** from 2 to 4094 (1 is reserved as the default VLAN tag and should not be used).

5. Enter a **VLAN Priority** level from 0 to 7 (or just leave it at the default value of 0).

6. Enter a brief **Description**.

7. When you are done, click on the **Save** button.

8. Click on the **Interface Assignments** tab.

9. In the **Available network ports** column, select the newly created VLAN in the drop-down box, and click on the **Add** button:

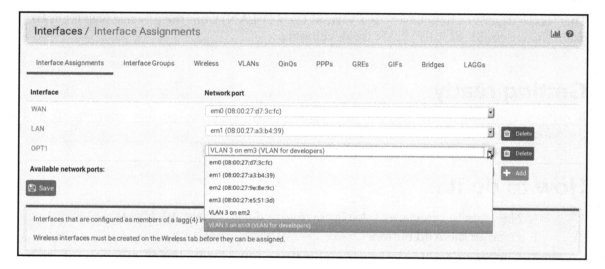

10. To configure the VLAN, click on the interface name in the **Interface** column.

11. On the **Interfaces** configuration page, check the **Enable Interface** checkbox.

12. Change the **Description** to an appropriate one for the VLAN (for example, DEV).

13. Set the **IPv4 Configuration Type** to an appropriate value (usually **Static IPv4**).

14. Set the **IPv6 Configuration Type**, or leave it set to **None**.

15. If you set the **IPv4 Configuration Type** to **Static IPv4**, you must enter the **IPv4 Address** and CIDR for the new VLAN. Use a subnet that has not yet been used (for example, 192.168.10.1/24).

16. Leave the **IPv4 Upstream gateway** set to **None**.
17. If you set the **IPv6 Configuration Type** to **Static IPv6**, you must enter the **IPv6 Address** and CIDR for the new VLAN.
18. Leave the **IPv6 Upstream gateway** set to none.
19. Leave the **Block private networks** and **Block bogon networks** checkboxes unchecked.
20. When you are done making changes, click on the **Save** button, and then, when the page reloads, click on the **Apply Changes** button.

How it works...

Up to now, we have contemplated networks that correspond to a single network interface. Sometimes, however, we want to decouple logical network groupings from physical interfaces. We may want to have more than one network on a single interface—or, less commonly, have a network span multiple interfaces. We can accomplish this with virtual LANs, or VLANs. By attaching a special header to an Ethernet frame, known as an 802.1Q tag, we can have VLANs. Since the VLAN tag is an integer from 1 to 4094, it would seem that we are limited to 4094 VLANs (or 4093, since we are not supposed to use 1 as a tag), but by using QinQ tagging, we can nest VLAN tags, making it possible to have a much greater number of VLANs on our private network (in fact, a much greater number of VLANs than we would probably ever need).

In step 5 of this recipe, we referenced the VLAN priority level. This is a feature added to pfSense with version 2.3 that allows you to define a class of service for your VLAN. It is a 3 bit field from 0 to 7. Somewhat counter-intuitively, 1 is the lowest priority level (background), while 7 is the highest, and 0 is best effort treatment, which is one step above the lowest priority level.

There's more...

In order to utilize VLANs on your network, you need one or more managed switches. These are switches that recognize 802.1Q tags placed in the Ethernet frame by pfSense, and which will forward the frames to the correct port. Managed switches are never *plug and play*, they always involve some configuration, so consult your switch's documentation for details on how to configure it.

See also

- The *Configuring VLANs from the console* recipe

Assigning interfaces from the console

This recipe describes how to assign interfaces using the console menu.

Getting ready

In order to complete this recipe, you will need at least one unassigned interface.

How to do it...

1. On the console menu, press *1* and press *Enter*.
2. The first option will be for setting up VLANs. Since we don't want to set up VLANs now, press *n* and *Enter*:

```
Do VLANs need to be set up first?
If VLANs will not be used, or only for optional interfaces, it is typical to
say no here and use the webConfigurator to configure VLANs later, if required.

Should VLANs be set up now [y|n]? n


VLAN interfaces:

em2.3              VLAN tag 3, parent interface em2

If the names of the interfaces are not known, auto-detection can
be used instead. To use auto-detection, please disconnect all
interfaces before pressing 'a' to begin the process.

Enter the WAN interface name or 'a' for auto-detection
(em0 em1 em2 em3 em2.3 or a): em0

Enter the LAN interface name or 'a' for auto-detection
NOTE: this enables full Firewalling/NAT mode.
(em1 em2 em3 em2.3 a or nothing if finished): em1

Enter the Optional 1 interface name or 'a' for auto-detection
(em2 em3 em2.3 a or nothing if finished): █
```

3. You will be prompted to enter the WAN interface name. Here, you must enter the device name for the interface that will be the WAN interface (for example, eth0, eth1, em0, em1, and so on). Enter the appropriate device name and press *Enter*.

4. You will be prompted to enter the LAN interface name, or nothing if finished. You only need to assign the WAN interface (in which case you will be able to log into pfSense using the WAN IP address). However, if you want to assign an interface to LAN, enter the device name and press *Enter*. Otherwise, just press *Enter*.

5. If there are more than two network interfaces, you can assign optional interfaces at the console. To do so, enter the device name and press *Enter*. Otherwise, just press *Enter*.

6. The interface assignments will be listed, and you will be asked whether you want to proceed. Pressing *n* and *Enter* will result in no changes being made, while pressing *y* and *Enter* will commit the changes.

7. If you pressed *y* and *Enter*, the changes will be written and the settings will be reloaded. You will then be returned to the console menu.

How it works...

In this recipe, we were able to assign interfaces (which was done earlier in the chapter via the web GUI) from the console. Many configurations can be done from the console—we can even restore earlier configurations and run utilities—and in this book, we will take advantage of this functionality.

See also

- The *Configuring a WAN interface from the console* recipe
- The *Configuring a LAN interface from the console* recipe
- The *Configuring optional interfaces from the console* recipe
- The *Configuring VLANs from the console* recipe

Configuring a WAN interface from the console

This recipe describes how to configure the WAN interface from the **Console** menu.

Getting ready

In order to complete this recipe, the WAN interface must have previously been assigned to one of the available network interfaces.

How to do it...

1. On the console menu, type **2** and press *Enter*.
2. pfSense will prompt you for the number of the interface you want to configure. For the WAN interface, this will be 1, so type 1 and press *Enter*.

3. pfSense will ask you if you want to configure the IPv4 WAN address through DHCP. In most cases, you will want to type *y*, because the WAN interface address will be assigned by your ISP via DHCP. Type *y* and press *Enter*. If you enter *n*, pfSense will prompt you for a WAN IPv4 address, and then the subnet bit count:

```
Available interfaces:

1 - WAN (em0 - dhcp, dhcp6)
2 - LAN (em1 - static)

Enter the number of the interface you wish to configure: 1

Configure IPv4 address WAN interface via DHCP? (y/n) y

Configure IPv6 address WAN interface via DHCP6? (y/n) y

Do you want to revert to HTTP as the webConfigurator protocol? (y/n) n

Please wait while the changes are saved to WAN...
  Reloading filter...
  Reloading routing configuration...
  DHCPD...

The IPv4 WAN address has been set to dhcp


The IPv6 WAN address has been set to dhcp6

Press <ENTER> to continue.
```

4. pfSense will ask you whether you want to configure the IPv6 WAN address through DHCP6. You can type y if your ISP supports IPv6 addressing, or type n, in which case IPv6 addressing for the WAN interface will be disabled.

5. pfSense will ask you whether you want to revert to HTTP for the webConfigurator protocol. Unless you have a reason for not using HTTPS for the web GUI, type *n* and press *Enter*.

6. The configuration process is now complete. The settings will be saved and pfSense will reload them.

How it works...

This recipe describes how to configure the WAN interface via the console instead of through the web GUI. Note that the options are much more limited than they are in the web GUI. For example, you only have the option to configure an IPv4 address via DHCP or use a static address. None of the other options, such as PPP or PPPoE are available. Also, with IPv6, the only option is DHCP6. If you require more options that are available here, use the web GUI.

See also

- The *Assigning interfaces from the console* recipe
- The *Configuring a LAN interface from the console* recipe
- The *Configuring optional interfaces from the console* recipe
- The *Configuring VLANs from the console* recipe
- The *Configuring a WAN interface* recipe

Configuring a LAN interface from the console

This recipe describes how to configure the LAN interface from the **Console** menu.

Getting ready

In order to complete this recipe, the LAN interface must have previously been assigned to one of the available network interfaces.

How to do it...

1. On the console menu, type **2** and press *Enter*.

2. pfSense will prompt you for the number of the interface you want to configure. For the LAN interface, this will be 2, so type 2 and press *Enter*.

3. pfSense will prompt you for the new LAN IPv4 address. Enter the new address and press *Enter*:

```
Available interfaces:

1 - WAN (em0 - dhcp, dhcp6)
2 - LAN (em1 - static)

Enter the number of the interface you wish to configure: 2

Enter the new LAN IPv4 address.  Press <ENTER> for none:
> 172.16.1.1

Subnet masks are entered as bit counts (as in CIDR notation) in pfSense.
e.g. 255.255.255.0 = 24
     255.255.0.0   = 16
     255.0.0.0     = 8

Enter the new LAN IPv4 subnet bit count (1 to 31):
> 16

For a WAN, enter the new LAN IPv4 upstream gateway address.
For a LAN, press <ENTER> for none:
>

Enter the new LAN IPv6 address.  Press <ENTER> for none:
>
```

4. pfSense will prompt you for the subnet bit count (the CIDR). Enter the bit count and press *Enter*.

5. pfSense will prompt you for the new LAN IPv4 upstream gateway address. You don't need to specify an upstream gateway, so just press *Enter*.

6. pfSense will prompt you for the new LAN IPv6 address. If you want to specify an IPv6 address, type it here; otherwise, just press *Enter*.

7. If you entered an IPv6 address, pfSense will prompt you for the subnet bit count (CIDR). Enter the bit count and press *Enter*.

8. If you entered an IPv6 address, pfSense will prompt you for the new LAN IPv6 upstream gateway address. You don't need to specify an upstream gateway, so just press *Enter*.

9. pfSense will ask whether you want to enable the DHCP server on LAN. If you enter y, you will then be prompted for the start and end addresses of the IPv4 client address range. You can enter y and type the start and end addresses, or just enter n and set up DHCP later on (recommended).

10. If you entered an IPv6 address, pfSense will ask if you want to enable the DHCP6 server on LAN. If you enter y, you will then be prompted for the start and end addresses of the IPv6 client address range. You can enter y and type the start and end addresses, or just enter n and set up DHCP6 later on (recommended).

11. pfSense will ask you whether you want to revert to HTTP for the webConfigurator protocol. Unless you have a reason for not using HTTPS for the web GUI, type n and press *Enter*.

12. The configuration process is now complete. The settings will be saved and pfSense will reload them.

How it works...

This recipe described how to set up a LAN interface's IP address using the console instead of the web GUI. Note that this option also allows you to set up the DHCP (or DHCP6) server, although it does not provide as many options as the web GUI. As with configuring a WAN interface, you may find it necessary to do the configuration via the web GUI, as the console only provides limited options.

See also

- The *Assigning interfaces from the console* recipe
- The *Configuring a WAN interface from the console* recipe
- The *Configuring optional interfaces from the console* recipe
- The *Configuring VLANs from the console* recipe
- The *Configuring a LAN interface* recipe

Configuring optional interfaces from the console

This recipe describes how to configure optional interfaces from the console menu.

Getting ready

In order to complete this recipe, at least one optional interface must have previously been assigned to one of the available network interfaces.

How to do it...

1. On the console menu, type 2 and press *Enter*.
2. pfSense will prompt you for the number of the interface you want to configure. Type the appropriate number and press *Enter*.
3. pfSense will prompt you for the new LAN IPv4 address. Enter the new address and press *Enter*.
4. pfSense will prompt you for the subnet bit count (the CIDR). Enter the bit count and press *Enter*.
5. pfSense will prompt you for the new LAN IPv4 upstream gateway address. You don't need to specify an upstream gateway, so just press *Enter*.
6. pfSense will prompt you for the new LAN IPv6 address. If you want to specify an IPv6 address, type it here; otherwise, just press *Enter*.
7. If you entered an IPv6 address, pfSense will prompt you for the subnet bit count (CIDR). Enter the bit count and press *Enter*.
8. If you entered an IPv6 address, pfSense will prompt you for the new LAN IPv6 upstream gateway address. You don't need to specify an upstream gateway, so just press *Enter*.
9. pfSense will ask whether you want to enable the DHCP server on LAN. If you enter y, you will then be prompted for the start and end addresses of the IPv4 client address range. You can enter y and type the start and end addresses, or just enter n and set up DHCP later on (recommended).

10. If you entered an IPv6 address, pfSense will ask whether you want to enable the DHCP6 server on LAN. If you enter y, you will then be prompted for the start and end addresses of the IPv6 client address range. You can enter y and type the start and end addresses, or just enter n and set up DHCP6 later on (recommended).

11. pfSense will ask you if you want to revert to HTTP for the webConfigurator protocol. Unless you have a reason for not using HTTPS for the web GUI, type n and press *Enter*.

12. The configuration process is now complete. The settings will be saved and pfSense will reload them. Repeat the process for as many optional interfaces as you wish to configure.

How it works...

This recipe describes how to set up interfaces such as an interface for a DMZ.

See also

- The *Assigning interfaces from the console* recipe
- The *Configuring a WAN interface from the console* recipe
- The *Configuring a LAN interface from the console* recipe
- The *Configuring VLANs from the console* recipe
- The *Configuring optional interfaces* recipe

Configuring VLANs from the console

This recipe describes how to add a VLAN from the console menu.

Getting ready

In order to complete this recipe, there must be at least one interface that was not previously assigned.

> Do not use the console if you don't want to have to reassign all the interfaces (for example, WAN, LAN, and any optional interfaces), because the only way to create VLANs from the console is to use the **Assign Interfaces** option.

How to do it...

1. From the console menu, type 1 and press *Enter*.
2. pfSense will ask if VLANs should be created now. Type *y* and press *Enter*.
3. pfSense will next warn you that if you proceed, all existing VLANs will be cleared. Type *y* and press *Enter*:

```
em0     08:00:27:d7:3c:fc   (up)   Intel(R) PRO/1000 Legacy Network Connection 1.
em1     08:00:27:a3:b4:39   (up)   Intel(R) PRO/1000 Legacy Network Connection 1.
em2     08:00:27:9e:8e:9c  (down)  Intel(R) PRO/1000 Legacy Network Connection 1.
em3     08:00:27:e5:51:3d  (down)  Intel(R) PRO/1000 Legacy Network Connection 1.

Do VLANs need to be set up first?
If VLANs will not be used, or only for optional interfaces, it is typical to
say no here and use the webConfigurator to configure VLANs later, if required.

Should VLANs be set up now [y|n]? y

WARNING: all existing VLANs will be cleared if you proceed!

Do you want to proceed [y|n]? y


VLAN Capable interfaces:

em0     08:00:27:d7:3c:fc   (up)
em1     08:00:27:a3:b4:39   (up)
em2     08:00:27:9e:8e:9c   (up)
em3     08:00:27:e5:51:3d   (up)

Enter the parent interface name for the new VLAN (or nothing if finished): em2
```

4. pfSense will list all the VLAN-capable interfaces. Although, technically, you can make a previously-assigned interface into the parent interface of a VLAN, it is not recommended. Type the name of one of the unassigned interfaces (for example, `eth0`, `eth1`, `em0`, or `em1`) and press *Enter*.

5. pfSense will next prompt you for the VLAN tag. Type the VLAN tag and press *Enter*.

6. Repeat steps 4 and 5 for as many VLANs as you wish to create. When you are done, press *Enter*.

7. pfSense will prompt you for the name of the WAN interface; type in the name and press *Enter*.

8. pfSense will prompt you for the name of the LAN interface; type in the name and press *Enter*.

9. pfSense will prompt you for the name of the Optional 1 interface. You can create a VLAN by using the name of the VLAN interface(s) assigned in steps 4 and 5. The name of the interface will have two numbers separated by a period. The first number will be the device number of the interface; the second number (after the period) will be the VLAN tag. Thus if the device name is `em`, and `em2` is the parent interface of a VLAN tag of `3`, the interface name will be `em2.3`. Type the interface name and press *Enter*.

10. When you are done assigning interfaces, press *Enter*.

11. pfSense will ask you whether you want to proceed. Type `y` and press *Enter*. Take note of the name of the newly created VLAN (for example, OPT1).

12. You now have assigned a VLAN, but the VLAN doesn't have an IP address. To set the VLAN's IP address, type `2` and press *Enter*.

13. Find the newly created VLAN in the list of interfaces and type the appropriate number and press *Enter*.

14. pfSense will prompt you for the VLAN's IPv4 address. Type in the address and press *Enter*.

15. pfSense will prompt you for the subnet bit count (CIDR) of the address. Type in the bit count and press *Enter*.

16. pfSense will prompt you for the IPv4 upstream gateway address. Since you don't need one, press *Enter*.

17. PfSense will prompt you for the VLAN's IPv6 address. You can type in an IPv6 address or just press *Enter*.

18. If you entered an IPv6 address, pfSense will prompt you for the subnet bit count (CIDR). Enter the bit count and press *Enter*. If you didn't enter an IPv6 address, skip to step 20.

19. If you entered an IPv6 address, pfSense will prompt you for the IPv6 upstream gateway address. Since you don't need one, press *Enter*.
20. pfSense will ask you whether you want to enable the DHCP server on the VLAN. Type y if you want to enable the DHCP server, and then type the range of available addresses. Otherwise, type n and press *Enter*.
21. If you entered an IPv6 address pfSense will ask you whether you want to enable the DHCP6 server on the VLAN. Type y if you want to enable the DHCP6 server, and then type the range of available addresses. Otherwise, type n and press *Enter*.
22. pfSense will ask you whether you want to revert to HTTP for the webConfigurator protocol. Unless you have a reason for not using HTTPS for the web GUI, type n and press *Enter*.
23. pfSense will save the changes, and reload them. VLAN configuration is now complete.

How it works...

This recipe describes how to set up VLANs from the console. The process is somewhat cumbersome, but if you need to create a VLAN and don't have access to the web GUI, it can be done.

See also

- The *Configuring VLANs* recipe

Essential Services 2

In this chapter, we will cover the following topics:

- Configuring the DHCP server
- Configuring the DHCP6 server
- Configuring static DHCP mappings
- Configuring the DHCP relay
- Specifying alternate DNS servers
- Configuring the DNS resolver
- Configuring a stand-alone DNS server
- Configuring dynamic DNS
- Adding a wireless access point

Introduction

At this point, we have installed pfSense and performed much of the basic configuration. We have already done the following:

- Determined our hardware requirements
- Installed pfSense
- Assigned and configured interfaces
- Set up SSH access
- Added VLANs, if necessary

Now we are ready to configure several of the essential services that our pfSense system will provide:

- The DHCP/DHCP6 service will enable clients to obtain IP addresses automatically.
- The DNS server will enable clients to resolve hostnames to IP addresses.
- The dynamic DNS service will allow pfSense to update a host's DNS record when that host's IP address changes.

Configuring the DHCP server

This recipe describes how to configure the DHCP server. The DHCP server assigns an IP address to anyone who requests one.

Getting ready

In order to enable the DHCP server on an interface, that interface must have a static IP address. If you have followed the recipes in order, you should have at least one interface with a static IP address (the LAN interface). This example will show how to configure the DHCP server on the LAN interface.

How to do it...

1. Navigate to **Services** | **DHCP Server**.
2. Click on the **LAN** tab, if it isn't selected already.
3. Under **General Options**, check the **Enable DHCP server on LAN interface** checkbox:

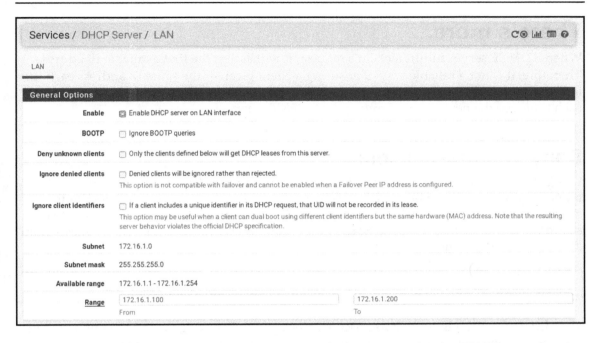

4. In the **Range** edit boxes, enter a range of IP addresses for the DHCP server to assign to clients. The range must be contiguous and within the range listed next to **Available range**.

5. If you do not need more than a single range of IP addresses, proceed to Step 6. Otherwise, perform the following steps to add multiple IP address pools:
    - Under **Additional Pools**, click on the **Add** pool button.
    - When the page reloads, add the new range, using the **Range** edit boxes.
    - Click on the **Save** button at the bottom of the page.
    - Click on the **LAN** tab to return to the DHCP configuration page for the LAN interface.
    - Repeat Step 5 for as many pools as you wish to add.

6. Click on the **Save** button, and the DHCP service will start.

7. Click on the **Apply Changes** button.

How it works...

A DHCP server accepts DHCP requests from clients and assigns them an available IP address.

There's more...

When a DHCP server fulfills a client's request, it will assign the first available IP address. Therefore, it is not a reliable way of ensuring a client receives the same IP address each time it sends out a DHCP request. To see how to ensure a client receives the same IP address each time, see the next recipe, *Creating static DHCP mappings*.

Deny unknown clients

Using this recipe will result in the DHCP server assigning an IP address to every client requesting one. This may not be what we want. Checking the **Deny unknown clients** checkbox will cause the DHCP server to assign IP addresses only to clients whose MAC addresses are listed under **DHCP Static Mappings for this Interface**. DHCP requests from all other clients will then be ignored:

Deny unknown clients	☐ Only the clients defined below will get DHCP leases from this server.

This differs from the **Enable Static ARP entries** option. Checking this option will result in unknown clients being assigned IP addresses even if **Deny unknown clients** is enabled (for that matter, they will be assigned an IP address even if the DHCP server is disabled), but only clients listed under **DHCP Static Mappings for this Interface** will be allowed to communicate with the firewall.

DNS servers

Under **Servers**, you can specify up to four DNS servers, which will be automatically assigned to DHCP clients. If you do not specify DNS servers here, pfSense will automatically assign DNS servers to clients in the following ways:

- If **DNS Forwarder** is enabled, then the IP address of the interface is used. This is because the **DNS Forwarder** turns the pfSense machine itself into a DNS server, so the IP address of the pfSense machine is assigned to each client.
- If **DNS Forwarder** is not enabled, then the DNS servers configured on the **General Setup** page are used. And if **Allow DNS server list to be overridden by DHCP/PPP on WAN** is enabled in **General Setup**, then the DNS servers obtained through the WAN will be used instead:

DNS servers	DNS Server 1	
	DNS Server 2	
	DNS Server 3	
	DNS Server 4	
	Leave blank to use the system default DNS servers: this interface's IP if DNS Forwarder or Resolver is enabled, otherwise the servers configured on the System / General Setup page.	

Gateway

The static IP address of the interface will serve as the gateway, but you can specify an alternate gateway in the **Gateway** edit box under **Other Options** if necessary (or type none for no gateway).

Domain name

The domain name specified in **General Setup** is used by default, but you can specify an alternate one in the **Domain name** edit box under **Other Options** if necessary.

Default lease time

An alternate lease time for clients who do not request a specific lease expiration time can be specified in the **Default lease time** edit box under **Other Options**. If left unspecified, the default lease time is 7,200 seconds.

Maximum lease time

An alternative maximum lease time can be specified for clients who request a specific expiration time in the **Maximum lease time** edit box under **Other Options**. If left unspecified, the default maximum lease time is 86,400 seconds.

Failover peer IP

CARP-configured systems can specify a failover peer IP address here. See the *Configuring CARP firewall failover* recipe in Chapter 7, *Redundancy, Load Balancing, and Failover* for more information.

Static ARP

Enabling static ARP entries will only allow clients with DHCP mappings to communicate with the firewall on this interface. Unknown clients will still receive an IP address, but all communication to the firewall will be blocked. This is different from *Deny Unknown Clients*, where unknown clients won't even receive an IP address.

Dynamic DNS

Checking the **Enable registration of DHCP client names** in DNS (which can be seen by clicking the **Show Advanced** button in the **Dynamic DNS** column in **Other Options**) will enable DHCP clients to register with the specified DDNS domain.

Additional BOOTP/DHCP options

Enter any custom DHCP options here. Visit `https://www.iana.org/assignments/bootp-dhcp-parameters/bootp-dhcp-parameters.xml` for a list of options.

See also

- The *Configuring the DHCP6 Server* recipe
- The *Configuring static DHCP mappings* recipe
- The *Configuring CARP firewall failover* recipe in *Chapter 7, Redundancy, Load Balancing and Failover*

Configuring the DHCP6 server

This recipe describes how to configure the DHCP6 server. The DHCP6 server accepts DHCP6 requests from clients and assigns them IPv6 addresses from the pool of available addresses.

Getting ready

In order to enable the DHCP6 server on an interface, you must have at least one interface configured with a static IPv6 address. This was an option in the *Configuring the LAN interface* and the *Configuring an optional interface* recipes. If you did not configure any of the non-WAN interfaces with a static IPv6 address, you must first reconfigure at least one of them. If necessary, use the recipes in `Chapter 1`, *Initial Configuration*, as a guide. In this recipe, we will describe how to enable the DHCP6 server on the LAN interface.

How to do it...

1. Navigate to **Services | DHCPv6 and RA**.
2. Click on the **LAN** tab, if it isn't selected already.
3. Click on the **DHCPv6 Server** tab, if it isn't selected already.
4. Under **DHCPv6 Options**, check the **Enable DHCPv6 Server on interface LAN** checkbox:

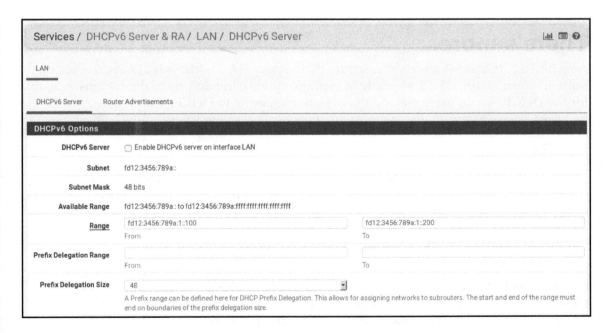

5. In **Range** edit boxes, enter a range of IPv6 addresses for the DHCP6 server to assign to clients. The range must be contiguous and within the range listed next to **Available** range.

6. Click on the **Save** button, and the DHCP6 server will start.
7. Click on the **Apply Changes** button.

 Note that there is no option to add multiple IP address pools, as there was with DHCP.

How it works...

The DHCP6 server accepts DHCP6 requests from clients and assigns them an available IPv6 address.

 Note that you can enable both the DHCP and DHCP6 server on an interface. In order to do so, the interface must be configured with both a static IPv4 address and a static IPv6 address.

There's more...

As with DHCP, there is a way of ensuring that certain MAC addresses always receive the same IP address (the **DHCPv6 Static Mappings** option). In addition to the options available for the DHCP server, there are additional options specific to DHCPv6.

Prefix delegation

Prefix delegation allows a delegating router—known as a prefix delegation server—to delegate IPv6 prefixes to requesting routers, known as prefix delegation clients. The clients can then use these prefixes to assign global IPv6 addresses to devices on their internal interfaces. Since it uses DHCPv6 messages to do this (defined in RFC 3633), it is sometimes referred to as DHCPv6 prefix delegation.

In order to utilize prefix delegation, enter the range in the **Prefix Delegation Range** edit boxes under **DHCPv6 Options**. You may also specify a size for the prefix in the **Prefix Delegation Size** drop-down box. Note that the start and end of the **Prefix Delegation Range** must end on the boundaries of the prefix delegation size.

See also

- The *Configuring the DHCP Server* recipe
- The *Configuring static DHCP mappings* recipe
- The *Configuring CARP firewall failover* recipe in Chapter 7, *Redundancy, Load Balancing and Failover*

Configuring static DHCP mappings

This recipe describes how to add a static (IPv4) DHCP mapping in pfSense. A static mapping ensures that a client always receives the same IP address from the DHCP server.

Getting ready

In order to create a static DHCP mapping, you must have at least one interface on which the DHCP server is enabled. (You can only create static DHCP mappings on interfaces using the DHCP server).

How to do it...

There are two ways of creating a static DHCP mapping.

1. Navigate to **Services | DHCP** and click on the **LAN** tab, if it isn't selected already.
2. Scroll to the bottom of the page. Beneath the **Save** button, there should be a section labeled **DHCP Static Mappings for this Interface**. Click on the **Add** button beneath this section:

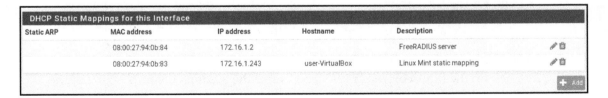

3. You are now in the **Edit Static Mapping** page. Enter a MAC address in the **MAC Address** edit box:

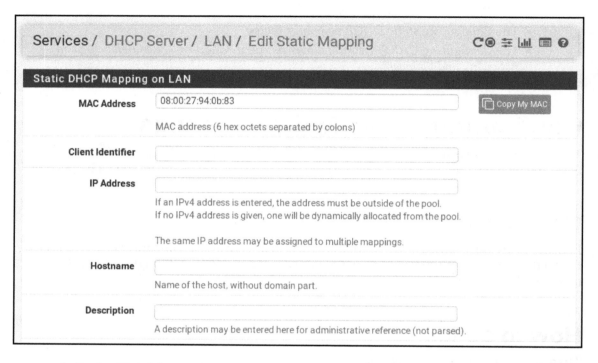

4. In the **IP Address** edit box, enter an IP address that is outside of the range of dynamically assigned IP addresses for this interface.
5. In the **Hostname** edit box, enter the host's name.
6. In the **Description** edit box, enter a brief (non-parsed) description.
7. Click on the **Save** button.
8. Click on the **Apply Changes** button. Scroll to the bottom of the **DHCP Server** page for the LAN interface and confirm that your new static mapping exists.

Another way to create a static DHCP mapping is to start at the **DHCP Leases** page.

1. Navigate to **Status | DHCP Leases**.
2. Click on the light-colored "plus" icon under the **Actions** column in one of the table entries.

3. You should now be in the **Edit Static Mapping** page. The **MAC address** field will be prefilled with the MAC address of the network interface on the system you are using.
4. In the **IP Address** edit box, enter an IP address that is outside of the range of dynamically assigned IP addresses for this interface.
5. The **Hostname** edit box may be prefilled. If not, enter the host's name.
6. In the **Description** edit box, enter a brief (non-parsed) description.
7. Click on the **Save** button.
8. Click on the **Apply Changes** button. Scroll to the bottom of the **DHCP Server** page for the LAN interface and confirm that your new static mapping exists.

How it works...

When a client connects to the DHCP server, the server will first check to see if there is a static mapping for the client's MAC address. If no such mapping exists, the server will use an IP address from its available range.

There's more...

Static mappings for each interface can be viewed by navigating to **Services** | **DHCP Server** and clicking on the appropriate interface tab.

See also

- The *Configuring the DHCP Server* recipe
- The *Configuring the DHCP6 Server* recipe
- The *Configuring the DHCP relay* recipe

Configuring the DHCP relay

This recipe describes how to configure pfSense to relay DHCP request between broadcast domains. This serves as an alternative to pfSense acting as a DHCP server.

Getting ready

pfSense can only be configured as a DHCP relay if the DHCP server has been disabled on all interfaces. If necessary, disable the DHCP server first. To disable the DHCP server, do the following:

1. Navigate to **Services** | **DHCP Server**.
2. Click on the tab for the interface on which the DHCP server is enabled (for example, LAN).
3. Uncheck the **Enable DHCP Server** on the interface checkbox.
4. Click on the **Save** button.
5. Repeat Steps 2 through 4 for each interface on which the DHCP server is enabled.

How to do it...

1. Navigate to **Services** | **DHCP Relay**.
2. Check the **Enable DHCP relay** on interface checkbox:

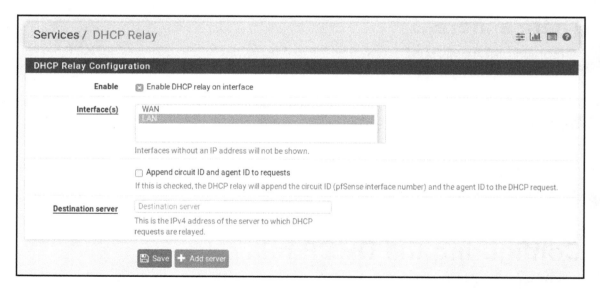

3. Select the interface on which the DHCP relay will be applied. Hold down the *Ctrl* key while clicking on an interface in the list box to select multiple interfaces.
4. If you want to append the circuit ID and agent ID to DHCP requests, check the **Append circuit ID and agent ID to requests** checkbox.
5. Enter the IP address of the existing DHCP servers to be used in the **Destination** server edit box. Multiple IP addresses may be entered, separated by commas.
6. Click on the **Save** button when done.

How it works...

When pfSense is configured to act as a DHCP relay, DHCP requests will be forwarded to the DHCP servers specified. The responses from the DHCP servers will be forwarded back to the client.

There's more...

The DHCP relay configuration allows you to append the circuit ID and agent ID to DHCP requests. The circuit ID identifies the circuit or port the DHCP request came in on, and the agent ID identifies the relay agent.

See also

- The *Configuring the DHCP Server* recipe
- The *Configuring the DHCP6 Server* recipe
- The *Configuring Static DHCP mappings* recipe

Specifying alternate DNS servers

This recipe describes how to configure pfSense to use DNS servers other than the ones provided by your WAN connection.

Getting ready

In most environments, routers rely on DHCP servers specified by the ISP through their WAN connection. For this reason, by default, pfSense has the **Allow DNS server list to be overridden by DHCP/PPP on WAN** option enabled. To specify alternate DNS servers manually, we will have to disable this option, which we will do in the following recipe.

How to do it...

1. Navigate to **System | General Setup**.
2. In the **DNS Servers** section, make the following changes:
   - Specify DNS servers in the **DNS Servers** edit boxes. You also have an option to select the gateway for each DNS server using the adjacent **Gateway** drop-down box. If you want to add more than two DNS servers, click on the **Add DNS Server** button, and another edit box will appear.
   - Uncheck the **Allow DNS server list to be overridden by DHCP/PPP on WAN** checkbox.
3. Click on the **Save** button.

How it works...

We have specified alternate DNS servers, which will be used instead of the ones specified by the ISP.

Using the DNS resolver

If the DNS forwarder is enabled, we can override the DNS servers for individual domains, or even override results for individual devices. For more information, see the following *Configuring the DNS Resolver* recipe. The DNS resolver takes precedence over all DNS requests.

Using your WAN DNS servers

When **Allow DNS server list to be overridden by DHCP/PPP on WAN** is enabled, pfSense will attempt to resolve DNS names using the DNS servers provided by the WAN, before falling over to the servers defined in the list. After the DNS resolver, this option takes precedence over DNS requests.

See also

- The *Configuring the DNS Resolver* recipe

Configuring the DNS resolver

This recipe describes how to configure the DNS resolver in pfSense. The DNS resolver allows pfSense to act as a DNS server.

Getting ready

The DNS resolver allows pfSense to resolve DNS requests using hostnames obtained by the DHCP service, statically obtained DHCP mappings, or manually obtained information. The DNS resolver can also forward all DNS requests for a particular domain to a server specified manually.

> Prior to pfSense Version 2.2, DNS forwarder was the default DNS server for pfSense. Version 2.2 and later iterations use Unbound (DNS resolver) as the default DNS server; however, DNS forwarder is still available.

How to do it...

1. Navigate to **Services | DNS Resolver**.
2. Check the **Enable DNS Resolver** checkbox.

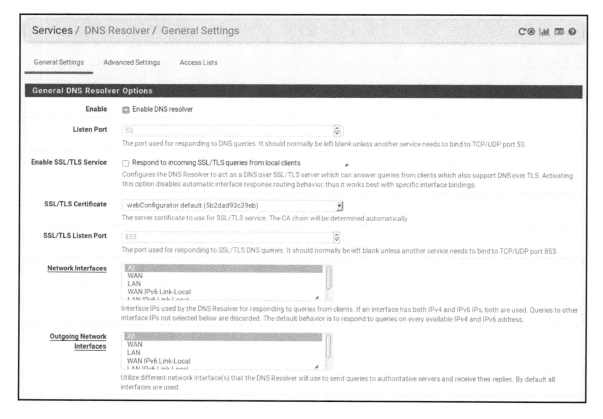

3. If you want to ensure that all nodes listed in **Status | DHCP Leases** that specified their hostname when requesting a lease are registered in the DNS resolver, check the **Register DHCP leases in the DNS Resolver** checkbox.
4. If you want to ensure that all nodes with a static DHCP mapping are registered with the DNS resolver, check the **Register DHCP static mappings in DNS Resolver** checkbox.

5. Specify individual hosts to be served as DNS records by scrolling down to **Host Overrides** and clicking on the **Add** button. Devices on this list will be checked first, so even if a record exists elsewhere, a record here takes precedence and is immediately returned. On the **Edit Host Override** page, you can enter the following parameters for a host:

    - The **Host** edit box is where you specify the host without the domain part.
    - The **Domain** edit box is where you specify the domain.
    - The **IP Address** edit box is where you specify the IP address of the host.
    - The **Description** edit box is where you may enter a brief (nonparsed) description.
    - You may also specify additional names for the host in the **Additional Names for this Host** section. Click on the **Save** button when you are done making changes.

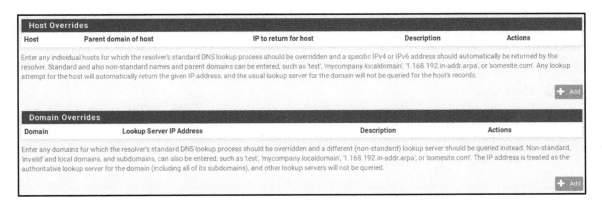

6. Specify a DNS server for a particular domain by scrolling down to **Domain Overrides** and clicking on the **Add** button. These records are checked immediately after the individual records are defined above, so a match here will take precedence over records that may exist elsewhere. On the **Edit Domain Override** page, you can enter the following parameters:

    - The **Domain** edit box is where you specify the domain to override.
    - The **IP Address** edit box is where you specify the IP address of the authoritative DNS server for the domain.

- The **Use SSL/TLS for DNS Queries forwarded to this server** checkbox will cause pfSense to send queries for this domain using SSL/TLS on port 853, thereby enabling the use of encrypted DNS traffic.
- The **Description** edit box is where you may enter a brief (nonparsed) description.

7. When you are done making changes, click on the **Save** button.
8. Click on the **Apply Changes** button.

How it works...

If enabled, the DNS resolver takes priority over all DNS requests and responds to them in the following order:

1. Individual device records
2. Domain-specific records
3. DHCP static mappings
4. DHCP leases

See also...

- The *Configuring the DHCP server* recipe
- The *Creating static DHCP mappings* recipe
- The *Configuring a stand-alone DHCP/DNS server* recipe

Configuring a stand-alone DHCP/DNS server

This recipe describes how to configure pfSense as a stand-alone DHCP and DNS server.

How to do it...

1. Configure pfSense as a DHCP server. See the *Configuring the DHCP server* recipe for details.
2. Create DHCP mappings for every device in the system that will obtain its IP address automatically through DHCP. See the *Creating static DHCP mappings* recipe for details.

3. Navigate to **System | General Setup**.

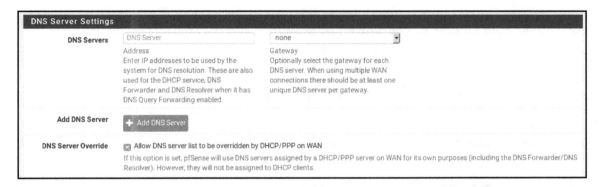

4. Ensure that no other DNS servers are specified.
5. Check the **Allow DNS server list to be overridden by DHCP/PPP on WAN** checkbox. This will enable pfSense to resolve external addresses using the DNS servers provided by your ISP through your WAN connection.
6. Click on the **Save** button.
7. Navigate to **System | DNS Resolver**.
8. Check the **Enable DNS Resolver** checkbox.

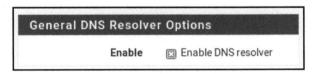

9. Check the **Register DHCP static mappings in the DNS Resolver** checkbox.

10. Create a **Host record** for any device that needs to be resolved but doesn't have a DHCP mapping (that is, devices that define their own IP).
11. Create a **Domain record** for any DNS requests you'd like to redirect for a particular domain.
12. When you are done, click on the **Save** button.
13. Click on the **Apply Changes** button.

How it works...

If the DNS resolver is enabled, every DNS request from every interface will be processed by pfSense. Individual host records will be checked first, and if a match is found, the associated IP address is returned immediately.

By enabling the **Register DHCP static mappings in the DNS Resolver** option, you won't have to worry about creating DNS records for these devices. This is advantageous, since as long as we create a static mapping for every device on our network, their hostnames will resolve automatically. Using this method, we will only have to add explicit hostname records for devices that specify their own IP addresses.

Register DHCP leases in DNS resolver

If the **Register DHCP Leases in DNS Resolver** option is enabled, pfSense will automatically register any devices that specify a hostname when submitting a DNS request. The downside, of course, is that not all devices submit a hostname, and when they do, it is sometimes cryptic. For this reason, it is probably good practice to register important devices using DHCP static mappings, and other (unimportant/unknown) devices can be referenced using their IP addresses.

See also

- The *Configuring the DHCP server* recipe
- The *Configuring the DHCP6 server* recipe
- The *Creating static DHCP mappings* recipe
- The *Configuring the DNS resolver* recipe

Configuring dynamic DNS

This recipe describes how to configure a dynamic DNS service in pfSense. pfSense's integrated dynamic DNS service allows you to update your dynamic DNS records automatically when you change an interface's IP address.

Getting ready

In order to use the DNS service, you must first register with a DDNS provider. Some of the more common DDNS providers are listed in the **Service Type** drop-down box on the Dynamic DNS configuration page. A quick web search should yield a list of DDNS providers that meet any specific criteria you might have.

How to do it...

1. Navigate to **Services | Dynamic DNS**.
2. Click on the **Dynamic DNS Clients** tab, if it isn't selected already.
3. Click on the **Add** button to add a new record.
4. Select a service type in the **Service Type** drop-down box (or choose **Custom** or **Custom v6**).

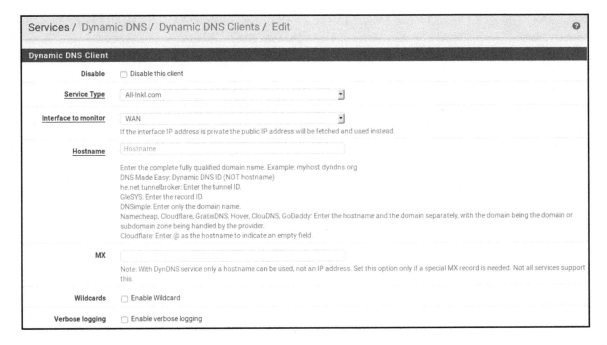

5. Choose an interface in the **Interface to Monitor** drop-down box (or just leave it at the default value of **WAN**).
6. Specify the fully qualified hostname in the **Hostname** edit box.

7. Check the **Enable Wildcard** checkbox, if applicable. Enabling this option will allow the use of wildcards appended to your hostname; for example, if your hostname is `myhostname.mydnsprovider.org`, then `x.myhostname.mydnsprovider.org` will work as well. Disabling this option will force the user to specify the exact hostname specified in the **Hostname** field.

8. Enter the username for your DDNS provider in the **Username** field.

9. Enter the password for your DDNS provider in the **Password** field. Retype the password in the **Confirm** field.

10. If you specified a custom entry, enter the update URL in the **Update URL** field.

11. You may optionally enter a brief (nonparsed) description in the **Description** field.

12. When you are done, click on the **Save** button.

How it works...

Whenever the IP address of our WAN interface changes, pfSense automatically connects to our dynamic DNS service and automatically updates the IP address.

Specifying an alternative service using RFC 2136

We may specify an alternative service that does not come preconfigured as long as it adheres to the RFC 2136 standard. Navigate to **Services | Dynamic DNS** and click on the **RFC 2136** tab. Then fill in the appropriate fields using the information provided by your RFC 2136-compliant DDNS provider.

For more information, refer to the Wikipedia Dynamic DNS page: `http://en.wikipedia.org/wiki/Dynamic_DNS` and to the official RFC 2136 Standard Documentation at `http://tools.ietf.org/html/rfc2136`

Adding a wireless access point

This recipe describes how to configure pfSense for use as a wireless access point.

Getting ready

In order to use pfSense as a wireless access point, you must meet the following prerequisites:

- Add a wireless card to your pfSense system that is supported by pfSense. You will likely want to consult the FreeBSD Hardware Notes first. You can find information about compatible wireless interfaces for FreeBSD 11.1 at: `https://www.freebsd.org/releases/11.2R/hardware.html#wlan`
- The wireless card must be detected by pfSense.

How to do it...

1. Navigate to **Interfaces | Assignments**.
2. Click on the **Wireless** tab.

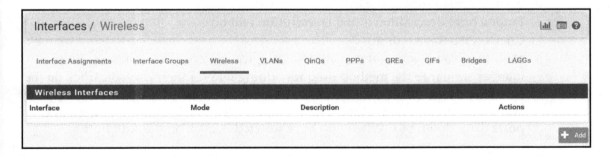

3. Click on the **Add** button to add a new interface.

4. Select the correct interface in the **Parent Interface** drop-down box. If your wireless card is not listed, then it was not detected by pfSense, and you will have to troubleshoot this issue.

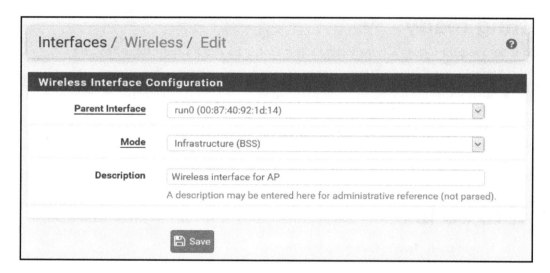

5. Select **Access Point** in the **Mode** drop-down box.

6. Enter a brief description in the **Description** edit box.

7. Click on the **Save** button.

8. Now that we have added the wireless card, we can assign the interface, in a manner similar to the method used for adding wired Ethernet cards. Click on the **Interface Assignments** tab.

9. Select the wireless card added in the previous steps in the **Available network ports** drop-down box. When you have selected it, click on the **Add** button.

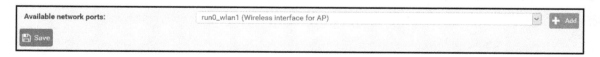

10. Click on the name of the newly assigned interface (for example, OPT1) in the Interface column. This will bring you to the wireless interface's configuration page.

11. In the **IPv4 Configuration Type** drop-down box, select **Static IPv4**.

12. In the **IPv6 Configuration Type** drop-down box, select **Static IPv6**, or just leave it at the default setting of **None**.

13. Scroll down to **Static IPv4 Configuration**. In this section, enter an IP address in the **IPv4 Address** edit box, and select the correct CIDR in the CIDR drop-down box.

14. If you chose **Static IPv6** as the **IPv6 Configuration Type**, you will need to enter an IPv6 address in the IPv6 Address edit box under **Static IPv6 Configuration**. You must also select the correct CIDR.

15. In the **Common Wireless Configuration** section, select the appropriate 802.11 standard in the **Standard** drop-down box.

16. Select a channel for your wireless card to use in the **Channel** drop-down box.

17. In the **Network-Specific Wireless Configuration** section, select **Access Point** in the Mode drop-down box.

18. Enter an SSID in the **SSID** edit box.

19. Check the **Force the card to use WME (wireless QoS)** checkbox.

20. In the WPA section, check the **Enable WPA** checkbox.

21. Enter a pre-shared key in the **WPA Pre-Shared Key** edit box.

22. When you are done making changes, click on the **Save** button.

23. Click on the **Apply Changes** button.

How it works...

Most SOHO networks incorporate some form of wireless access. One of the ways of accomplishing this with pfSense is to use a separate wireless access point and connect it to one of the interfaces on your pfSense firewall/router. If you find it preferable to use pfSense as a wireless access point, however, you can, provided that you add a compatible wireless card to your pfSense system, ensure that pfSense has detected the card, and follow the preceding recipe. If you are using a thin client as your pfSense system, then in all likelihood, using a separate wireless access point is the better option, as you are likely to be hindered by the lack of spare expansion slots on the thin client (although using a USB wireless adaptor is also an option). If you are using a desktop or laptop system to host pfSense, however, you may find it easier to add a wireless card to your configuration and use pfSense as an access point.

See also

- The *Configuring the LAN interface* recipe in `Chapter 1`, *Initial Configuration*
- The *Configuring optional interfaces* recipe in `Chapter 1`, *Initial Configuration*

Firewall and NAT

3

In this chapter, we will cover the following recipes:

- Creating and using aliases
- Creating a firewall rule
- Setting a firewall rule schedule
- Creating a floating rule
- Creating a NAT port forwarding entry
- Creating an outbound NAT entry
- Creating a 1:1 NAT entry
- Creating an NPt entry
- Enabling UPnP and NAT-PnP

Introduction

In any deployment scenario, it is likely you will be using your pfSense system to filter traffic—after all, filtering traffic is the core function of a firewall. In order to do so, you will find it necessary to create and edit firewall rules. pfSense supports the creation of two types of firewall rules. Standard firewall rules work on a per-interface basis and filter traffic leaving the interface. Floating rules, on the other hand, can be applied to more than one interface, and can apply to traffic both entering and leaving the interface.

Network Address Translation (**NAT**) is useful in scenarios in which we have a fixed number of external IP addresses and a series of internal addresses. This is often the case in home and SOHO deployments, and, as a result, we will cover them in this chapter. Finally, in some cases, it is useful to automate NAT port mapping, and to this end, we will cover UPnP and NAT-PnP.

Creating and using aliases

This recipe describes how to create, edit, and delete aliases. Aliases provide a degree of separation between firewall/NAT rules and values that may change in the future, such as IP addresses, networks, and ports. Using aliases whenever possible makes it much easier to maintain firewall rules.

How to do it...

1. Navigate to **Firewall** | **Aliases**.
2. Click on the **Add** button.
3. Enter a name for the alias in the **Name** text field:

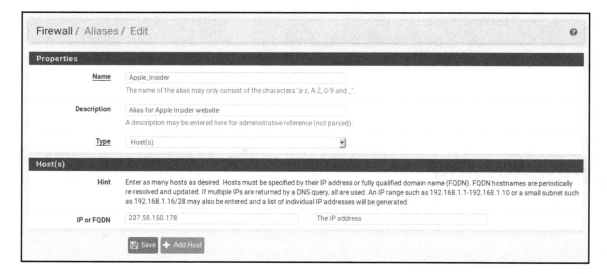

4. Enter a brief (non-parsed) description in the **Description** text field.
5. Select the type of alias to create in the **Type** drop-down menu (the choices are **Host(s)**, **Network(s)**, **Port(s)**, **URL (IPs)**, **URL (Ports)**, **URL Table (IPs)**, **URL Table (Ports)**. The differences between these types will be explained in the *There's more* section.

6. Finish the configuration based on the **Type** selection. For **Host(s)**, you should enter a host; for **Network(s)**, you should enter a network and CIDR, and for **Port(s)**, you should enter a port or port range. If you need to specify more than one entry, click on the **Add** button. There should be an **Add** button for all types except **URL Table (IPs)** and **URL Table (Ports)**.
7. When you are done, click on the **Save** button.
8. Click on **Apply Changes**.

How it works...

An alias is a placeholder for information that may change. For example, you may have a printer that has an IP address of 172.16.1.100. By creating an alias for this IP address, we can then create firewall and NAT rules that refer to the printer without having to change all the rules if the IP address of the printer changes. If the IP address does change, we just need to change the alias.

There's more...

When creating an alias, you can choose different types. You can choose from the following options:

- **Host(s)**: This option allows you to specify one or more IP addresses or hostnames. Hostnames will be periodically re-resolved.
- **Network(s)**: You can specify a network by specifying the network portion of an IP address and the CIDR (for example, 172.16.0.0/16).
- **Port(s)**: You can specify a port or a range of ports (the first and last port should be separated by a colon).
- **URL (IPs)**: You can specify one or more URLs that, in turn point to text lists of IP addresses. Lists should be limited to 3,000 or fewer addresses.
- **URL (Ports)**: You can specify one or more URLs that, in turn, point to text lists of ports. Lists should be limited to 3,000 entries.
- **URL Table (IPs)**: Similar to **URL (IPs)**, but you can only specify a single URL, and the text list loaded will be refreshed at an interval of your choosing. Lists can be longer than 3,000 addresses.
- **URL Table (Ports)**: Similar to **URL (Ports)**, but you can only specify a single URL, and the text list loaded will be refreshed at an interval of your choosing. As with URL Table (IPs), lists can be longer than 3,000 entries.

As you can see, there are several options, including options to have the alias utilize a list or lists of IPs or ports, which in turn can be edited. Another way we can organize our aliases is to nest them, so we have aliases of aliases. For example, we might have several identical printers, each with their own IP address. We can create an alias for each printer, and then create an alias that refers to all the printers.

> You can also utilize lists of IP addresses and/or networks by using the bulk import option, as described later in this recipe.

Using an alias

You can generally use an alias wherever you would be allowed to input whatever type the alias is. For example, if an alias refers to an IP address and the field you are entering requires a hostname or IP address, you should be able to use the alias. You will be able to tell if this is the case, because if you start typing the alias and aliases are allowed in the field, the auto-complete functionality of pfSense should cause all the valid aliases to appear.

Editing an alias

To edit an alias, do the following:

1. Navigate to **Firewall** | **Aliases**.
2. Click on the **Edit** icon (the pencil) for the alias you wish to edit.
3. Make the necessary changes.
4. When you are done making changes, click on the **Save** button.
5. Click on the **Apply Changes** button.

Deleting an alias

To delete an alias, do the following:

1. Navigate to **Firewall** | **Aliases**.
2. Click on the **Delete** icon (the trash can) for the alias you wish to delete.
3. When the dialog box that reads **Are you sure you wish to delete alias?** appears, click on **OK**.
4. Click on the **Apply Changes** button.

Bulk importing aliases

To import a list of multiple IP addresses, do the following:

1. Navigate to **Firewall** | **Aliases**.
2. Click on the **Import** button to bulk import aliases.
3. Enter a name in the **Name** text field:

4. Enter a brief non-parsed description in the **Description** text field.
5. In the **Aliases to import** textbox, enter or paste in a list of IP addresses and/or networks.
6. When you are done, click on the **Save** button.
7. Click on the **Apply Changes** button.

See also

- The *Creating a firewall rule* recipe
- The *Creating a NAT port forwarding rule* recipe
- Official documentation at: https://www.netgate.com/docs/pfsense/firewall/aliases.html

Creating a firewall rule

This recipe describes how to create a firewall rule. We will create a firewall rule on the LAN interface to block the website http://appleinsider.com/ (207.58.150.178).

How to do it...

1. Navigate to **Firewall | Rules**.
2. Since we want to create a rule that applies to the LAN interface, click on the **LAN** tab:

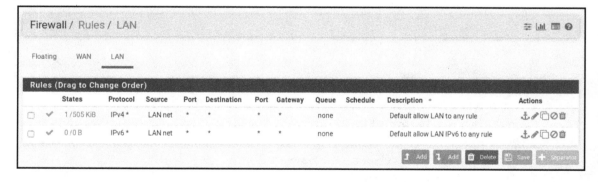

3. The table on the page will list all the current rules for the LAN interface. There will be two **Add** buttons below the table. Since we want to create a rule that will be appended to the top of the table, click on the **Add** button with the up arrow.

4. Set the action in the **Action** drop-down menu to **Block**:

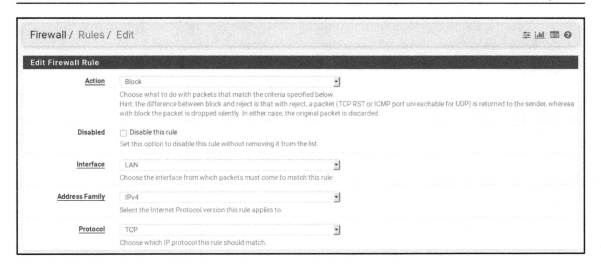

5. You can leave **Interface** set to **LAN**, Address Family set to **IPv4,** and Protocol set to **TCP**.

6. In **Destination**, select **Single host or alias** in the drop-down menu and enter 207.58.150.178 in the adjacent text field:

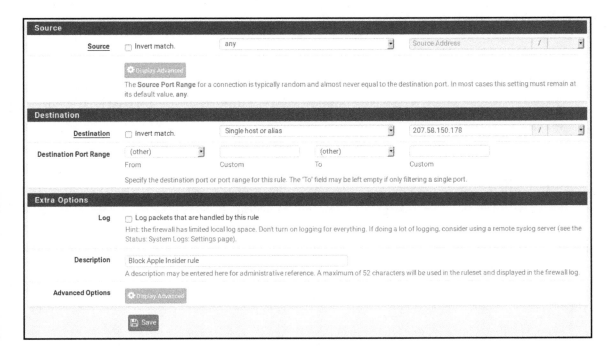

7. In the **Extra Options** section, enter a description in the **Description** text field.
8. When you are done, click on the **Save** button.
9. Click on the **Apply Changes** button to reload the firewall rules.

How it works...

All LAN traffic passes through the list of LAN firewall rules. If traffic matches all of the rule's criteria, the rule will be executed.

 Firewall rules are evaluated on a top-down basis. Thus, pfSense will apply the rule to traffic that matches the rule's criteria that is closest to the top of the list. The rest of the rules will be skipped.

There's more...

Firewall rules are highly configurable. Here are some of the more common options:

- **Action**: This determines what happens if the traffic matches the rule's criteria. The options are as follows:

    - **Pass**: Let the traffic pass.
    - **Block**: Drop the packet silently.
    - **Reject**: Drop the packet, but send back either a TCP RST error (for TCP packets), or an ICMP port unreachable error (for UDP packets).

- **Disabled**: Enabling this option allows you to disable the rule without deleting it, which is handy when troubleshooting.
- **Interface**: Traffic originating from the specified interface will be subject to the rule. The default value is whatever interface's tab you are on when you add the rule, but you can change it to any interface you choose using the interface drop-down menu.

- **Protocol**: This specifies the protocol to be matched. Usually the default of TCP is sufficient, but in some cases, we may want to match a different protocol (for example, to match ping traffic, we would use ICMP).
- **Source**: This is typically left at the default value of any for incoming traffic.
- **Source port range**: This is also typically left set to any.

- **Destination**: This is typically the alias or IP address of the computer servicing the request.
- **Destination port range**: This is typically the specific port on the computer servicing the request.
- **Log**: Enable logging to record packets that match this rule. Usually this option is disabled, since logging packets that match rules is a good way to generate unreasonably large log files. Enabling logging, however, can be helpful when troubleshooting.
- **Description**: You can enter a brief description that explains the purpose of the rule here.

The source port

When creating a firewall rule, it is important to remember that the source port is often chosen by the system's implementation of the networking protocol being used from a range of ports. Since we rarely know what this port is in advance, it is usually correct to leave the source set to any. To understand why this is the case, consider the example of a user requesting a simple web page. Port 80 is the default port for HTTP traffic, but this refers to the port requested on the remote server. The port used on the client will be chosen from a range of ports (typically from 1024 to 65535); this port is often a seemingly arbitrarily chosen one. If the router uses NAT, this internal port will be translated to a different (external) port number, and then the request will be sent. The return traffic will flow the opposite way, first to the external port number on the router, then to the client's internal port number. Thus, while we know the port to which traffic will be directed on the destination server, it is almost a certainty that we do not know the source port. Therefore, we should avoid the mistake of specifying the source port, except for rare cases in which we know the source of the traffic in advance.

Ordering firewall rules

As mentioned earlier, firewall rules are evaluated on a top-down basis. The first rule that matches a packet is executed, and the rest are skipped. It is important to consider the order of firewall rules. Often specific rules will proceed more general rules. For example, consider the LAN interface. When pfSense is initially installed, it generates two default Allow LAN to any rules – one for IPv4 traffic and the other for IPv6 traffic. The purpose of these rules is to allow internet traffic on the LAN interface, thus allowing LAN nodes to communicate with other local networks and with the internet. If we had placed our newly created rule to block `appleinsider.com` after these rules, it would always be ignored, since the Allow LAN to any rules will match all traffic (any protocol and any destination). Therefore, it must be placed before these rules.

The easiest way to re-order rules in pfSense using the web GUI is to click your mouse on the rule you wish to move and drag it into place. You can also move rules around by checking the checkbox in the leftmost column of a rule's entry, and then clicking on the **Move selected rules above/below this one** icon (the anchor icon) for the appropriate rule. Use *Shift + Click* to move rules below the rule.

Duplicating firewall rules

Often, we want to make a new firewall rule that is very similar to an existing one. In such cases, it is usually easier to make a copy of the original rule and then edit it to suit our purposes. To copy a rule, click on the **Copy** icon (the icon that looks like two sheets of paper).

Advanced features

There is also a section on the firewall edit page called **Advanced Options**. These options only appear if you click on the **Display Advanced** button. In this section, you will find a series of less commonly used matching criteria. As with the other criteria, the rule will apply if the packets match the criteria. Here are some of the more useful options:

- **Source OS**: This will attempt to match the operating system of the source traffic.
- **Diffserv Code Point**: A mechanism for providing **Quality of Service** (**QoS**) of network traffic. Systems can prioritize traffic based on their code point values.
- **TCP Flags**: Matches traffic based on whether certain TCP flags are set.
- **State Type**: Specifies a particular state tracking mechanism.

- **No XMLRPC Sync**: This prevents a rule from being synced on other CARP members.
- **Schedule**: Allows you to specify the time when this rule is valid. You must define a schedule entry to use this option; once you do, the schedules defined will appear here.
- **Gateway**: Gateways other than the default one may be specified here.
- **In/Out:** Allows you to specify alternative queues and virtual interfaces. This option is useful if you want to redirect matched traffic into a traffic shaping queue.
- **Ackqueue/Queue**: Specifies alternative acknowledge queues.

Having a separate queue for TCP ACK packets can be an effective way of ensuring that ACK packets are received by a remote server in a timely manner, thus improving download speeds.

See also

- The *Creating an alias* recipe
- The *Creating a NAT port forward rule* recipe
- The *Setting a firewall rule schedule* recipe

Setting a firewall rule schedule

This recipe describes how to create a schedule. Schedules allow us to control when firewall rules are enabled. They are primarily used with firewall rules, but their generic design allows them to be used with many present and future pfSense features. If a firewall rule specifies a schedule, the rule will only be enabled during those hours. In this example, we will create a schedule so that the rule we created in the previous section will only be enabled during work hours (9 AM-5 PM).

When creating and using schedules, it is important to have your NTP time sync settings properly configured, and to synchronize with a reliable server. Also take into account time-zone differences and daylight savings time, when applicable.

How to do it...

1. Navigate to **Firewall | Schedules**.
2. Click on the **Add** button.
3. On the Schedules **Edit** page, enter a name in the **Schedule Name** text field:

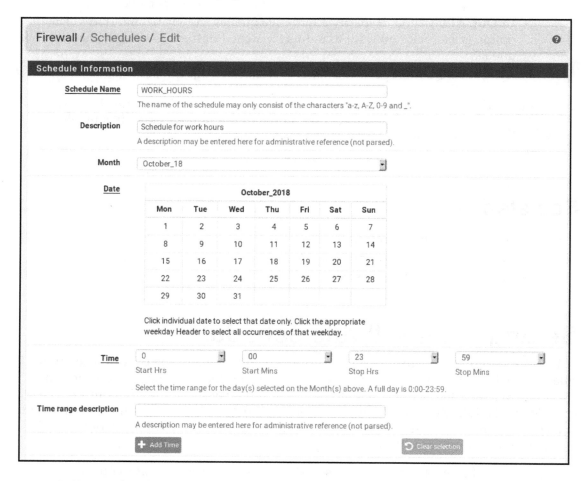

4. Enter a brief non-parsed description in the **Description** text field.
5. You can leave the **Month** set to the current month.

6. On the calendar, click on each of the column headings for weekdays (**Mon, Tue, Wed, Thu, Fri**) to select all weekdays.

7. In the **Time** drop-down menus, select **9:00** as the start time and **17:00** (5:00 PM) as the end time:

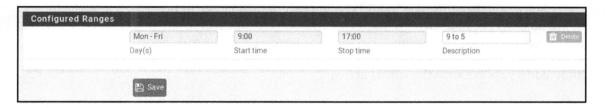

8. You can enter a brief description of the time range in the **Time range description** text field.

9. Click on the **Add Time** button. Note that the time range is now added to the **Configured Ranges** section.

10. Click on the **Save** button.

How it works...

Features associated with a schedule will only be active during the schedule specified. We still have to associate a firewall rule with the schedule entry we just created. To associate the rule that we created in the previous recipe with this schedule entry, we can do the following:

1. Navigate to **Firewall | Rules**.

2. Click on the **LAN** tab to display the LAN firewall rules.

3. Click on the edit icon (the pencil) for the **Block Apple Insider rule**.

4. On the edit page for the firewall rule, click on the **Display Advanced** button.

5. Under **Advanced Options**, scroll down to Schedule. Select the newly created schedule in the drop-down menu.

6. Click on the **Save** button.

7. Click on the **Apply Changes** button to reload the firewall rules.

There's more...

Note that the **Schedule** column for the rule we edited now has the schedule we just added. In the preceding screenshot, the column currently has an icon of a yellow cross, indicating that the rule is currently inactive because it is not between 9 AM and 5 PM on a weekday. If the rule were active, this icon would change to a red stop icon, indicating that traffic is being blocked because this is a block rule (the same result would occur if we selected **Reject** in the **Action** drop-down menu). However, if we create a pass rule and the rule becomes active, the icon will change from yellow to a green play icon, indicating that traffic is allowed to pass because the rule is active.

Selecting dates or days of the week

To select individual dates on which a schedule entry will apply, click on individual dates on the calendar on the **Schedule** edit page. Note that you can select different months using the **Month** drop-down menu if you want to select a date from a future month. To select all instances of a weekday, regardless of the month, click on the appropriate weekday header on the calendar.

See also

- The *Creating an alias* recipe
- The *Creating a firewall rule* recipe
- The Creating a floating rule recipe
- The *Creating a NAT port forward rule* recipe

Creating a floating rule

This recipe describes how to create a floating rule.

Floating firewall rules have several distinct advantages over non-floating rules:

- They can apply to more than one interface at a time. This saves us from having to make copies of essentially identical rules on different interfaces, and is handy in a number of situations in which we want a rule to be in effect on multiple interfaces.

- Whereas conventional firewall rules are only invoked when packets leave an interface, floating firewall rules may be invoked when traffic enters an interface (**in**), when it leaves an interface (**out**), or either direction (**any**).

- In the **Action** drop-down menu, in addition to the **Pass**, **Block**, and **Reject** options that are available for conventional firewall rules, there is a fourth option called **Match**. If this option is selected, the rule will be applied to packets matching the rule, but the pass/block status of the packets will not be affected. This option is often used for traffic shaping, as we can use a **Match** rule to divert certain packets into different queues.

- There is also an option called **Quick**. If we enable the **Quick** checkbox, the rule will be applied to packets that match the rule criteria immediately. If this option is not enabled, however, the rule will not be applied until the conventional per-interface rules have been applied. This option should be used with care, as enabling it will cause a floating rule to supersede per-interface rules.

In this recipe, we will create a floating rule that will recreate the default Allow LAN to any rule, but we will apply it to all local interfaces.

How to do it...

1. Navigate to **Firewall** | **Rules**.
2. Click on the **Floating** tab. The page should display a table of all floating rules:

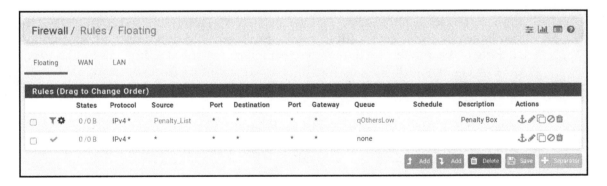

3. Click on the **Add** button with the down arrow to add a new rule to the end of the list.

4. Leave the **Action** set to **Pass**:

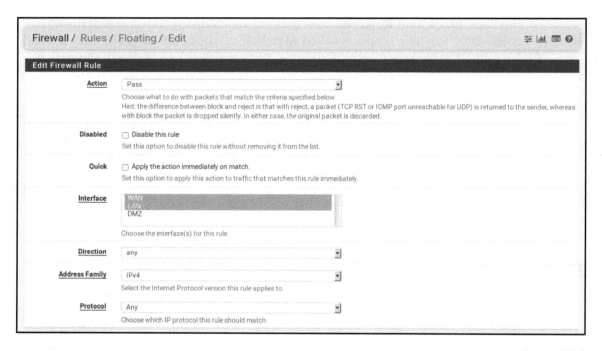

5. In the **Interface** list box, select all local (non-WAN) interfaces, except the DMZ if you have one. To select multiple interfaces, either hold down the *Shift* key while clicking on each interface name (to select interfaces one at a time), or hold down the *Ctrl* key while clicking on the first and last interface (to select multiple interfaces).

6. Change the protocol in the **Protocol** drop-down menu to **Any**.

7. Leave both **Source** and **Destination** set to **any**:

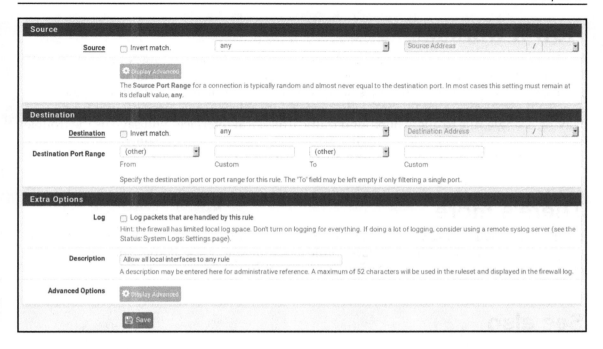

8. Add an appropriate description in the **Description** text field (for example, `Allow all local interfaces to any rule`).
9. When you are done making changes, click on the **Save** button.
10. Click on the **Apply Changes** button to reload the firewall rules.

If you have a DMZ interface, do not select it when selecting interfaces. We generally only want to allow inbound access to the DMZ, not outbound access.

How it works...

We have created a floating rule that replaces all the per-interface **Allow N to any** (when N is the interface) with a single allow rule. Since we did not enable the **Quick** option, it will be invoked after any per-interface rules have been invoked, which is what we want; more specific firewall rules should almost always take precedence over more general rules. Having a single rule to allow outbound traffic from local interfaces will save us the trouble of having to recreate the rule every time we add a new interface (we will just have to edit this rule instead).

There's more...

Floating rules will be used extensively when we are configuring traffic shaping, as they are the primary means by which we place traffic into different traffic shaping queues, as will be demonstrated in Chapter 6, *Traffic Shaping*.

See also

- The *Creating an alias* recipe
- The *Creating a firewall rule* recipe
- The *Setting a firewall rule schedule* recipe
- The *Creating a NAT port forwarding entry* recipe

Creating a NAT port forwarding entry

This recipe will describe how to create a NAT port forwarding entry.

The complexity of **Network Address Translation** (**NAT**) rules varies greatly. In this recipe, we will only cover port forwarding rules. There are actually three other types of NAT rules available in pfSense:

- **Outbound NAT:** As the name implies, this form of NAT applies to outbound traffic and involves replacing local IP addresses and port numbers with the WAN IP and port, so packets can be sent out over the public internet. By default, pfSense is configured to automatically generate outbound NAT rules for local interfaces, but you may have to manually configure outbound NAT rules if you are using a VPN, or in other scenarios in which the automatic rules do not produce the desired result. This form of NAT will be covered in a recipe later in this chapter.

- **1:1 NAT:** This form of NAT is typically invoked when you have a set of public IP addresses (for example, for a web or file server) that need to be mapped to a set of private IP addresses (for example, the local addresses of your servers) in a 1:1 manner. This form of NAT will be covered in a recipe later in this chapter.

- **NPt:** Stands for **Network Prefix Translation**. This is similar to 1:1 NAT, but for IPv6 addresses instead of IPv4 addresses.

Getting ready

In this recipe, we will create a rule that will allow us to SSH into a Raspberry Pi on our DMZ network. Assume the DMZ network's network address is `192.168.2.0/24`, and the Raspberry Pi's IP address is `192.168.2.2`.

How to do it...

1. Navigate to **Firewall | NAT**.
2. If the **Port Forward** tab isn't selected by default, click on **Port Forwarding:**

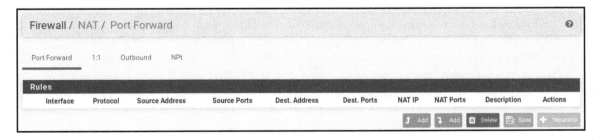

3. Click on the **Add** button with the down arrow to add a new port forwarding rule.

4. Leave the **Interface** set to **WAN:**

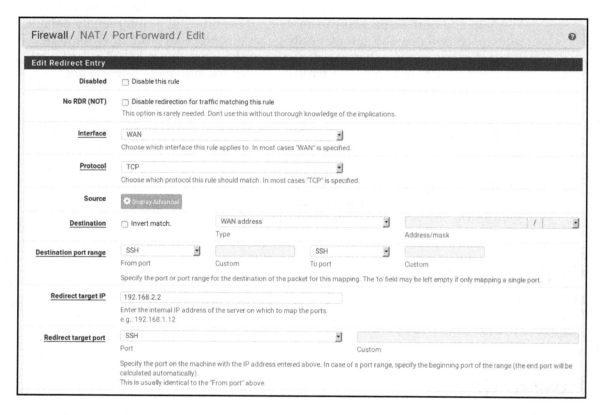

5. Leave the **Protocol** set to **TCP.**
6. For **Destination port range**, select **SSH** in the **From port** drop-down box.
7. In the **Redirect target IP** text field, enter 192.168.2.2.
8. For **Redirect target port**, select **SSH** in the **Port** drop-down menu.
9. You can enter a brief description in the **Description** edit box (for example, NAT rule for Raspberry Pi):

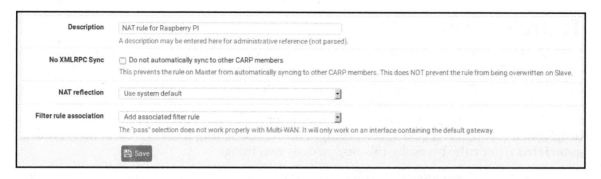

Description	NAT rule for Raspberry PI
	A description may be entered here for administrative reference (not parsed).
No XMLRPC Sync	☐ Do not automatically sync to other CARP members
	This prevents the rule on Master from automatically syncing to other CARP members. This does NOT prevent the rule from being overwritten on Slave.
NAT reflection	Use system default
Filter rule association	Add associated filter rule
	The "pass" selection does not work properly with Multi-WAN. It will only work on an interface containing the default gateway.
	💾 Save

10. Leave **Filter rule association** set to **Add associated filter rule**.
11. Click on the **Save** button when done.
12. Click on the **Apply Changes** button.

Selecting SSH in the drop-down menus for destination port range and redirect target port causes pfSense to insert the default SSH port (22) as the port to which the rule applies. You could also enter 22 in the adjacent edit box and it would have the same effect.

How it works...

All traffic passes through the list of NAT rules. Packets that meet the rule's criteria (interface, protocol, source port range, and destination port range) will be redirected to the **Redirect target IP** and **Redirect target port** specified.

Like all rules in pfSense, NAT rules are evaluated from the top down, and the first rule to match the traffic will be applied. The rest of the rules will be ignored.

There's more...

It should be noted that NAT port forwarding rules and firewall rules are two separate entities. NAT port forwarding forwards traffic, while firewall rules allow or deny traffic. Just because a port forwarding rule exists to forward traffic does not mean that the firewall rule will allow the traffic. If we want to allow traffic, we must create a corresponding firewall rule. Fortunately, pfSense makes life easier for us with the Filter rule association drop-down menu in NAT port forwarding. The default setting for this parameter is **Add associated filter rule**. Invoking this option does two things:

- It will automatically create a firewall rule to allow the traffic (in our case, it will create a WAN interface rule allowing traffic to pass on port 22).
- Because it is an associated filter rule, if we edit the port forwarding rule, pfSense will automatically update the corresponding firewall rule. For example, if we change the destination port range to a different port, pfSense will automatically update the rule to apply to that port.

The other options for filter rule association are as follows:

- **Add unassociated filter rule:** pfSense will create a corresponding firewall rule, but the rule will not be updated if and when you make changes to the port forwarding rule.
- **Pass:** pfSense will pass traffic that matches the port forwarding rule through the firewall rule without creating a corresponding firewall rule. (Thus, we could say pfSense creates an implicit firewall rule.)
- **None:** pfSense will not create a corresponding firewall rule, explicit or implicit.

 Using the **Pass** option could create confusion if you later have to troubleshoot NAT and firewall rules, since there will be an implicit firewall rule that does not appear in any of the firewall tables.

NAT rules can be configured using a variety of options. Here are some of the more commonly used options:

- **Disabled:** You can enable or disable a NAT port forwarding rule with this option.

- **No RDR (NOT):** Enabling this option will disable traffic redirection for this rule. This option can come in handy if you create a port forwarding rule that covers a range of ports, but need to disable port forwarding for a subset of this range. For example, assume we create a NAT port forwarding rule for **Direct Client-to-Client (DCC)**, a subprotocol for file transfers commonly associated with **Internet Relay Chat**, or **IRC**). The rule enables port forwarding on ports 5000 to 5010. For some reason, we want to disable port forwarding on ports 5003 through 5005. By creating a port forwarding rule covering these ports, enabling the No RDR option, and placing it ahead of the original port forwarding rule, we can disable port forwarding on ports 5003-5005.

- **Interface**: Allows you to specify the interface for the NAT rule (usually WAN).

- **Protocol**: Specifies the protocol for the NAT rule. Usually, this is set to TCP (the default), or TCP/UDP, but there are many other options. For example, if you want to create a port forwarding rule for ping traffic, you could set this option to ICMP. Any is also an option.

- **Source:** Typically, the source is set to the default value of any (as with firewall rules, we generally do not care about the source of the traffic). You can, however, specify the source of the traffic here.

- **Source Port Range**: This is also set to any by default, but you can specify your own port range here.

- **Destination**: Most often, destination is set to the WAN address, but you can set it to another address here.

- **Destination Port Range**: This is the port the traffic will be requesting. If we are, for example, creating a port forwarding rule for a web server, we would select HTTP, or just type 80. If we are creating a rule for a custom port, an alias can help clarify the purpose of the rule.

- **Redirect Target IP**: This is the IP address of the internal node to which traffic will be forwarded.

- **Redirect Target Port**: This is the port on the internal node to which traffic will be forwarded

- **Description**: You can enter a brief description here; it will be copied into any associated firewall rules.

- **NAT reflection**: Enabling NAT reflection allows you to use the rule's external IP address (usually the WAN address) on internal networks.

- **Filter Rule Association:** Enables the creation of a corresponding firewall rule.

Port redirection

A port forwarding rule can be used to redirect traffic to an internal node on the same port that was requested. However, we can also redirect traffic to a different port on the internal node. These are a couple of reasons why we might want to do this:

- **Security through obscurity:** The port commonly used for HTTP is port 80. We might have a website that we want to make accessible on the public internet, but we want to keep it secret. By setting the destination port range to a different port, we can have an accessible website that is also secret. In this section, we will use this principle to change the external port of the SSH server to make it less hackable.

- **Single public IP address:** People in environments with only a single IP address may find themselves stuck; for example, they may want to remote access two separate computers using **Remote Desktop Protocol** (**RDP**) on port 3389, but there is only a single IP address. By using port redirection, you can set up one port for one computer and another port for the second computer (for example, 51000 and 51001).

Port redirection example

To provide an example of port redirection, we will modify the rule created in this recipe so it uses a destination port other than 22. To modify the rule, do the following:

1. Navigate to **Firewall | NAT**.
2. Click on the **Edit** icon for the rule we previously created.
3. Change the **Destination port range** to a port other than 22 (select **Other** in the drop-down menu and then type an arbitrary port number in the custom edit box; for example, 12345).
4. When you are done making changes, click on the **Save** button.
5. Click on the **Apply Changes** button.

By changing the Raspberry Pi SSH port forwarding rule, we can now SSH into our Raspberry Pi using whatever port we entered in step 3. Thus, anyone running a port scanner on our site will not see port 22 open and won't know what service is running on the open port.

See also

- The *Creating an alias* recipe
- The *Creating a firewall rule* recipe
- The *Setting a firewall rule schedule* recipe
- The *Creating an outbound NAT entry* recipe

Creating an outbound NAT entry

This recipe will describe how to create an outbound NAT entry.

Outbound NAT is responsible for taking outbound traffic from internal networks and translating internal addresses and ports into external ones. For example, assume that a node with an internal address of 172.16.1.2 requests a web page from a remote site. 172.16.1.2 is an internal address; thus, if it is left as the source IP address in our packet, the web server will not know where to send the web page. In fact, our packet won't even reach the web server, as a properly configured router will block packets with private addresses from reaching the public internet. Outbound NAT solves this problem by performing two tasks:

- Outbound NAT will strip the private, internal address from the packet and replace it with the WAN IP address. Since the WAN IP address is a public IP address, the remote web server will know where to send the web page.
- Outbound NAT has an option to keep the same source port (static), or to change the port (randomize source port). By changing the source port to a random value, the chances of a port conflict on a network with multiple users is reduced.

Outbound NAT is not something you normally have to configure. By default, pfSense will automatically generate outbound NAT rules for all local interfaces and localhost (127.0.0.0/8) addresses. If you navigate to **Firewall** | **NAT** | **Outbound**, you can confirm that this is the case. If you have not altered any of the outbound NAT settings since installing pfSense, there should be two rules for each internal interface (and for localhost):

- A generic [a]uto created rule to translate internal addresses to the WAN address
- An [a]uto created rule for ISAKMP for **Internet Key Exchange** (**IKE**) during the establishment of IPsec VPN tunnels

Given the fact that pfSense can generate outbound NAT rules for us automatically, you might wonder why we would ever have to create our own outbound NAT rules. But there are some cases when we may have to add new rules—for example, a custom VPN configuration, where certain traffic has to be directed to a static port. Altering the outbound NAT rules might also be helpful in certain circumstances. In this recipe, we will consider one such case. Assume that we suspect certain LAN subnet users are using up a disproportionate amount of bandwidth. We can more easily find the total bandwidth used on LAN if we create a virtual IP address for the WAN address and direct outbound NAT traffic to it.

How to do it...

1. Navigate to **Firewall** | **Virtual IPs**.
2. Click on the **Add** button.
3. For **Type**, select **IP Alias**:

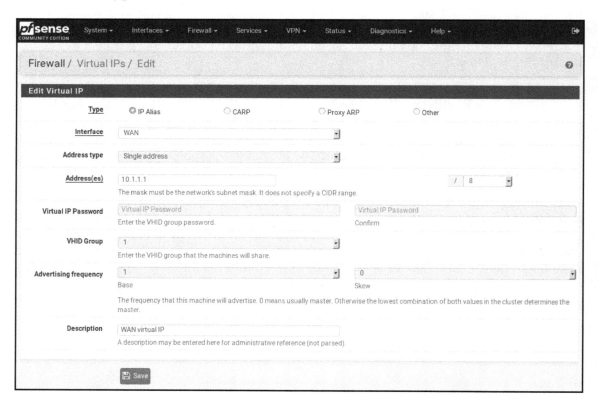

4. Keep the **Interface** set to **WAN** and the **Address type** set to **Single address**.

5. In the **Address** text field, enter a virtual IP for the WAN address (for example, `10.1.1.1/8`). Select the appropriate number of bits in the drop-down box for the subnet mask.

6. Enter a description in the **Description** edit box (for example, `WAN virtual IP`).

7. Click on the **Save** button.

8. Click on the **Apply Changes** button.

9. Navigate to **Firewall | NAT**.

10. Click on the **Outbound** tab.

11. In the **Outbound NAT Mode** section, select **Manual Outbound NAT.**

12. Click on the **Save** button, and then click on **Apply Changes**.

13. You should now have a table with a series of manual outbound NAT rules. Find the Auto created rule – LAN to WAN and click on the **Edit** icon for the rule.

14. In the **Translation** section, change the **Address** to the virtual IP we just created:

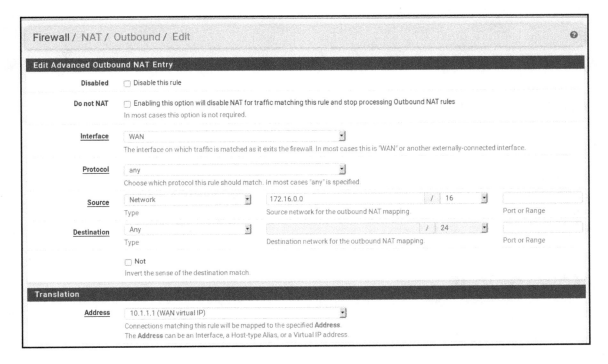

15. Click on the **Save** button.

16. Click on the **Apply Changes** button.

How it works...

We have changed the outbound NAT settings to translate outbound NAT traffic on the LAN interface to the virtual IP address we created for the WAN address. This will make it easier to track LAN traffic.

There's more...

We can track outbound LAN traffic by navigating to **Diagnostics | pfTop** and typing `src` and the virtual IP address for the WAN interface into the filter expression text field.

See also

- The *Creating an alias* recipe
- The *Creating a firewall rule* recipe
- The *Setting a firewall rule schedule* recipe
- The *Creating a 1:1 NAT entry* recipe

Creating a 1:1 NAT entry

This recipe will describe how to create a 1:1 NAT entry.

1:1 NAT allows us to map a single external IP address to a single internal IP address, or we can map an external network to an internal network. We might have a scenario in which we acquired public IP addresses for different resources—for example, a web server. If the web server is a node on one of our private networks, then we must map the public address to the web server's private address.

How to do it...

1. Navigate to **Firewall | NAT**.
2. Click on the **1:1** tab.

3. Click on one of the **Add** buttons to add a new rule.
4. In the **External subnet IP** text field, enter the public IP address:

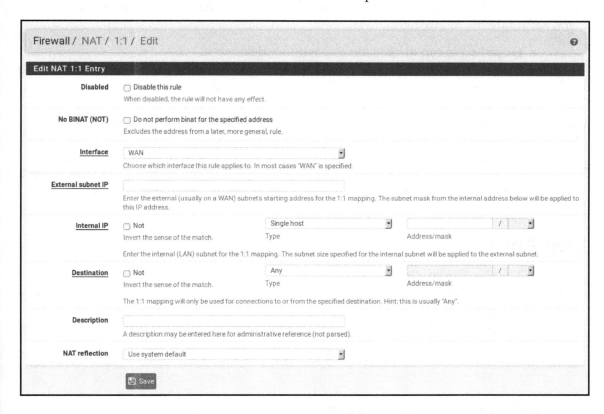

5. Enter the private IP address in the **Internal IP** text field. Leave the drop-down menu set to **Single host**.
6. Leave **Destination** set to **Any**.
7. Enter a brief description in the **Description** text field.
8. When you are done making changes, click on the **Save** button.
9. Click on the **Apply Changes** button.

By adding a 1:1 NAT entry, we can translate an external IP address (or network) to an internal one.

There's more...

There are several other options not mentioned in the recipe that can be helpful in some cases, including the following:

- **Disable:** We can disable the rule without deleting it.
- **No BINAT (NOT):** As with port forwarding, we can disable 1:1 NAT for the specified address or network, thus excluding a subset of addresses from a later, more general rule.
- **Destination**: If we use this option, the 1:1 mapping will only be used for connections to and from the specified destination.
- **NAT reflection**: We can enable or disable NAT reflection, which, if enabled, allows us to use the external IP address specified in the 1:1 mapping from behind the firewall. We can also disable this option, or use the system default.

See also

- The *Creating an alias* recipe
- The *Creating a firewall rule* recipe
- The *Setting a firewall rule schedule* recipe
- The *Creating a port forwarding rule* recipe
- The *Creating an outbound NAT entry* recipe

Creating an NPt entry

This recipe will describe how to create an NPt entry. **NPt**, or **Network Prefix Translation**, allows you to map one IPv6 prefix to another. It is similar to 1:1 NAT, except that with IPv6, translation is more often used with entire prefixes and not single IP addresses.

How to do it...

1. Navigate to **Firewall** | **NAT**.
2. Click on the **NPt** tab.

3. Click on one of the **Add** buttons to add a new entry.
4. Choose the appropriate interface in the **Interface** drop-down menu (you can usually leave this set to **WAN**):

5. In the first **Address** text field, enter the internal IPv6 prefix, and select the correct CIDR in the corresponding drop-down menu.
6. In the second **Address** edit box, enter the external IPv6 prefix, and select the correct CIDR in the corresponding drop-down menu.
7. Enter a brief description in the **Description** text field.
8. When you are done making changes, click on the **Save** button.
9. Click on the **Apply Changes** button.

How it works...

NPt enables you to map an internal IPv6 prefix to an external one. It should be noted, however, that NPt does not function like traditional network address translation or port address translation, and you cannot use NPt to map an internal prefix to a prefix in use on a WAN interface. Rather, NPt must be used with a routed subnet.

Enabling UPnP and NAT-PnP

UPnP and NAT-PnP are different implementations of the same concept. They both allow for automated port mapping. These protocols are both designed to make it easy for clients to automatically configure port mapping. UPnP is commonly associated with Microsoft-based systems, while NAT-PnP is more commonly associated with Apple.

In this recipe, we will describe how to enable UPnP and NAT-PnP.

How to do it...

1. Navigate to **Services** | **UPnP and NAT-PnP**.
2. Check the **Enable UPnP and NAT-PnP** checkbox.
3. Check the **Allow UPnP Port Mapping** checkbox, or the **Allow NAT-PnP Port Mapping** checkbox, or both:

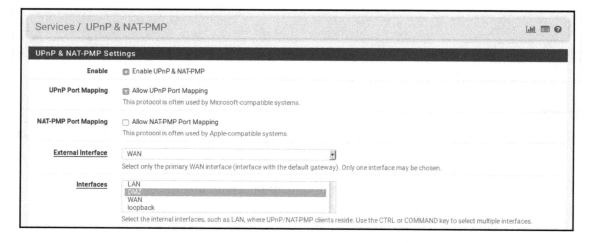

4. In the **Interfaces** list, select the interfaces to which UPnP/NAT-PnP will be applied.
5. When you are done making changes, click on the **Save** button.

How it works...

Enabling UPnP and NAT-PnP allows certain devices (for example, game consoles) to function properly on your network without having to define specific port forwarding rules.

There's more...

The following options are also available when configuring UPnP and NAT-PnP:

- Specify a **Maximum Download Speed** for devices
- Specify a **Maximum Upload Speed** for devices
- Specify the **Override WAN Address** for devices (you can specify a virtual IP here)
- Specify the **Traffic Shaping Queue** for devices
- **Enable Log Packets handled by UPnP and NAT-PnP clients**
- **Use System Uptime instead of UPnP and NAT-PnP uptime**
- **Default Deny access to UPnP and NAT-PnP**
- Define one or more **ACL Entries** to allow or deny entry to certain clients
- Define a **Custom presentation URL** for UPnP and NAT-PnP clients
- Define a **Custom model number** instead of the pfSense firmware version for UPnP and NAT-PnP clients

Security warning

Allowing external devices to make and modify their own port forwarding rules has security implications. If you plan to use these services, be aware of the risk. In such circumstances, it might be a good idea to dedicate a separate interface for these services (and other risky traffic). If you aren't using your DMZ for any other services, you might consider using the DMZ.

See also

- pfSense UPnP and NAT-PnP documentation: `https://www.netgate.com/docs/pfsense/services/configuring-upnp-and-nat-pmp.html`
- Wikipedia UPnP article: `https://en.wikipedia.org/wiki/Universal_Plug_and_Play`
- Wikipedia NAT-PnP documentation: `https://en.wikipedia.org/wiki/NAT_Port_Mapping_Protocol`

Additional Services 4

In previous chapters, we covered everything essential to the core functionality of pfSense. In Chapter 1, *Initial Configuration*, and Chapter 2, *Essential Services*, we covered the steps necessary for maintaining a fully-functional pfSense system, and in Chapter 3, *Firewall and NAT*, we covered firewall and NAT rules, which allow pfSense to act as a firewall.

In this chapter, we will cover services that are not as essential as those already covered but are nonetheless services that many homes and SOHO users will likely want to utilize. Demonstrating how to set up a captive portal covers a large portion of this chapter. There are several different ways of configuring a captive portal in pfSense, and we will cover all of them. In this chapter, we will cover the following recipes:

- Creating a captive portal without authentication
- Creating a captive portal with voucher authentication
- Creating a captive portal with User Manager authentication
- Creating a captive portal with RADIUS authentication
- Configuring NTP
- Configuring SNMP

Introduction

When a captive portal is enabled on a network, a user trying to access that network will first be directed to a web page. That web page, at a minimum, will usually require the user to agree to the terms of service for a network, and may require some form of authentication. Although captive portals can be used with both wired and wireless networks, they are more commonly used to provide a gateway to a wireless network.

Implementing a captive portal is potentially beneficial for several reasons. First, they provide an easy way of separating guest traffic from other network traffic, thus keeping guests away from sensitive company data. Second, we can collect data on individual captive portal users, making it easy to identify users that are over-utilizing resources (for example, users downloading large files or constantly streaming video). The captive portal page is a good place to put your **End User Licence Agreement** (**EULA**); a captive portal user's assent to such an agreement potentially protects you or your company from legal liability. Finally, a captive portal page can be a good way to market your company's product to customers. You can place special offers on this page, as well as links to your company's social media pages.

pfSense provides several ways of implementing a captive portal on your network. You can have a captive portal page that does not require authentication. You can also perform authentication through either vouchers or the **User Manager**. Finally, you can perform authentication through a separate RADIUS server.

Creating a captive portal without authentication

In this recipe, we will demonstrate how to create a captive portal that requires no user authentication.

A captive portal provides a means of controlling access to a network. Captive portals are typically used to redirect users of a network that provides outbound internet access to a web page that displays the company's terms of service. For that reason, it is often used when companies provide WiFi access to their customers. In some cases, you may only want to display the terms of service and not require any user authentication. In other cases, you may want to require authentication; fortunately, pfSense supports several types of authentication.

In this recipe, we will demonstrate the simplest form of captive portal configuration—setting up a captive portal that requires no authentication.

Getting ready

In order to set up a captive portal on an interface, the DHCP (or DHCP6) server must be running on the interface. To enable the DHCP or DHCP6 server, see `Chapter 2`, *Essential Services, Configuring the DHCP server* and the *Configuring the DHCP6 server* recipes. It is generally good practice to set up a separate interface for captive portal traffic.

How to do it...

1. Navigate to **Services** | **Captive Portal:**

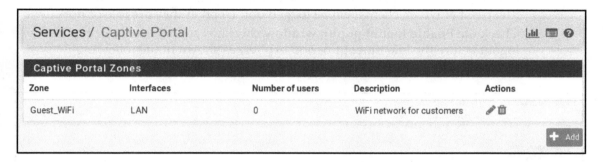

2. Click on the **Add** button.
3. Enter a name into the **Zone name** edit box and a brief description into the **Zone description** edit box.
4. When done, click on the **Save and Continue** button.
5. When the page loads, it should default to the **Configuration** tab. Check the **Enable Captive Portal** checkbox to display other captive portal configuration options.
6. In the **Interfaces** list box, select the interface(s) on which the captive portal will be enabled. If you do not have a separate interface for captive portal traffic and you have added a DMZ, you can select **DMZ**, as shown in the following screenshot:

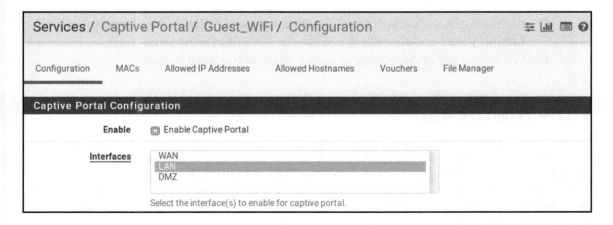

7. In the **Idle timeout** edit box, enter a reasonable value for the idle timeout (for example, 10 minutes).

8. In the **Hard timeout** edit box, enter a reasonable value for the hard timeout (for example, 60 minutes), or leave this field blank if you do not want a hard timeout (the point at which clients will be logged out, whether they are idle or not).

9. Check the **Enable logout popup window** checkbox so that users can explicitly logout before the idle timeout period expires, as shown in the following screenshot:

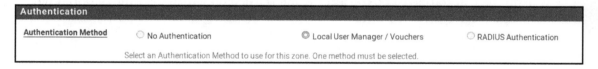

10. In the **After authentication Redirection URL** edit box, enter a redirection URL (for example, `www.google.com`).

11. Scroll down to the **Authentication** section, and make sure **No Authentication** is selected as the authentication method, as shown in the following screenshot:

Authentication		
Authentication Method	○ No Authentication ◉ Local User Manager / Vouchers ○ RADIUS Authentication	
	Select an Authentication Method to use for this zone. One method must be selected.	

12. For the moment, we will leave the **Portal** page, **Authentication error** page, and **Logout** pages undefined; we can use the default pfSense pages.

13. When you are done making changes, click on the **Save** button.

How it works...

By creating a captive portal, any user who attempts to connect to one of the networks on which the captive portal is enabled will first have to click on the **Accept** button on the **Portal** page to pass through the captive portal. The user will then be redirected to the Google home page, after which they will have access to the network and will be able to use the internet. This is enabled until the hard timeout limit is reached or a user logs out; whichever comes first.

There's more...

All three captive portal pages (the portal page, authentication error page, and logout page) can be customized to fit your organization's styling. The easiest way to do this is to edit the page in the HTML editor of your choice, save the file, and then upload the page to pfSense using the appropriate **Browse** button in the **HTML Page Contents** section. If the authentication method selected is **No Authentication**, the portal page does not need to have fields for the username and password; it only needs a button for accepting the terms of service, for example `<input name="accept" type="submit" value="Continue">`. A logout page only needs a message indicating the user has logged out of the network, but you can add your company's logo on this page if desired. The authentication error page needs only a message indicating that the login attempt has failed.

If you are not experienced in coding web pages, there are many sites that have sample captive portal login pages that you can customize to fit your needs. We have included several example captive portal login pages you can use at: `https://github.com/dzient/learn_pfsense/tree/master/ch4`.

In subsequent captive portal recipes, we will customize the captive portal HTML pages using the pages contained in our GitHub repository.

See also

- The *Creating a captive portal with voucher authentication* recipe
- The *Creating a captive portal with User Manager authentication* recipe
- The *Creating a captive portal with RADIUS authentication* recipe

Creating a captive portal with voucher authentication

In this recipe, we will create a captive portal with authentication through pfSense's voucher system. Vouchers are an ideal form of authentication in scenarios where you want to provide access to one of your networks on a temporary basis. Setting up access via vouchers involves generating a series of voucher codes that are then issued to users. These vouchers are good for a fixed period of time (you can define this period). You can also track network usage by keeping track of which voucher codes are given to certain users.

How to do it...

1. Navigate to **Services** | **Captive Portal**.
2. Click on the **Add** button.
3. Enter a name into the **Zone name** edit box and a brief description into the **Zone description** edit box.
4. When done, click on the **Save and Continue** button.
5. When the page loads, it should default to the **Configuration** tab. Check the **Enable Captive Portal** checkbox to display other captive portal configuration options.
6. In the **Interfaces** list box, select the interface(s) on which the captive portal will be enabled.
7. Enter reasonable values in the **Idle timeout** and **Hard timeout** edit boxes.
8. Check the **Enable logout popup window** checkbox so that users can explicitly log out before the idle timeout period expires.
9. In the **After authentication Redirection URL** edit box, enter a redirection URL (such as `www.google.com`).
10. Scroll down to the **Authentication** section and make sure **Local User Manager/Vouchers** is selected, as shown in the following screenshot:

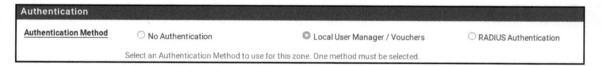

11. Scroll down to **HTML Page Contents**. For voucher authentication, we will define a custom page. In the **Portal page** contents section, click on the **Browse** button and upload a page for voucher authentication. The page must have the two following fields:
    - `<input name="auth_voucher" type="text">`
    - `<input name="accept" type="submit" value="Continue">`

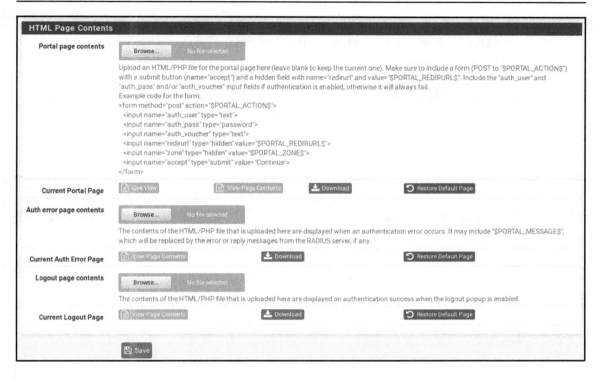

12. When you are done making changes, click on the **Save** button.
13. Voucher authentication is now configured, but we still need to generate voucher codes. To do this, click on the **Vouchers** tab, as shown in the following screenshot:

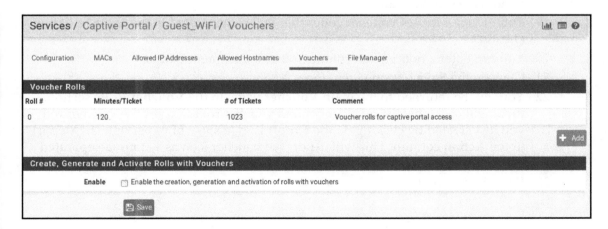

14. Check the **Enable the creation, generation and activation of rolls with vouchers** checkbox to begin the voucher creation process.

15. Click on the **Save** button.

16. When the page reloads, there will be a new section at the top of the page, **Voucher Rolls**. Click on the **Add** button in this section to add a voucher roll.

17. Enter a 16-bit number in the **Roll** # edit box (0-65535). This number will be found on the top of the generated voucher roll, as shown in the following screenshot:

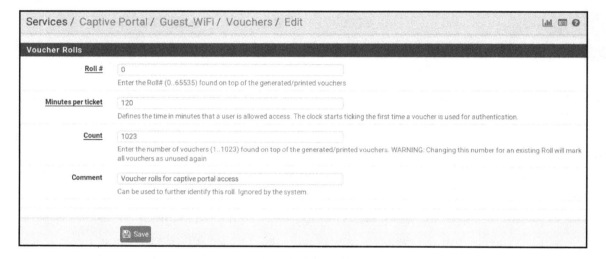

18. Enter the number of minutes each user is allowed per voucher code in the **Minutes per ticket** edit box.

19. Enter the number of voucher codes that will be generated in the **Count** edit box (1-1023).

20. You can enter a non-parsed comment in the **Comment** edit box.

21. Click on the **Save** button when done.

22. You will be returned to the main **Voucher** page. In the **Voucher Rolls** section, there will be a table listing all generated voucher rolls. Export the voucher roll you just created by clicking on the **Export** icon (a sheet of paper with an X on it) in the **Action** column. This will export the voucher icon as a **comma-separated value** (CSV) file that can be opened with a text editor or spreadsheet.

23. Repeat steps 16 through 22 for as many voucher rolls as you wish to generate.

How it works...

In the preceding recipe, we performed two separate tasks. The first was to enable a captive portal on one or more interfaces, using **Local User Manager/Vouchers** as the authentication method. The second task was to generate one or more voucher rolls containing voucher codes for use with the captive portal. Once the voucher rolls are generated, we can use those voucher codes for authentication. If voucher codes are the only form of authentication we use, then we don't have to maintain a database of captive portal users, making voucher authentication the easiest form of authentication available.

There's more...

On the **Vouchers** tab, there were several options available that are worthy of further explanation:

- **Voucher Public Key/Voucher Private Key:** In these two text boxes, you may enter an RSA public/private key pair of your choice – or you can use the pair that pfSense has generated for you. You can also click on the **Generate new keys** button in the **Voucher Public Key** section to generate a new public/private key pair.
- **Character set:** This field allows you to define the character set used in generated voucher codes.
- **# of Roll bits/# of Ticket bits/# of Checksum bits:** You can change the numbers in these fields to redefine the range of each. For example, the default number of roll bits is 16; the default number of ticket bits is 10. This allows us to define roll numbers from 0 to 65535, and each voucher roll can have up to 1,023 codes. If we needed to generate a greater number of codes per roll, we could change the number of ticket bits to 12, thus allowing us up to 4,096 codes per roll. The only restriction is that the sum of the roll, ticket, and checksum (the checksum field defines the size of the checksum over roll and ticket) bits must be one less than the RSA key size, as shown in the following screenshot:

# of Roll bits	16
	Reserves a range in each voucher to store the Roll # it belongs to. Allowed range: 1..31. Sum of Roll+Ticket+Checksum bits must be one Bit less than the RSA key size.
# of Ticket bits	10
	Reserves a range in each voucher to store the Ticket# it belongs to. Allowed range: 1..16. Using 16 bits allows a roll to have up to 65535 vouchers. A bit array, stored in RAM and in the config, is used to mark if a voucher has been used. A bit array for 65535 vouchers requires 8 KB of storage.
# of Checksum bits	5
	Reserves a range in each voucher to store a simple checksum over Roll # and Ticket#. Allowed range is 0..31.

- **Voucher Database Synchronization:** This section allows you to define the IP address, port, username, and password for the master voucher database node. Setting up a voucher database that is synchronized over multiple pfSense nodes allows you to ensure that used voucher codes are marked as used on all nodes. You can leave these fields blank in the following instances:
    - There is only one pfSense node on your network, thus eliminating the need for synchronization
    - This is the only pfSense node on which the captive portal is enabled
    - This is the master voucher database node (the page warns us that this option should only be used on slave nodes)

See also

- The *Creating a captive portal without authentication* recipe
- The *Creating a captive portal with User Manager authentication* recipe
- The *Creating a captive portal with RADIUS authentication* recipe

Creating a captive portal with User Manager authentication

In this section, we will demonstrate how to create a captive portal with **User Manager** authentication. In some circumstances, we may want to maintain a database of users allowed to use the captive portal on our system. In such cases, we have two options: authentication through pfSense's built-in **User Manager**, or authentication through an external RADIUS server. Since authentication through the User Manager is by far the easier option, we will demonstrate how to authenticate with the **User Manager** first.

How to do it...

1. Navigate to **Services | Captive Portal**.
2. Click on the **Add** button.
3. Enter a name in the **Zone name** edit box and a brief description into the **Zone description** edit box.
4. When done, click on the **Save and Continue** button.

5. When the page loads, it should default to the **Configuration** tab. Check the **Enable Captive Portal** checkbox to display other captive portal configuration options.

6. In the **Interfaces** list box, select the interface(s) on which the captive portal will be enabled.

7. Enter reasonable values in the **Idle timeout** and **Hard timeout** edit boxes, as shown in the following screenshot:

Idle timeout (Minutes)	
	Clients will be disconnected after this amount of inactivity. They may log in again immediately, though. Leave this field blank for no idle timeout.
Hard timeout (Minutes)	
	Clients will be disconnected after this amount of time, regardless of activity. They may log in again immediately, though. Leave this field blank for no hard timeout (not recommended unless an idle timeout is set).

8. Check the **Enable logout popup window** checkbox so that users can explicitly log out before the idle timeout period expires.

9. In the **After authentication Redirection URL** edit box, enter a redirection URL (such as www.google.com).

10. Scroll down to the **Authentication** section and make sure **Local User Manager/Vouchers** is selected.

11. Check the **Allow only users/groups with "Captive portal login" privilege** checkbox.

12. Scroll down to **HTML Page Contents**. We will upload a custom page for authentication (**Portal page contents**). If desired, you can use a portal page that allows entering a voucher code or a username/password combination. At a minimum, your portal page must contain the following fields:
    - `<input name="auth_user" type="text">`
    - `<input name="auth_pass" type="password">`
    - `<input name="accept" type="submit" value="Continue">`

    You can also click on the **Restore Default Page** button in the **Portal** page's contents section to use pfSense's default captive portal login page.

13. When you are done, click on the **Save** button.

14. We have set up the captive portal, but we now need to add one or more users using the **User Manager**, allowing authorized users to log in. Only users with the captive portal login privilege enabled will be able to use our captive portal. Navigate to **System | User Manager**.

15. Click on the **Groups** tab, as shown in the following screenshot:

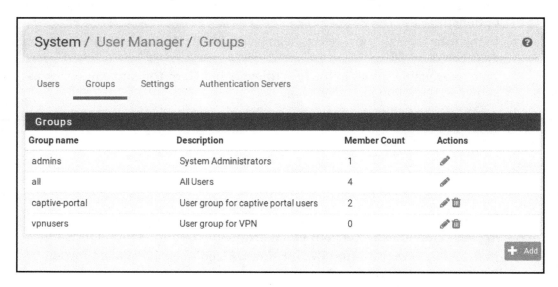

16. Click on the **Add** button to add a new group.
17. Enter a name in the **Group name** edit box (such as `captive-portal`):

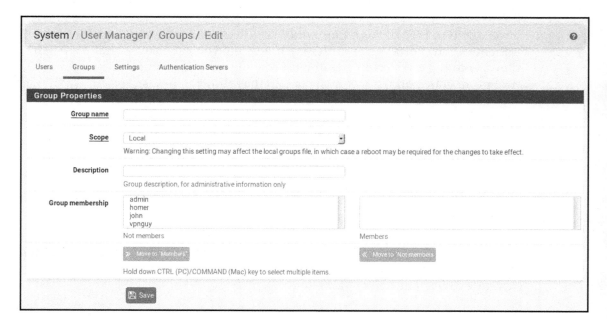

18. Enter a brief description in the **Description** edit box, as shown in the preceding screenshot.
19. Click on the **Save** button.
20. We must now edit the newly-created group and add the necessary permissions. Click on the **Edit** icon for the group.
21. There will be a new section on the edit page for the group called **Assigned Privileges**. In this section, click on the **Add button**.
22. The **Assigned privileges** list box should have an entry called **User – Services: Captive Portal login**. Click on this entry to select it, as shown in the following screenshot:

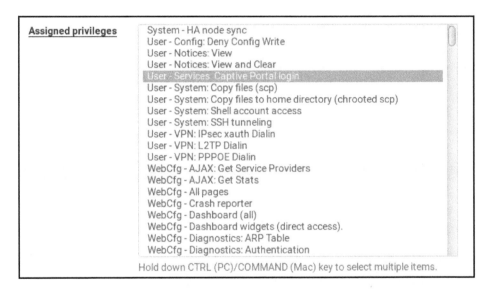

23. Click on the **Save** button when you are done. The captive portal login should now be in the **Assigned Privileges** list, as shown in the following screenshot:

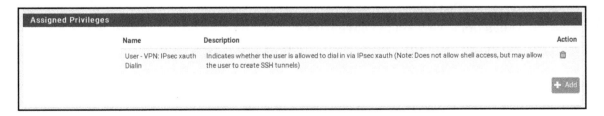

24. Click on the **Users** tab.

25. Click on the **Add** button.
26. Enter a username and password combination in the **Username** and **Password** edit boxes, as shown in the following screenshot:

27. Enter the user's full name in the **Full name** edit box.
28. In the **Group membership** section, make the user a member of the newly-created captive portal group by clicking on the group in the leftmost list box and clicking on the **Move to "Member of" list** button. The group should move to the rightmost list box.
29. When done, click on the **Save** button.
30. Repeat steps 25 to 29 for as many users as you wish to add.

How it works...

In the first section, we added a captive portal that accepts authentication via the **User Manager.** Since there is a single option for both **User Manager** and voucher authentication, we could accept authentication from both at the same time.

 If **Local User Manager/Vouchers** is selected as the authentication method, voucher authentication can be used even if the **Allow only users/groups with "Captive portal login"** privilege set is enabled. You will need a portal page that has fields for a user's username, password, and voucher code in order to accept both forms of authentication.

See also

- The *Creating a captive portal without authentication* recipe
- The *Creating a captive portal with voucher authentication* recipe
- The *Creating a captive portal with RADIUS authentication* recipe

Creating a captive portal with RADIUS authentication

This recipe describes how to create a captive portal that will use a RADIUS server for authentication. **RADIUS**, which stands for **Remote Authentication Dial-In User Service**, is a network protocol that provides centralized **Authentication, Authorization, and Accounting** (**AAA**) management. It is implemented on a number of different platforms, including UNIX and Microsoft Windows servers. It is also often used by **internet service providers** (**ISP**) to provide access to the internet and email services. RADIUS operates on port 1812 and is an application-layer protocol. Although it was initially developed by a private company (Livingston Enterprises, Inc.), it now exists as an IETF standard. Authentication and authorization are described in RFC 2865, while accounting is described in RFC 2866.

Getting ready

Creating a captive portal that uses RADIUS is not that difficult. You can either use an external RADIUS server installed on a separate computer, or you can use a RADIUS server installed on your pfSense system. If you choose the latter, setup is relatively easy, as FreeRADIUS, an implementation of RADIUS licensed under the GNU General Public License version 2, is available as an installable package. In this recipe, we will install this package and use it as our RADIUS server.

How to do it...

1. Navigate to **System | Package Manager**.
2. Click on the **Available Packages** tab.
3. Scroll down to find the **freeradius3** package. Click on the corresponding **Install** button.
4. You will be redirected to the **Package Installer** tab. Confirm the installation by clicking on the **Confirm** button. A text box will appear that updates you on the installation status; installation should not take more than a couple of minutes.
5. When the installation is complete, you can begin RADIUS configuration by navigating to **Services | FreeRADIUS**.
6. Click on the **Interfaces** tab. Here, you will set up the ports for **Accounting, Authentication**, and **Status,**, as shown in the following screenshot:

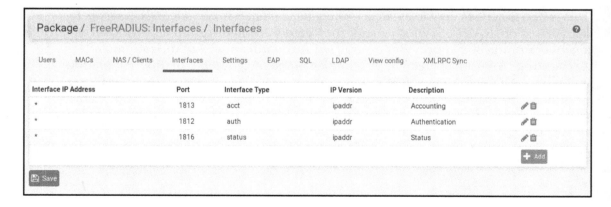

7. Click on the **Add** button and set up the authentication port, keeping the following things in mind:
   - You can keep the **Interface IP Address** as * (in which case the RADIUS server will listen on all interfaces).
   - **Port** should be kept at its default value of **1812**.
   - Keep **Interface Type** set to its default value of **Authentication**.
   - Keep **IP Version** set to its default value of **IPv4**, unless your system is using IPv6, in which case you can select **IPv6** in the **IP Version** dropdown box.
   - Enter a brief description in the **Description** edit box.
   - Click on the **Save** button when you are done.

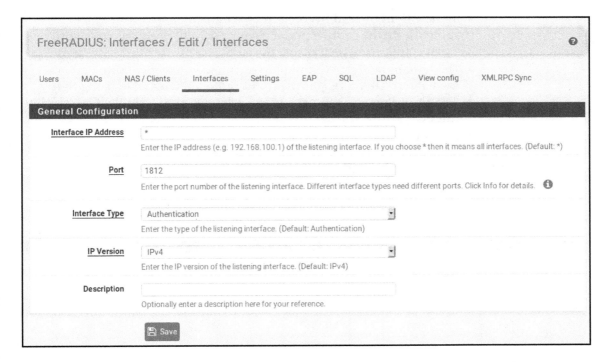

8. Repeat step 7 for the other two ports. Set one port's **Interface Type** to **Accounting** with a **Port** value of **1813**. Set another port's **Interface Type** to **Status** with a **Port** value of 1816. If there are other ports you wish to configure, you can repeat this process, but once the **Accounting**, **Authentication**, and **Status** ports are added, we have set up the bare minimum we need to for RADIUS to work.

9. Click on the **NAS / Clients** tab. We must add the pfSense captive portal as a client.

10. Click on the **Add** button. Now we can begin client configuration with the following steps:

- Enter the pfSense system's IP address in the **Client IP Address** edit box. Since we installed the RADIUS server onto the pfSense system, we can enter the loopback address here (127.0.0.1).

- The **Client IP Version** can be kept at its default value of **IPv4**, unless you are using IPv6 on your system, in which case change the value to **IPv6**.

- Enter a name in the **Client Shortname** edit box (such as Captive-portal).

- In the **Client Shared Secret** edit box, enter a password that will authenticate the captive portal client. You will need this password later when configuring the captive portal.

- The remaining fields can remain unchanged for now (note that you can use either UDP or TCP as the client protocol, with UDP being the default protocol). You may enter a brief description in the **Description** edit box.

- When you are done, click on the **Save** button:

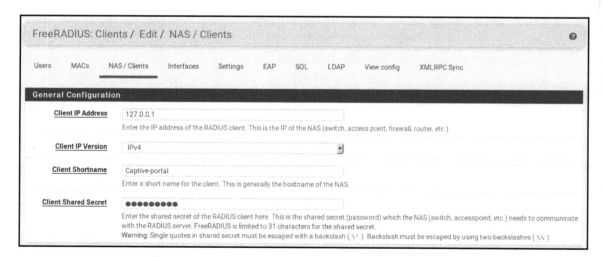

11. Click on the **Users** tab. Here, we can add one or more captive portal users.
12. Click on the **Add** button and configure the following:
    - Add a username/password combination in the **Username** and **Password** edit boxes.
    - You can leave **Password Encryption** set to **Cleartext-Password**, unless you need to have encrypted passwords; in which case, you can change this setting to **MD5**.
    - Click on the **Save** button when you are done.

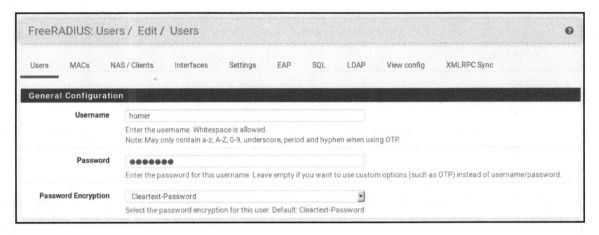

13. Repeat step 12 for as many users as you wish to add.
14. Navigate to **Services | Captive Portal**.
15. Click on the **Add** button.
16. Enter a name into the **Zone name** edit box and a brief description into the **Zone description** edit box.
17. When done, click on the **Save and Continue** button.
18. When the page loads, it should default to the **Configuration** tab. Check the **Enable Captive Portal** checkbox to display other captive portal configuration options.
19. In the **Interfaces** list box, select the interface(s) on which the captive portal will be enabled.
20. Enter reasonable values in the **Idle timeout** and **Hard timeout** edit boxes.

21. Check the **Enable logout popup window** checkbox so that users can explicitly log out before the idle timeout period expires.

22. In the **After authentication Redirection URL** edit box, enter a redirection URL (such as `www.google.com`).

23. Scroll down to the **Authentication** section and set **Authentication Method** to **RADIUS Authentication**, as shown in the following screenshot:

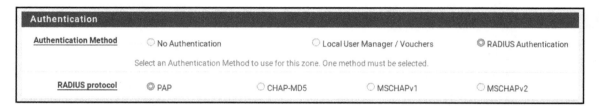

24. You can keep **RADIUS Protocol** set to **PAP**, unless you set **Password Encryption** to **MD5** in step 12, in which case you should select **CHAP-MD5**.

25. For the **Primary RADIUS Server**, enter the **IP Address** (`127.0.0.1`), **RADIUS port** (`1812`), and **RADIUS shared secret** (whatever you entered as the `Client Shared Secret` in step 10):

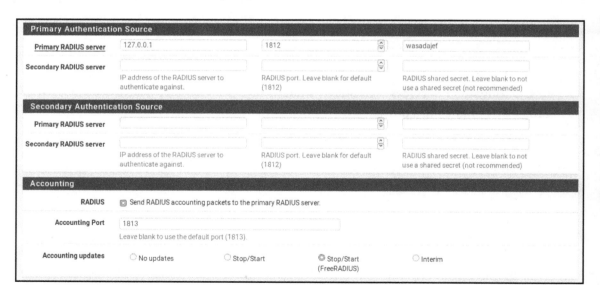

26. Scroll down to **Accounting**. You don't have to set up accounting, but it will potentially make troubleshooting easier if you do. To set up accounting, do the following:
    - Check the **Send RADIUS accounting packets to the primary RADIUS server** checkbox.
    - Set the **Accounting port** to 1813.
    - Set **Accounting updates** to **Stop/Start (FreeRADIUS)**.

27. Set the **RADIUS NAS IP Attribute** to the IP address of the interface on which the captive portal is running.

28. You can enable MAC authentication by checking the **RADIUS MAC Authentication** checkbox. If you enable this option, the RADIUS server will use the end user's MAC address as the username and the value entered in the MAC authentication secret edit box as the password. This is a useful option if you don't want to configure separate user accounts but still want to keep track of different users. If this option is used, any username entered in the **Username** field on the captive portal login page will be ignored, as shown in the following screenshot:

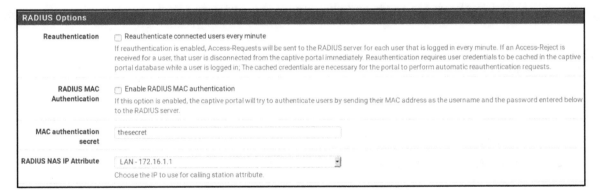

29. Scroll down to **HTML Page Contents** and make sure an appropriate page is configured for **Portal page contents** (it must have a username and password field), or just use the pfSense default page by clicking on the **Restore default page** button.

30. When you are done making changes, click on the **Save** button.

How it works...

We have configured a captive portal that uses a RADIUS server for authentication. Thus, logging in to the captive portal involves the following steps:

1. The end user enters their credentials on the captive portal login page and clicks on the **Login** button
2. The pfSense captive portal takes these credentials, logs into the RADIUS server, and passes on the credentials to the RADIUS server
3. The RADIUS server either authenticates or rejects the login attempt, depending on whether the credentials are valid

In this recipe, we installed freeradius3, the FreeRADIUS package, one of many third-party packages available for pfSense which can be used to extend the functionality of your pfSense system beyond what the base installation provides. If the base installation does not provide the functionality you require, be sure to check what packages are available before assuming it is a lost cause. You can do this by browsing to **System | Package Manager** and clicking on the **Available Packages** tab.

See also

- The *Creating a captive portal without authentication* recipe
- The *Creating a captive portal with voucher authentication* recipe
- The *Creating a captive portal with User Manager authentication* recipe
- The Wikipedia RADIUS page: https://en.wikipedia.org/wiki/RADIUS

Configuring NTP

This recipe describes how to configure NTP on your pfSense system. **Network Time Protocol** (**NTP**), is an application-layer protocol. The purpose of NTP is to synchronize internet-connected devices to within a few milliseconds of Coordinated Universal Time (UTC). In most cases, the minimal configuration done when pfSense is initially set up is enough to ensure that the time on your pfSense system is accurate. You may, however, want to perform additional configuration under some circumstances. For example, if your system is part of a certificate-validating infrastructure, or if you're running pfSense on an embedded system that does not have its own clock.

In this recipe, we will configure NTP and add several more NTP pools.

How to do it...

1. Navigate to **Services | NTP**. You should be on the default **Settings** tab, as shown in the following screenshot:

2. In the **Interface** list box, select **WAN** as the interface on which to listen.
3. Click on the **Add** button to add a new pool or server.
4. Type `0.pool.ntp.org` in the hostname edit box for the new server. Leave the **Is a Pool** checkbox checked.
5. Repeat steps 3 and 4 for `1.pool.ntp.org`, `2.pool.ntp.org`, and `3.pool.ntp.org`.

We have added several pools to our NTP configuration. The system will now try to find the closest available servers for us.

There's more...

Google has made available a set of public NTP servers. They can be found at the following hostnames and IP addresses:

Hostname	IP Address
time.google.com	216.239.35.0
time2.google.com	216.239.35.4
time3.google.com	216.239.35.8
time4.google.com	216.239.35.12

Configuring SNMP

In this recipe, we will configure **Simple Network Management Protocol** (**SNMP**) for use in pfSense. **SNMP** is a standard protocol that enables SNMP clients to query status information on devices that support SNMP.

Getting ready

SNMP-managed networks consist of managed devices, software that runs on managed devices (known as agents), and software running on the manager, known as the **network management station** (**NMS**). Management data is stored in **management information bases** (**MIBs**), which are hierarchical structures.

Enabling SNMP on pfSense enables it to act as a network management station. SNMP is implemented on pfSense/FreeBSD via the bsnmpd service.

How to do it...

1. Navigate to **Services | SNMP**.
2. Check the **Enable SNMP Daemon** checkbox, as shown in the following screenshot:

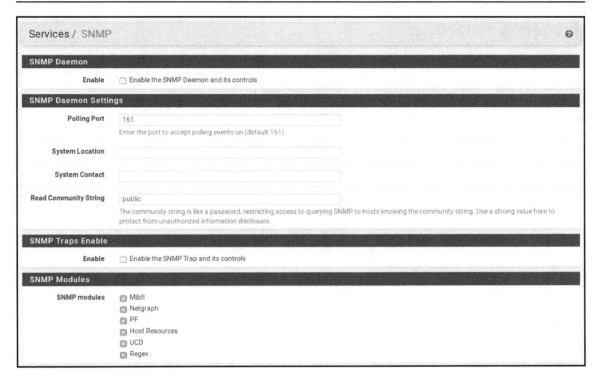

3. Leave the **Polling Port** set to the default value of 161.

4. Optionally, enter a location and contact name in the **System Location** and **System Contact** edit boxes.

5. In the **Read Community String** edit box, enter a passphrase. This string is roughly equivalent to a password, restricting access to querying SNMP to devices specifying the correct community string.

6. In the **SNMP Modules** section, specify the modules to be queried by checking the appropriate checkboxes.

7. In the **Interface Binding** section, choose the interfaces on which to listen (the default value is **All**).

8. When you are done making changes, click on the **Save** button.

By enabling SNMP on pfSense, the system can now query vital SNMP information from different SNMP agents.

There's more...

SNMP traps are sent by SNMP-capable devices to specified servers when a significant event occurs. SNMP trap servers then decide how to process and handle the event. For example, a trap server can e-mail a network administrator. This is useful for network administrators who want to receive alerts quickly, rather than wait for a potentially long polling cycle to complete.

To specify a trap server in pfSense, take the following steps:

1. Navigate to **Services | SNMP**.
2. Check the **Enable SNMP Traps** checkbox.
3. Enter the trap server hostname in the **Trap Server Name** edit box.
4. Enter the port in the **Trap Server Port** edit box.
5. Enter a string in the **Trap Server String** edit box.
6. Click on the **Save** button.

See also

- pfSense SNMP documentation: `https://www.netgate.com/docs/pfsense/services/snmp-daemon.html`
- Wikipedia's SNMP page: `https://en.wikipedia.org/wiki/Simple_Network_Management_Protocol`

5
Virtual Private Networking

In this chapter, we will cover the following:

- Configuring the IPsec VPN service – peer-to-peer
- Configuring the IPsec VPN service – client/server
- Connecting to the IPsec VPN service
- Configuring the OpenVPN service
- Connecting to the OpenVPN service
- Configuring the L2TP VPN service

Introduction

In recent years, **Virtual Private Networks** (**VPNs**) have come to play a key role in connecting to private networks over the public internet and connecting private networks at different locations to each other over the internet. They allow us to connect to private networks remotely and access resources as if they are local. At one time, such functionality was only available via private WAN circuits. Such circuits offer low latency and high reliability, but the high monthly costs make this option prohibitively expensive for many users.

Fortunately, we have the option of configuring a VPN. The downside of using a VPN, rather than a private WAN circuit, is that VPNs establish tunnels over the internet. As a result, they must be encrypted, and encrypting traffic requires processing power. Therefore, establishing and maintaining a VPN tunnel will require a system with more resources than the minimum pfSense specifications. This should be taken into consideration when selecting hardware for your system. In some cases, purchasing specialized hardware to offload some of the processing overhead from the CPU may be an economical decision, though in many cases, buying the most powerful CPU that fits your budgets will yield the biggest bang for your buck.

Hardware considerations aside, configuring VPN services in pfSense is a relatively easy process. In this chapter, we will first consider the process of choosing whether to use IPsec, OpenVPN, or L2TP. We will then cover recipes for all three of these protocols.

Choosing the right VPN server

There are several factors you will likely want to consider when choosing which VPN protocol to use. Some of the more crucial factors include the following:

- Interoperability with other routers and firewalls
- The type of authentication used
- Operating systems supported
- Security needs

Interoperability is something that comes into play when configuring a peer-to-peer VPN tunnel (in other words, one that connects to another firewall). In many cases, there may be a pfSense firewall at both ends of the tunnel, but in other cases, you may want to connect to a non-pfSense firewall. In such cases, IPsec is probably the best choice, since it is included with virtually every VPN-capable device. OpenVPN, being an open source protocol, is gaining acceptance, but it is not nearly as ubiquitous as IPsec.

The type of authentication used may also be a factor to consider. IPsec works with both username/password combinations, pre-shared keys, and certificates. L2TP does not have any built-in authentication. Therefore, if you require authentication, you either won't be using L2TP, or you'll be using it in combination with another protocol, such as IPsec. OpenVPN supports both pre-shared keys and certificates.

Another relevant consideration is what operating systems you will be supporting. If you will be primarily supporting Windows clients, IPsec is a good choice, as support for IPsec has been built into every version of Windows starting with Windows Vista. There are also third-party IPsec clients available for Windows, such as the Shrew Soft VPN client.

If you will be primarily supporting Linux clients, the choice is not quite as obvious, as built-in support for VPN protocols under Linux is limited. Ubuntu has built-in support for **Point-to-Point Tunneling Protocol** (**PPTP**), which is no longer supported by pfSense. OpenVPN has a client for Linux, and is probably your best choice. There are also IPsec clients available for Linux, which are of varying degrees of reliability and ease of use.

If you are supporting macOS clients, IPsec is likely the best option, as macOS has had built-in support for IPsec for many years. Snow Leopard (10.6) and later even has a built-in Cisco VPN client that provides a graphical interface. Although earlier versions of macOS do not come with this client pre-installed, you can install the Cisco Remote Access IPsec client on them.

If you must support a mixture of OSes, your choice of which protocol to use becomes more complicated. IPsec is the one protocol for which all three major OSes—Windows, Linux, and macOS—have clients available. L2TP is also a possible choice, although it is often implemented in combination with another protocol, Windows supports L2TP, either in conjunction with IPsec or L2TP alone. OpenVPN is a possibility if you are supporting both Windows and Linux; unfortunately, as of this writing, there is no OpenVPN client for macOS.

Finally, you likely want to consider cryptographic security. As L2TP has no encryption, this is essentially a choice between OpenVPN and IPsec. OpenVPN uses the SSL encryption library, which provides several different cryptographic ciphers. One disadvantage of OpenVPN is that it seems to favor backward compatibility over security. In addition, OpenVPN operates on the application layer of the seven-layer OSI model, whereas IPsec operates at the network layer, giving it a slight edge over OpenVPN.

Configuring the IPsec OpenVPN server – peer-to-peer

In this recipe, we will configure the IPsec server to connect to another IPsec server (peer-to-peer).

The purpose of this recipe is to set up an IPsec VPN tunnel that is similar to a tunnel we might set up if we wanted to connect two private networks separated by a considerable distance, as would be the case if we had networks in separate facilities. For example, we might have to connect a company's headquarters with a satellite office. Fortunately, there are pfSense firewalls at the boundary of each network. The endpoint for each tunnel will be the WAN interface of each firewall.

In order to set up this VPN tunnel, we must complete several steps:

1. Phase 1 and phase 2 configuration must be completed on the first firewall.
2. Firewall rules must be added to allow VPN traffic to pass through the firewall.
3. We must repeat the first two steps on the second firewall.

How to do it...

1. Navigate to **VPN** | **IPsec**.
2. On the default **Tunnels** tab, click on the **Add P1** button:

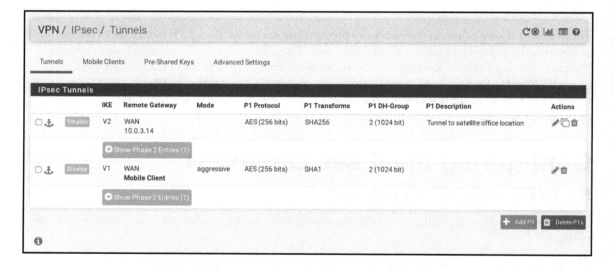

3. In the **General Information** section of the **Edit Phase 1** page, change the **Key Exchange version** to **IKEv2**:

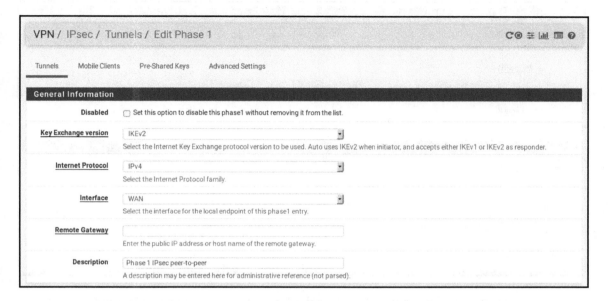

4. Set **Remote Gateway** to the IP address of the second pfSense firewall.
5. Enter a brief description in the **Description** text field.

6. Enter a key in the **Pre Shared Key** text field:

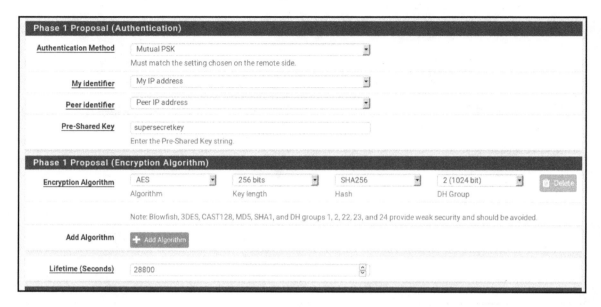

7. Change the **Hash Algorithm** to **SHA256**. All other values can be kept at their default values.
8. When the page reloads, click on the **Show Phase 2 Entries** button. This should make the Add P2 button visible.
9. Click on the **Add P2** button.
10. In the **General Information** section of the page, keep **Local Network** set to **LAN subnet**.
11. Set **Remote Network** to the LAN subnet and CIDR of the remote network's LAN.
12. Enter a brief description in the **Description** text field.
13. In the **Phase 2 Configuration (SA/Key Exchange)** section, **AES256-GCM** is selected as an Encryption Algorithm.
14. Select **SHA256** as the **Hash Algorithm**.
15. When you are done making changes, click on the **Save** button.
16. When the page reloads, click on **Apply Changes**.

17. Now we need to add a firewall rule to allow VPN tunnel traffic to pass:
    1. Navigate to **Firewall | Rules** and click on the **IPsec** tab (**Firewall | Rules | IPsec**).
    2. Click on one of the **Add** buttons at the bottom of the page to add a rule.
    3. On the **Edit** page for this rule, select **Network** in the **Source** drop-down menu. Enter the subnet and CIDR of the remote network. This should be the same information entered for **Remote Network** in the **Phase 2 IPsec** configuration.
    4. Click on the **Save** button.
    5. Click on **Apply Changes** to reload the firewall rules:

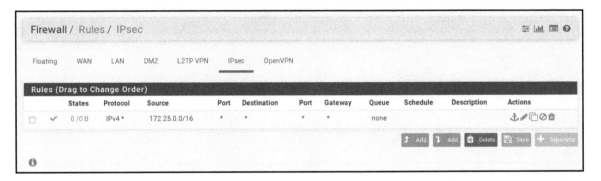

18. The configuration of the first firewall is now complete. We need to repeat the process for the second firewall:
    1. On the second firewall, navigate to **VPN | IPsec**.
    2. On the **Tunnels** tab, click on the **Add P1** button.
    3. Repeat the process followed for phase 1 configuration of the first firewall, but set **Remote Gateway** to the IP address of the first firewall.
    4. Create the phase 2 entry on the second firewall. Again, the process should be identical to the process followed for the first firewall, the exception being that **Remote Network** should be set to the LAN network behind the first firewall.
    5. Navigate to **Firewall | Rules | IPsec**, and create a firewall rule that is identical to the rule created on the first firewall.

19. Now that phase 1, phase 2 and the firewall configuration are complete on both ends of the tunnel, navigate to **Status | IPsec** on either firewall. There should be a table of currently configured IPsec connections.

20. Click on the **Connect VPN** button for the newly configured connection. In the table, the IPsec tunnel status should change from **Disconnected** to **ESTABLISHED**. The **Status** column will also indicate how long the tunnel has been up. The IPsec tunnel should remain up until you click on the **Disconnect** button on either firewall (or otherwise terminate the IPsec service on either end):

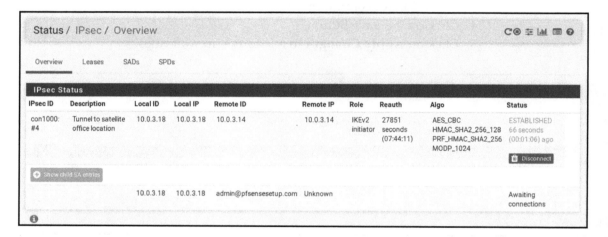

 Now that the IPsec tunnel has been established and access to the LAN network has been granted to IPsec clients on either end of the tunnel, a user on one network who wishes to use resources on the remote LAN network (for example, an FTP server) should be able to do so.

How it works...

We configured a peer-to-peer IPsec tunnel between two pfSense firewalls by creating essentially identical phase 1 and phase 2 configurations on either end. We also added firewall rules to both ends to allow IPsec traffic to pass to the LAN. As a result, now users on either end can access LAN resources on the remote end as if they are local resources on a local subnet.

There's more...

In this recipe, we left out any explanation of a number of options available for configuring IPsec connections in pfSense. Here are some of the more useful options:

- Phase 1 configuration:
    - **Key Exchange**: We can choose between IKEv1 (V1), IKEv2 (V2), or Auto. If Auto is chosen, IPsec will use IKEv2 when initiating a connection, but will use either IKEv1 or IKEv2 when accepting a connection.
    - **Internet Protocol**: pfSense currently supports both IPv4 and IPv6 for IPsec.
    - **Interface**: Usually, the endpoint of our tunnel is the WAN interface, but we can set this parameter to any interface we choose.
    - **Remote Gateway**: This is the IP address of the remote firewall, and is usually the same as the WAN IP address of that firewall.
    - **Authentication Method**: We can choose between Mutual PSK (authentication using a pre-shared key) and Mutual RSA (authentication using certificates). If you choose Mutual PSK, you will have to enter a pre-shared key during phase 1 configuration. If you choose Mutual RSA, you will have to enter a certificate and a **Certificate Authority (CA)**.
    - **Negotiation Mode**: If you selected Auto for Key Exchange, you will be able to choose what level of authentication security is used when the VPN tunnel is down and has to be rebuilt. **Main** forces the peer to re-authenticate, while **Aggressive** will rebuild the tunnel quickly, without forcing re-authentication.
    - **My identifier/Peer identifier**: These parameters determine how each side identifies itself to the other side of the connection. Usually you can leave both set to IP address, but there are several other options, such as Distinguished name (which you will then have to enter in an adjacent text field).
    - **Encryption Algorithm**: Here you can select the encryption method. If you require strong encryption, you should probably use AES or Blowfish.
    - **DH Group**: DH stands for **Diffie-Hellman**; this parameter allows you to choose the Diffie-Hellman group that is used to generate session keys.
    - **Disable Rekey**: If this option is enabled, IPsec will not renegotiate a connection that is about to expire.

- **Responder Only**: If this option is enabled, IPsec will only be able to accept connections, not initiate them.
- **Dead Peer Detection (DPD)**: If this option is enabled, IPsec will try to detect if the other end of the connection is having problems, and try to rebuild the tunnel if necessary.
- Phase 2 configuration:
  - **Mode**: You can choose between **Tunnel** mode and **Transport** mode. Tunnel mode will encrypt the entire IP packet and add a new IP header, while Transport mode will encrypt the payload but not the IP header. If you choose Tunnel mode you have a choice between IPv4 and IPv6; this setting should match whatever you set for internet protocol in the phase 1 configuration.
  - **Local Network**: This setting allows you to choose what local network is accessible from the other end of the tunnel (you usually want this set to LAN subnet).
  - **NAT/BINAT translation**: If NAT/BINAT translation is required on the network specified in Local Network, you can specify the translation here.
  - **Protocol**: This is the protocol for key exchange. The de facto standard is **Encapsulating Security Payload** (**ESP**), which provides for both encryption and authentication of IPsec data, but you can also select **Authentication Header** (**AH**), which provides for authentication only. If you select ESP, you must also select one or more encryption algorithms.
  - **Encryption Algorithm**: The algorithm for tunnel encryption; the default is AES. You can choose more than one algorithm.
  - **Hash Algorithms**: Algorithms used when calculating hashes. You may choose more than one algorithm.
  - **PFS Key Group**: If this option is selected, IPsec will perform a **PFS** (**Perfect Forward Security**) key exchange when establishing a tunnel.
  - **Automatically ping host**: Here, you can specify an IP address at the remote end of the connection that IPsec will ping. If IPsec gets responses to the pings, it will keep the tunnel up; otherwise, it will disconnect.

Configuring the IPsec VPN service – client/server

In this recipe, we will configure the IPsec service to allow multiple clients to connect to our network.

In the previous recipe, we showed how IPsec can be used to create a VPN tunnel between two pfSense firewalls. In this recipe, we will demonstrate how IPsec can be used for a different purpose. Sometimes, we want to allow individual clients to access our network over the internet. Fortunately, pfSense enables us to do this, via IPsec mobile client configuration. In order to configure mobile clients, we must set up individual user accounts, and as was the case when we were configuring Captive Portal in pfSense, the User Manager provides a means for adding user accounts.

How to do it...

1. Navigate to **VPN | IPsec**.
2. Click on the **Mobile Clients** tab.
3. Check the **Enable IPsec Mobile Client Support** checkbox:

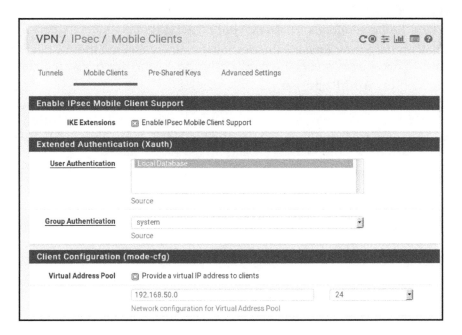

4. In the **User Authentication** listbox, select **Local Database**.
5. In the **Group Authentication** drop-down menu, select **system**.
6. Check the **Provide a virtual IP address** to clients checkbox.
7. Enter a network and CIDR for the virtual address pool.
8. Check the **Save Xauth Password** checkbox.
9. Check the **DNS Default Domain** checkbox, and enter localdomain as the default domain.
10. Check the **Provide a DNS server list** checkbox and enter 1.1.1.1 and 1.0.0.1 as the DNS servers.
11. Check the **Login Banner** checkbox and enter an appropriate login banner.
12. When you are done, click on the **Save** button.
13. When the page reloads, click the **Create Phase 1** button.
14. Keep the **Key Exchange** set to **IKEv1**.
15. Set the **Authentication Mode** to **Mutual PSK + XAuth**.
16. Change **Peer identifier** to **User distinguished name**. Enter something unique for this field, such as an email address.
17. In the **Pre-Shared key** text field, enter an appropriate pre-shared key.
18. Scroll down to **Advanced Options**, and change **NAT Traversal** to **Force**. This will force the use of **NAT-T** on port 4500.
19. When you are done, click on **Save**.
20. When the page reloads, click on **Apply Changes**.
21. Click on the **Show Phase 2 Entries** for the newly created mobile client phase 1 entry. This should reveal the **Add P2** button for the newly created connection.
22. Click on the **Add P2** button.
23. Most of the default values on the **Edit Phase 2** page can be kept at their default values. It is recommended, however, that you change the **Encryption Algorithm** to **AES256-GCM**, and that you change the **Hash Algorithm** to **SHA256**.

24. When you are done making changes, click on the **Save** button.
25. Phase 1 and phase 2 configuration is complete; now we must add one or more users via the User Manager. Navigate to **System** | **User Manager** to begin the process. First, add a group for VPN users:
    1. Click on the **Groups** tab.
    2. Click on the **Add** button to add a new group.
    3. Enter a group name of `vpnusers`:

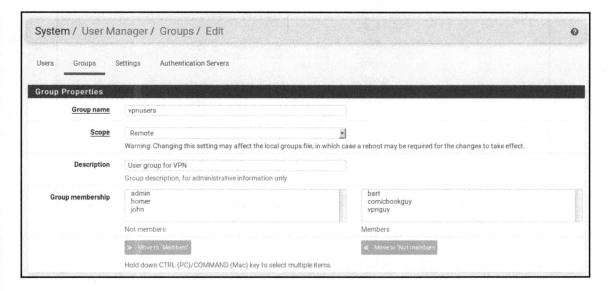

    4. In the **Scope** drop-down menu, select **Remote**.
    5. Click on the **Save** button.
    6. When the page reloads, the **vpnusers** group should be listed in the table. Click on the **Edit** icon for **vpnusers**.
    7. There will now be a section on the configuration page for the group called **Assigned privileges**. Click on the **Add** button in this section.

5. In the **Assigned privileges** box, select **User – VPN: IPsecxauthDialin** and click on **Save**:

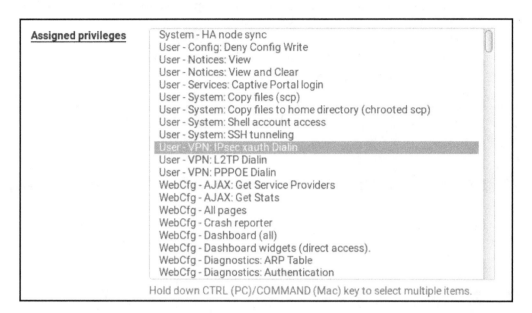

9. On the main configuration page, click on **Save**.

26. Now we can add users to the **vpnusers** group, which we can do by clicking on the **Users** tab:

1. From the **Users** tab, click on the **Add** button.

2. Set an appropriate **Username** and **Password** combination for the new user.

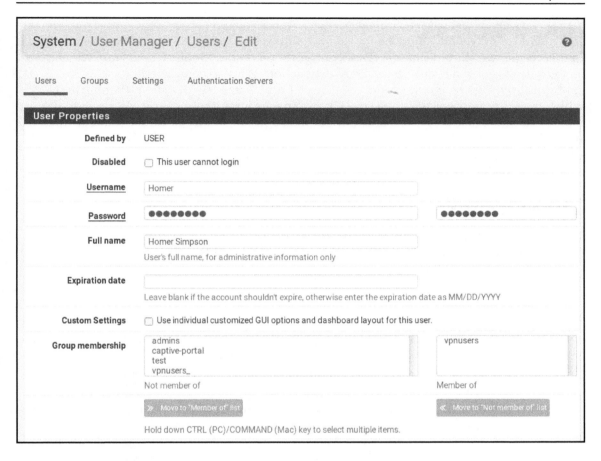

3. Under **Group Memberships**, select the **vpnusers** group.
4. For the **IPsec Pre-Shared Key**, enter the key you entered during phase 1 configuration.
5. Click on the **Save** button.
6. Repeat these steps for as many users as you wish to add.

How it works...

In this recipe, we started phase 1 IPsec configuration on the Mobile Clients tab, which enables us to set up a client-server IPsec connection. We also completed phase 2 configuration. During configuration, we chose Local Database for user authentication, which means that pfSense will use the User Manager for authentication. As a result, we also had to create users that have as one of their privileges the ability to create an IPsec tunnel, which is what we did when we created a user group that had **User – VPN: IPsecxauthDialin** as one of its privileges, and added users to it.

There's more...

This recipe demonstrated how to set up a client-server IPsec connection on the server side, but we deliberately left out how to set up the IPsec client. This we will do in the next recipe, *Connecting to the IPsec VPN service*.

IPsec mobile client configuration has several options that we did not cover in this recipe. Here are some of the more useful options:

- **Provide virtual IPv6 addresses to clients**: pfSense supports IPv6; thus, we can assign virtual IPv6 addresses if we enable this option.
- **Provide a list of accessible networks to clients**: If enabled, remote clients will receive a list of accessible local networks.
- **Provide a list of split DNS domain names to clients**: If enabled, you may specify different DNS zones for IPsec users. If a client connects through an IPsec tunnel, they will be accessing internal resources as if they are on the internal network, and therefore they may have to use different IP addresses than they would if they were trying to access them externally.
- **WINS Servers**: If this option is enabled, you can specify WINS servers for name resolution.
- **Phase2 PFS Group**: If this option is enabled, you can configure a Perfect Forward Security group for clients that will override PFS settings in phase 2.

There are two additional tabs on the IPsec settings page:

- **Pre-Shared Keys**: This page contains a table with all IPsec pre-shared keys, including ones corresponding to users created in the **User Manager**. You can also add pre-shared keys from this tab.
- **Advanced Settings**: The first section of the **Advanced Settings** tab is devoted to logging controls, which allows you to control the log verbosity for a number of different elements related to the IPsec Daemon. The second section is devoted to various parameters that you most likely will not need to change, but they are configurable here nonetheless.

Connecting to the IPsec VPN service

This recipe demonstrates how to connect to the IPsec service configured in the previous recipe. We will be connecting as a remote client. For this recipe, we will be using the Shrew Soft VPN client, which works with most versions of Windows (2000 and later). You can download this client at `https://www.shrew.net/download/vpn`.

Getting ready

You will need to download the most recent Shrew Soft VPN client that is compatible with your version of Windows. Once you do this, run the installer. When the installer presents a choice between the **Professional** and **Standard Edition** of the client, choose **Standard Edition**. You can use the default options for everything else, unless you want to change the installation location.

How to do it...

1. Launch **VPN Access Manager** (the Shrew Soft client).
2. On the **VPN Access Manager** main menu, click on the **Add** button to add a new connection.

3. On the **General** tab, enter the **Host Name or IP Address** of the IPsec server configured in the previous recipe. Generally, this will be the same as the WAN interface of the firewall where we configured the IPsec client-server tunnel. All other settings can remain at their default values:

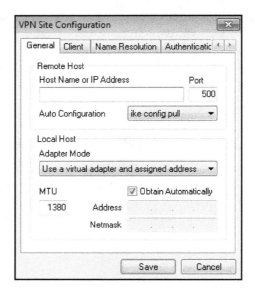

4. Click on the **Authentication** tab (it is the fourth tab in the most recent version).
5. In the **Authentication Method** drop-down menu, select **Mutual PSK + XAuth**, to match what we set in phase 1 of the previous recipe:

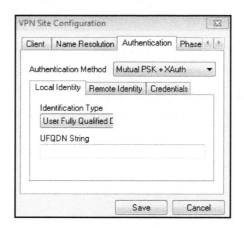

6. On the **Local Identity** sub tab, select **User Fully Qualified Domain Name** in the **Identification Type** drop-down menu, again matching what we entered in phase 1 of the previous recipe.

7. In the **UFQDN String** text field, enter the user distinguished name used in step 16 of the previous recipe.

8. On the **Credential** sub tab, enter the pre-shared key we entered in the previous recipe into the **Pre-Shared Key** text field.

9. Click on the **Phase 1** tab.

10. Keep **Exchange Type** set to **aggressive** and **DH Exchange** set to **group 2**:

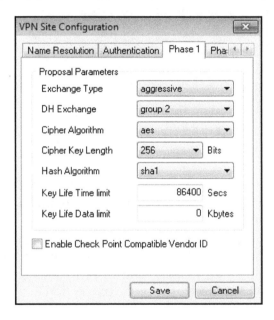

11. Set **Cipher Algorithm** to **aes**, **Cipher Key Length** to **256**, and **Hash Algorithm** to **sha1**. Keep all other settings on this tab at their default values.

12. Click on the **Phase 2** tab.

13. Set **Transform Algorithm** to **esp-aes**, **Transform Key Length** to **256**, and **HMAC Algorithm** to **sha1**. Keep all other settings on this tab at their default values:

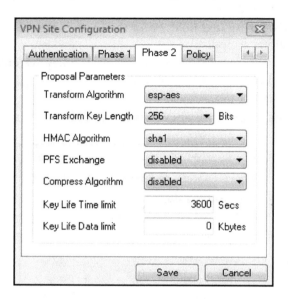

14. When you are done making changes, click on the **Save** button.
15. Select the newly created connection in **Shrew Soft's VPN Access Manager** and click on **Connect**.
16. A dialog box will appear prompting you for a username and password. Enter the credentials for one of the IPsec mobile users created in the previous recipe.
17. If the **Connect** tab indicates that the tunnel was enabled (tunnel enabled should be the last update to the status list), the connection to the remote firewall is complete.

You can check on the status of the VPN by navigating to **Status | IPsec** on the remote firewall. There should be a listing in the table for each of the mobile clients along with information about which encryption algorithms are being used, how long the connection has been active, and much more.

Configuring the OpenVPN service

This recipe demonstrates how to set up an OpenVPN connection from the server side.

As with IPsec, OpenVPN can be used in both site-to-site mode (creating an OpenVPN tunnel between two firewalls) and client-server mode (one side accepts a connection from the other side). The implementation of OpenVPN in pfSense allows us to set up peer-to-peer and client-server connections, but in a slightly different way than IPsec. With IPsec, if we wanted to connect two firewalls, we had to use peer-to-peer mode. With OpenVPN, to connect two firewalls we must connect them in client-server mode. Thus, the client can be either (a) another firewall, or (b) a mobile client who needs to connect to our network (and we can have multiple clients connecting to the same server).

In this recipe, we will describe how to set up pfSense to act as an OpenVPN server. This requires seven separate steps:

1. Creating the CA and certificates
2. Configuring the OpenVPN server
3. Creating firewall rules to allow OpenVPN traffic to pass
4. Importing the CA and user certificate to the client
5. Configuring the OpenVPN client
6. Creating a firewall rule to allow OpenVPN traffic to pass on the client
7. Verifying the functionality of the OpenVPN tunnel

How to do it...

First, we must create the CA and certificates on the server:

1. Navigate to **System | Cert. Manager**.
2. From the default tab, **CAs**, click on the **Add** button to create the CA.

3. In the **Descriptive name** text field, enter a brief name:

4. In the **Method** drop-down menu, select **Create an Internal Certificate Authority**.
5. In the **Internal Certificate Authority** section, make sure the required fields are completed. You can also complete the optional fields **(Country Code, State or Province**, and so on).

6. When you are done, click on the **Save** button.
7. Click on the **Certificates** tab. We need to create two certificates: one for the server, and one for the client.
8. Click on the **Add/Sign** button to add a new certificate.
9. Enter a name in the **Descriptive Name** text field (for example, `OpenVPN server certificate`):

10. In the **Certificate Authority** drop-down menu, select the CA we created in the earlier steps.
11. Make sure the **Certificate Type** is set to **Server Certificate**:

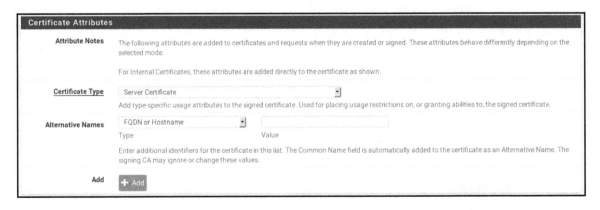

12. Click on the **Save** button.
13. Click on the **Add/Sign** button to add a new certificate.

14. Enter a name in the **Descriptive Name** text field (for example, `OpenVPN client certificate`).

15. In the **Certificate Authority** drop-down menu, select the CA we created in the earlier steps.

16. Make sure the **Certificate Type** is set to **User Certificate**.

17. Click on the **Save** button.

18. The table on the **Certificates** tab should list both the newly created server certificate and user certificate. Click on the **Export Certificate** button for the user certificate and save the certificate to a safe place:

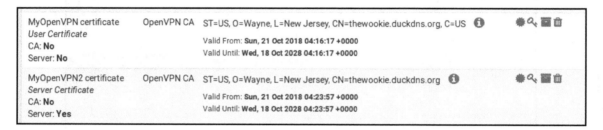

19. Click on the **Export Key** button for the user certificate and save the key to a safe place. You will need to import both the certificate and the key onto the client later.

20. Click on the **CA** tab and click on the **Export CA** button for the CA we created earlier. Save the CA.

21. Repeat this process for the CA's key. We will need to import the CA onto the client, and we need both the CA and the key.

Now we can begin configuration of the OpenVPN server:

1. Navigate to **VPN | OpenVPN**.

2. From the **Servers** tab, click on the **Add** button.

3. In the **General Information** section, we can leave all settings at their default values. Be sure that **Server** mode is set to **Peer to Peer (SSL/TLS)**. You can keep **Local port** set to **1194** (the default OpenVPN port) unless you have reason to select a different port. You can enter a brief description in the **Description** text field:

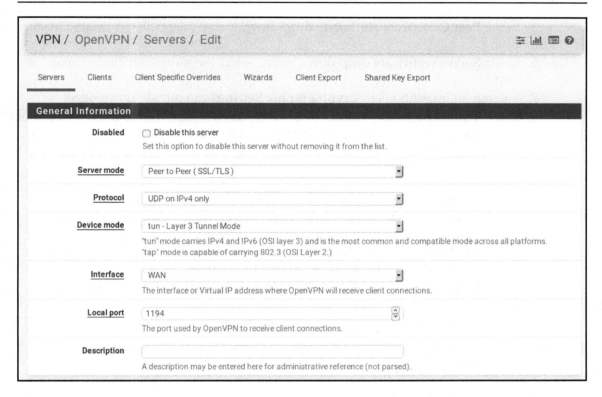

4. In the **Cryptographic Settings** section, make sure the **Use a TLS Key** and **Automatically Generate a TLS Key** checkboxes are checked. You will need to paste the autogenerated key into the client settings later:

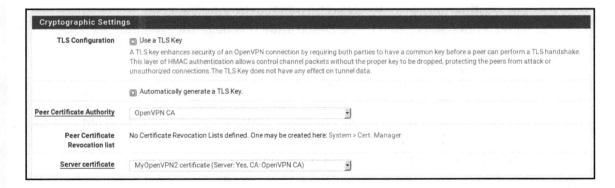

5. In the **Peer Certificate Authority** drop-down menu, select the CA created in step 1.
6. In the **Server certificate** drop-down menu, select the server certificate created in step 1.
7. The remaining settings in **Cryptographic Settings** can remain unchanged.
8. In the **Tunnel Settings** section, specify a virtual IPv4 network in the **IPv4 Tunnel Network** text field. The virtual network must be big enough to accommodate the server virtual address and at least one client, so the smallest IPv4 network you can specify is a /30 network.
9. In the **IPv4 Local network(s)** text field, specify the IPv4 networks that will be accessible from the remote endpoint. Usually you should just specify the LAN network, but you may specify more than one network, separated by commas.
10. In the **IPv4 Remote network(s)** text field, specify the IPv4 remote networks that will be routed through the tunnel. As with **IPv4 Local network(s)**, you can specify more than one network, separated by commas.
11. In the **Client Settings** section, for **Topology**, select **net30** in the drop-down menu.
12. When you are done making changes, click on the **Save** button.

OpenVPN server configuration is complete, but we still need to create firewall rules to allow OpenVPN traffic to pass:

1. Navigate to **Firewall | Rules**.
2. On the **WAN** tab, click on the first **Add** button (the one with the up arrow). The **Firewall Edit** page will load.
3. For **Protocol**, select **UDP** in the drop-down menu.
4. For **Destination**, select **WAN** address in the drop-down menu.
5. Enter a brief description in the **Description** text field (for example, `OpenVPN rule for WAN`).
6. When you are done, click on the **Save** button.
7. Click on the **Apply Changes** button.
8. Click on the **OpenVPN** tab.
9. We only need to create one rule for the OpenVPN tunnel, so click on either **Add** button. The **Firewall Edit** page will load.
10. For **Protocol**, select any in the drop-down menu.
11. Enter a brief description in the **Description** text field.
12. Click on the **Save** button.

13. Click on the **Apply Changes** button:

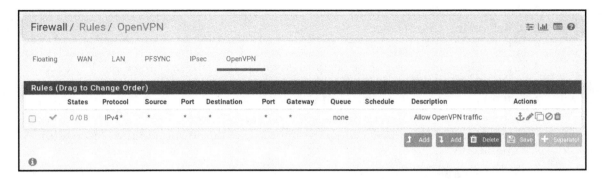

Next, we switch to the other firewall and import the CA and client certificate:

1. Navigate to **System | Certificate Manager**.
2. From the CAs tab, click on the **Add** button.
3. In the **Descriptive** name text field, enter the same name for the CA as you did on the server.
4. Make sure **Import an existing Certificate Authority** is selected in the **Method** drop-down menu.
5. **Paste Certificate data** and **Certificate Private Key** into the corresponding text boxes.
6. When done, click on the **Save** button.
7. Click on the **Certificates** tab.
8. Click on the **Add/Sign** button to add the client certificate.
9. For **Method**, make sure **Import** an existing **Certificate** is selected.
10. In the **Descriptive** name text field, enter the name used when the certificate was created on the server.
11. Paste **Certificate data** and **Certificate Private Key** (for the user certificate) into the corresponding text boxes.
12. When done, click on the **Save** button.

Next, we begin OpenVPN client configuration:

1. Navigate to **VPN | OpenVPN**.
2. Click on the **Clients** tab.
3. Click on the **Add** button.
4. In the **General Information** section, enter the IP address of the OpenVPN server in the **Server host or address** text field.
5. All other settings in the **General Information** section can be kept at their default values. Make sure **Server mode** is set to **Peer to Peer (SSL/TLS)**, and make sure **Server port** is set to **1194**. You may enter a brief description in the **Description** edit box.
6. In **Cryptographic Settings**, make sure **Use a TLS Key** is checked. Uncheck **Automatically Generate a TLS Key**; this will cause the **TLS Key** text box to appear. Paste the **TLS Key** generated by the OpenVPN server into this box.
7. In the **Peer Certificate Authority** drop-down menu, select the CA created in step 1 (and imported to the client in step 4) as the CA.
8. In the **Client Certificate** drop-down menu, select the client (user) certificate created in step 1 (and imported to the client in step 4).
9. In the **Tunnel Settings** section, in the **IPv4 Tunnel Network** edit box, specify the same virtual IPv4 network you specified for this setting on the server side in step 2.
10. In the **IPv4 Remote network(s)** text field, specify the remote IPv4 networks that will be routed through the VPN tunnel. This is typically identical to the IPv4 networks specified for **IPv4 Remote network(s)** on the server side in step 2.
11. In the **Topology** drop-down menu, select **net30**.
12. When you are done making changes, click on the **Save** button.

Next, we need to create a firewall rule to allow OpenVPN traffic to pass:

1. Navigate to **Firewall | Rules** and click on the **OpenVPN** tab.
2. Click on one of the **Add** buttons to add a new rule.
3. Keep the **Action** set to **Pass**.
4. Set the **Protocol** to **any**.
5. Leave the **Source** and **Destination** set to **any**.
6. Enter a brief description in the **Description** text field (for example, `Allow OpenVPN traffic`).
7. Click on the **Save** button.

8. Whereas we have to explicitly connect IPsec tunnels, with OpenVPN, the tunnel will connect automatically as soon as we complete configuration, assuming the OpenVPN service is running. To verify that this is the case, navigate to **Status** | **OpenVPN** on the client. The newly created tunnel should be listed in the table with a **Status** of **up**. If the tunnel is not up, there are several possible reasons:

   - The OpenVPN service is not running.
   - The CA and certificates were set up incorrectly.
   - A configuration error was made.

 Note that when we added firewall rules for the server, we had to add a rule to allow traffic through the WAN interface on the server side, but we did not have to add such a rule on the client side. This is because the client is initiating the VPN connection; therefore, the client's traffic must be allowed through the WAN interface. Return traffic is allowed, so we don't need a corresponding client-side rule; rather, we only needed a rule to allow OpenVPN traffic on the client.

There's more...

In this recipe, we deliberately kept the encryption settings at their default values in order to simplify the process. If your organization has more stringent security standards, however, feel free to change these settings to meet your requirements. Just make sure that the settings are the same on the server and client sides.

If you were unable to establish a VPN connection, there are a number of reasons why it might fail. In order to troubleshoot such a problem, we must first gather information, and a good place to start is the system logs. Navigate to **Status** | **System Logs** | **VPN** to begin. The latest log entries should provide a clue as to why a VPN tunnel cannot be established.

If you are having problems with authentication, make sure the CA and certificates were set up correctly. Remember, the CA should be the same on both ends of the connection, while the server side should be using a server certificate and the client side should be using a user certificate. Both server and user certificates should be internal certificates using the same CA. Another reason authentication may fail is that the TLS key does not match on client and server.

It is possible that the connection attempt may fail before reaching the authentication phase. If so, you may want to make sure that the server can reach the client and the other way around. To do so, you could ping the client from the server and the server from the client. Before you do so, you should make sure there is a rule on the WAN interface for each side to allow **Internet Control Message Protocol** (**ICMP**) traffic. If not, you can add such rules. You may want to disable these rules later for security reasons.

Connecting to the OpenVPN service

In this recipe, we will demonstrate how to set up an OpenVPN client connection.

In circumstances in which we need to support one or more clients in the field connecting to our network through a VPN tunnel, we will find it necessary to set up an OpenVPN client connection. Fortunately, pfSense makes the process easy—the OpenVPN Client Export Utility package greatly simplifies the process of setting up a client connection from both the server and client side, as we shall see.

Getting ready

In order to complete this recipe, you will first need a valid CA and a valid server certificate, which you will have done already if you followed the previous recipe, *Configuring the OpenVPN service*. If you have not created a CA and server certificate, you will create them in as the first two steps in this recipe.

How to do it...

1. Make sure you have a valid CA. If not, create one by following step 1 in the *Connecting to the OpenVPN service* recipe.
2. Make sure you have a valid server certificate. If not, create one by following step 1 in the *Connecting to the OpenVPN service* recipe.

3. Add an OpenVPN client with the User Manager:
    1. Navigate to **System** | **User Manager**.
    2. Click on the **Group** tab.
    3. Click on the **Add** button to add a new group.
    4. Enter a name in the **Group name** text field (for example, `Remote VPN Users`).
    5. Enter a brief description in the **Description** text field.
    6. When you are done making changes, click on **Save**.
    7. Click on the **Users** tab.
    8. Click on **Add** to add a VPN client.
    9. Enter a **Username** and **Password** in the appropriate text field.
    10. Enter the user's full name in the **Full name** text field, if desired. In the **Group membership** section, add the user to the newly created user group.
    11. Check the **Click to create a user certificate** checkbox.
    12. Click on the **Save** button.
    13. Repeat the process for as many VPN clients as you wish to add.
4. Next, we need to install the the **OpenVPN Client Export Utility**:
    1. Navigate to **System** | **Package Manager**.
    2. Click on the **Available Packages** tab.
    3. Find **openvpn-client-export** in the list, and click on the **Install** button for this package.
    4. Clicking on the **Install** button will take you to the **Package Installer** tab; click on the **Confirm** button on this tab.
    5. Wait for **openvpn-client-export** to install.

5. Now we can configure the OpenVPN server:
   1. Navigate to **VPN | OpenVPN**.
   2. Click on the **Wizards** tab. This will take you through the OpenVPN server setup.
   3. Leave **Type of Server** set to **Local User Access**. Click on the **Next** button:

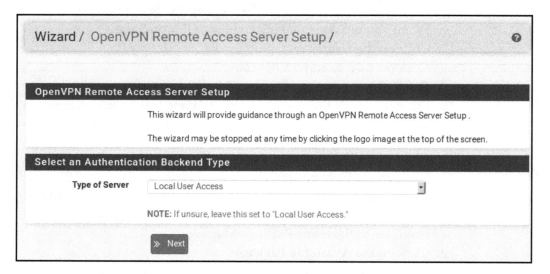

4. In the **Certificate Authority** drop-down menu, select the CA created in step 1 (or earlier if you followed the *Connecting to the OpenVPN service* recipe). You may also click on the **Add new CA** button to generate a new CA; otherwise, click on the **Next** button.
5. In the **Certificate** drop-down menu, select the server certificate created in step 1 (or earlier if you followed the *Connecting to the OpenVPN service* recipe). You may also click on the **Add new certificate** button to generate a new server certificate; otherwise, click on the **Next** button.
6. On the **Server Setup** page, scroll down to **Tunnel Settings**. In the **Tunnel Network** text field, enter a virtual network for private communications between the client and server. You can make this network as big or as small as you wish. For example, if you know you will never have more than a dozen clients connecting and 192.168.1.0 is not being used by any of the subnets on your network, you can set it to `192.168.1.0/28`.

7. In the **Local Network** text field, enter the local network that will be accessible from the remote endpoint (usually the LAN network).
8. Scroll down to **Client Settings**. In **DNS Default Domain**, enter the default domain name for clients, if there is one.
9. You may also enter up to four DNS servers in the DNS Server text field.
10. You may enter up to two NTP servers in the **NTP Server** edit boxes.
11. When you are done making changes, click on the **Next** button.
12. On the **Firewall Rule Configuration** page, make sure both **Firewall rule** and **OpenVPN Rule** are checked. Once you confirm this, click on the **Next** button:

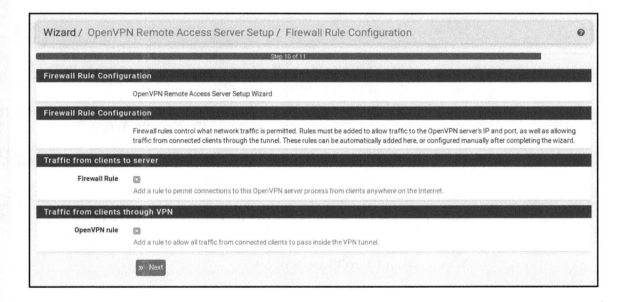

13. The final page of the wizard should inform you that configuration is complete. Click on the **Finish** button to complete the wizard:

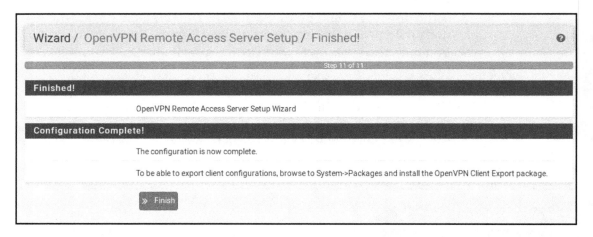

6. Confirm that the configured server appears on the **Servers** tab. Once you do, you can begin using the **Client Export Utility**:
   1. Click on the **Client Export** tab.
   2. Make sure the correct server is selected in the **Remote Access Server** drop-down menu.
   3. Check the **Password Protect Certificate** checkbox.
   4. Enter a password in the **Certificate Password** text field (the password must be entered twice).
   5. Scroll down to the **OpenVPN Clients** section and download the appropriate config file or client for the appropriate user (you should see different options for each user configured earlier) iOS, Android, Windows, and macOS are supported:

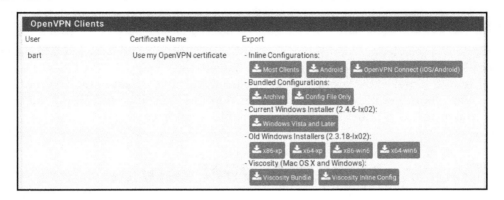

7. Now that we have the OpenVPN client software, we can move over to the remote system and connect to the remote firewall:

    1. Install the downloaded OpenVPN client on the client's computer.

    2. Run the installed client. The client interface will prompt you for the username and password. Enter the username and password entered in the **User Manager** for the client earlier. When you are done, click on **OK**.

    3. The client should now be connected to the server via OpenVPN:

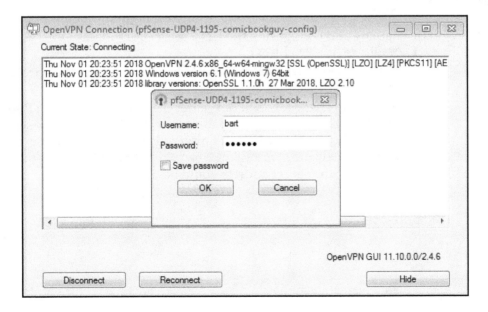

There's more...

In this recipe, we enabled and configured the OpenVPN server and connected to the server remotely using the OpenVPN client. You don't have to use the OpenVPN Client Export Utility, although it makes the process of setting up the client software much easier. The client software should work with all versions of Windows starting with Vista, and can also be made to work with Windows 2000/XP with some tweaking.

Configuring the L2TP VPN service

In this recipe, we will demonstrate how to set up an L2TP connection. L2TP is rarely used alone, but is often used in combination with IPsec. There are three steps to configuring an L2TP connection in pfSense:

1. Configuring the L2TP server
2. Adding L2TP users
3. Adding an L2TP firewall rule

How to do it...

1. Begin by enabling and configuring the L2TP server:
    1. Navigate to **VPN | L2TP**.
    2. Check the **Enable L2TP server** checkbox. The rest of the settings will appear.
    3. In the **Server address** edit box, enter the IP address the L2TP server should give to clients as the gateway. It should be an address just outside the range of addresses reserved for the clients. For example, if you plan to use 192.168.1.10 to 192.168.1.60 for client IP addresses, the server address could be 192.168.1.61:

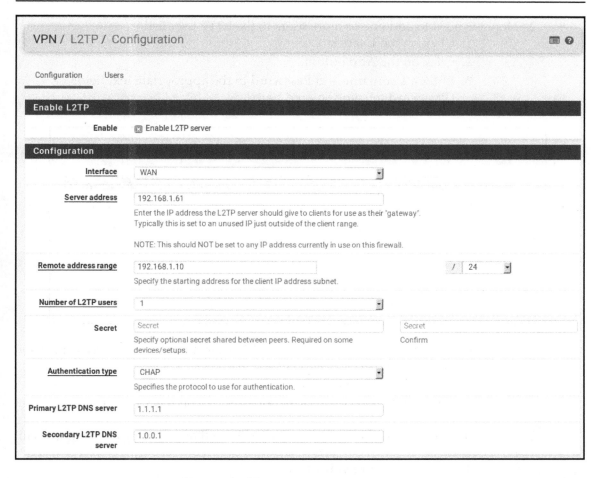

VPN / L2TP / Configuration

Configuration   Users

Enable L2TP

Enable   ☒ Enable L2TP server

Configuration

Interface   WAN

Server address   192.168.1.61

Enter the IP address the L2TP server should give to clients for use as their "gateway".
Typically this is set to an unused IP just outside of the client range.

NOTE: This should NOT be set to any IP address currently in use on this firewall.

Remote address range   192.168.1.10   / 24

Specify the starting address for the client IP address subnet.

Number of L2TP users   1

Secret   Secret   Secret

Specify optional secret shared between peers. Required on some   Confirm
devices/setups.

Authentication type   CHAP

Specifies the protocol to use for authentication.

Primary L2TP DNS server   1.1.1.1

Secondary L2TP DNS
server   1.0.0.1

4. In the **Remote address range** edit box, enter the starting IP address for the client IP address subnet. Select the correct CIDR in the adjacent drop-down menu.

5. Select the appropriate number of users in the **Number of L2TP users** drop-down menu.

6. In the **Primary L2TP DNS server** text field, enter 1.1.1.1.

7. In the **Secondary L2TP DNS server** text field, enter 1.0.0.1.

8. When you are done making changes, click on the **Save** button.

2. Now we need to add one or more users to the L2TP user list:
   1. Click on the **Users** tab.
   2. Click on the **Add** button.
   3. Enter a **Username** and **Password** in the appropriate text fields (**Password** must be entered twice):

   4. You may enter an IP in the **IP address** text field, in which case the user will be assigned a specific IP address.
   5. Click on the **Save** button.
   6. Repeat this process for as many users as you wish to add.

3. Finally, we need to create a pass rule for L2TP, so that incoming connections will not be blocked:
   1. Navigate to **Firewall | Rules**.
   2. Click on the **L2TP VPN** tab.
   3. Click on one of the **Add** buttons to add a rule.
   4. Set the **Protocol** to **any**.
   5. Leave the **Source** and **Destination** set to **any**.
   6. Enter a brief description in the **Description** edit box (for example, L2TP pass rule).
   7. When you are done making changes, click on the **Save** button.
   8. Click on the **Apply Changes** button to reload the firewall rules.

6
Traffic Shaping

In this chapter, we will cover the following:

- Configuring traffic shaping using the traffic-shaping wizard
- Configuring traffic shaping using floating rules
- Configuring traffic shaping using Snort

Introduction

Regardless of the size or purpose of your network, you will derive benefits from optimizing the performance of your network. One of the means we have of optimizing the performance is through traffic shaping, which allows us to manage traffic in such a way that some packets are prioritized over others. Without traffic shaping, packets are processed on a **first-in, first-out** (**FIFO**) basis. While this might be adequate in many cases, in other cases it can lead to saturated connections and increased latency.

The traffic shaper does its job by examining packets leaving network interfaces. If packets meet certain criteria, they are treated differently. In this sense, implementing traffic shaping is similar to implementing firewall rules. Yet rather than pass, block, or reject packets, we place packets that match the traffic-shaping criteria into separate queues. Priority traffic goes into a priority queue, where it is sent immediately. Lower priority traffic is held back until the higher priority packets pass.

As you may have imagined, traffic shaping can be used in a variety of scenarios:

- When low latency is required, we can employ traffic shaping to make sure this happens. This is typically the case if we are using **Voice over IP** (**VoIP**) applications or online games.
- In many cases, latency is not important—we want as much excess bandwidth as is possible, but we don't care as much about when the packets arrive. This is typically the case when we are using peer-to-peer file sharing applications.

- We may have asymmetric internet connections that we want to even out. In North America, it is fairly commonplace to have more download bandwidth than upload bandwidth. Your maximum download bandwidth may seem unattainable in some cases. This may be because the download client is sending ACK packets (packets acknowledging receipt of data), but these packets are in a FIFO queue with all other outbound traffic. Setting up a separate outbound queue just for ACK packets will potentially increase the speed of downloads.
- If we are running pfSense at a business, we may want to deprioritize non-business-related traffic (for example, streaming video or file downloads).

These are just a few of the possible scenarios we may encounter when setting up traffic shaping on our networks.

Traffic shaping also plays a large role in the current debate on **net neutrality**. Advocates of net neutrality argue that internet data should be treated equally. Opponents of net neutrality argue in favor of multiple tiers of service, and that forcing internet providers to treat all data packets equally will result in fewer choices for consumers. Fortunately, the net neutrality debate is focused primarily on the public internet, and since we are mainly concerned with our private networks, we can sidestep this controversy.

As you become more involved with implementing traffic shaping with pfSense, you will become aware of the limitations of the built-in traffic shaper. The traffic shaper is capable of creating queues with varying levels of priority (levels 1 to 7, to be exact). Identifying which traffic should go into a certain queue can be challenging. We can assume that traffic coming in on a certain port is used by a certain application, and act accordingly. We can also make assumptions based on what protocol is being used (for example, VoIP traffic will tend to use **User Datagram Protocol** (UDP). In some cases, we need to examine the contents of a packet to determine which application has generated the packet. Since we are examining the contents of the packet in order to determine what application the packet originated from, and the seven-layer OSI model considers layer 7 the application layer, we call such an examination **Layer 7 packet inspection**. The pfSense traffic shaper lacks the ability to do any kind of layer 7 packet inspection (also known as **deep packet inspection**). Earlier versions of the traffic shaper attempted to implement this, but apparently it never really worked, and also caused other traffic-shaping functionality to break. As a result, more recent versions of pfSense do not implement layer 7 traffic shaping, and in order to get this done, we must use third-party packages.

In this chapter, we consider three separate scenarios. In the first, we will use the traffic shaping wizard to prioritize certain traffic and deprioritize other traffic. In the second, we will create a floating rule to deal with a more specific traffic shaping scenario. In the third, we will use Snort to implement layer 7 traffic shaping.

Configuring traffic shaping using the traffic-shaping wizard

In this recipe, we will use the pfSense traffic-shaping wizard to prioritize Skype traffic and deprioritize BitTorrent traffic. Assume that we have both the Skype client and one or more BitTorrent clients already installed on one or more nodes on our network.

How to do it...

1. Navigate to **Firewall | Traffic Shaper**.
2. Click on the **Wizards** tab.
3. Click on the **Multiple Lan/Wan** link:

4. Enter the **Number of WAN type connections** and the **Number of LAN type connections** in the appropriate text fields. Leave the latter set to **1** to apply traffic shaping only to LAN interface traffic:

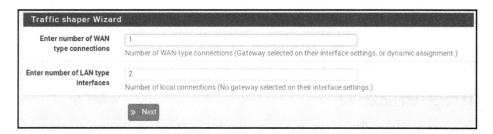

5. Click on the **Next** button.
6. On the next page, select the interface and scheduling algorithm for each of the **LAN** and **WAN** interfaces. If you only have one LAN interface, no changes need to be made here:

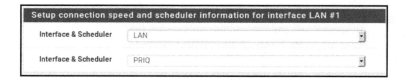

7. Select the correct upload and download bandwidth in the **Upload** and **Download** text fields. You can select the appropriate upload and download rates in the corresponding drop-down menus (choices are **Kbit/s**, **Mbits/s**, and **Gbits/s**):

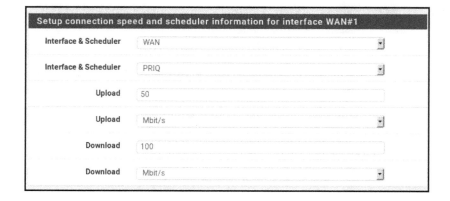

8. Click on the **Next** button.
9. Check the **Prioritize Voice over IP traffic** checkbox.
10. Keep the **Provider** set to **Generic** (Skype isn't listed):

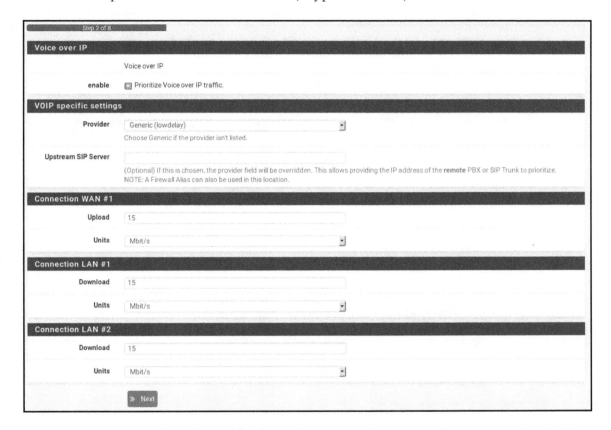

11. In the text fields for the **WAN** and **LAN** interfaces, enter the amount of upload and download bandwidth you want to reserve for Skype calls. A high definition Skype video call requires at least 1.2 Mbits/s of both upload and download bandwidth, so you'll likely want to reserve at least that much and possibly more, depending on how many simultaneous Skype calls you anticipate occurring on your network.
12. Click on the **Next** button when done.

13. The next page controls settings for the **Penalty Box**, which allows you to penalize an IP address or alias. Since we don't need to penalize anyone, click on the **Next** button:

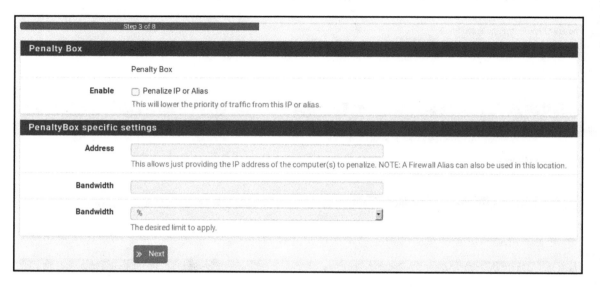

14. The next page controls settings for peer-to-peer networking. Check the **Lower priority of Peer-to-Peer networking** checkbox:

15. Check the **When enabled, all uncategorized traffic is fed to the p2p queue** checkbox. Enter 10 into the **Bandwidth** edit box to limit P2P traffic to 10% of the total bandwidth:

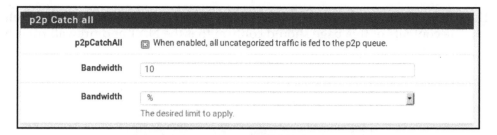

16. In the **Enable/Disable specific P2P protocols** section, check the **BitTorrent** checkbox to enable the BitTorrent protocol:

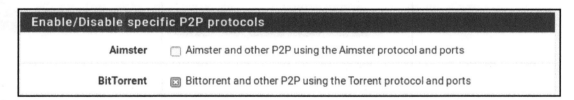

17. Click on the **Next** button.
18. The next page of the wizard is for prioritizing network games. Since we don't want to prioritize any games, click on the **Next** button.
19. The next page of the wizard is for raising and lowering the priority of software, such as remote desktop applications and messengers. Since we don't want to raise or lower the priority of these applications, click on the **Next** button.
20. We have now reached the end of the wizard. Click on the **Finish** button to load the new profile:

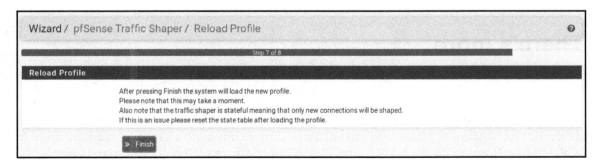

21. You will now be redirected to the **Filter Reload** page at **Status | Filter Reload**. The contents of this page should confirm that the NAT and firewall rules have reloaded:

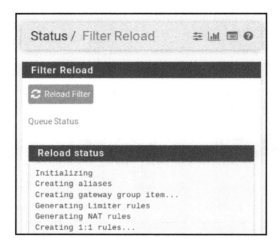

How it works...

Using the traffic shaping wizard, we have defined a set of rules that prioritize Skype traffic and deprioritize BitTorrent traffic. As a result, even if we have multiple Skype connections, they should not suffer even if we are using BitTorrent or otherwise downloading files. As we shall see, however, the manner in which pfSense determines which traffic is Skype traffic and which traffic is BitTorrent traffic is not necessarily foolproof.

There's more...

There are two variants of the traffic-shaping wizard: Multiple LAN/WAN, which is what we used in this recipe, and Dedicated Links, which we did not use. **Dedicated Links** is for cases in which certain LAN/WAN pairings do not mix with other traffic. This would be the case if users on a certain subnet have a different internet connection (and, therefore, a different WAN gateway) than other users. For example, imagine a network configuration in which traffic flows from the LAN to the WAN, but traffic from the demilitarized zone (**DMZ**) goes to WAN2. In such a case, each LAN-WAN connection has its own traffic-shaping requirements, and using the Dedicated Links wizard helps us take this into account.

On the Shaper configuration page of the wizard, you must choose the queuing discipline for each of the interfaces. In this recipe, we left the discipline set to PRIQ, but there are several choices:

- **Priority Queuing (PRIQ)**: The simplest of all queuing disciplines supported by pfSense. Packets are assigned different priority levels, with higher priority levels being favored over lower priority levels. This guarantees lower latency for high priority traffic, but lower priority traffic can become starved of bandwidth.
- **Class-Based Queuing (CBQ)**: Each class has an upper and lower bound for bandwidth, and classes can be subdivided. No guarantees are made concerning latency.
- **Hierarchical Fair Service Curve (HFSC)**: This type of queue utilizes two separate curves. The fairness portion of the curve provides a minimum latency, while the service portion determines the amount of bandwidth allocated. This queuing discipline tries to balance the competing interests of latency and bandwidth, but no guarantees concerning latency are made.

There is also a page of the wizard devoted to the **Penalty Box**. Very simply, the penalty box takes traffic from an IP or alias and places it into a queue that is limited to a percentage of the total bandwidth.

To see the rules the traffic-shaping wizard has generated, navigate to **Firewall** | **Rules** and click on the **Floating** tab. There should be three new rules: one to prioritize VoIP traffic, and two to lower the priority of BitTorrent traffic (one for BitTorrent TCP traffic and the other for BitTorrent UDP traffic). Note that these rules do not use the **Pass**, **Block**, or **Reject** actions, but instead use the Match action, and simply place traffic that match the rule criteria into different queues. Also, note the limitations of the traffic shaping wizard: the only criteria for the VoIP rule is that it uses the UDP protocol—yet there may well be other traffic that uses UDP that will now be placed in the VoIP queue. even though it is not VoIP traffic. The rules for BitTorrent, on the other hand, will match traffic that uses either UDP or TCP, and ports 6881 to 6999. We can easily circumvent these rules by using other ports for BitTorrent traffic.

☐	▼✿	0 /869 B	IPv4 UDP	*	*	*	*	*	qVoIP	DiffServ/Lowdelay/Upload	⬓✎⬚⊘🗑
☐	▼✿	0 /0 B	IPv4 TCP	*	*	*	6881 - 6999	*	qP2P	m_P2P BitTorrent outbound	⬓✎⬚⊘🗑
☐	▼✿	0 /0 B	IPv4 UDP	*	*	*	6881 - 6999	*	qP2P	m_P2P BitTorrent outbound	⬓✎⬚⊘🗑

One of the ways to prevent circumvention of the traffic-shaping rules is to identify traffic based on the content of the packets. This is referred to as layer 7 traffic shaping, or deep packet inspection. Unfortunately, the pfSense traffic shaper no longer supports layer 7 traffic shaping. Therefore, if you want to implement this form of traffic shaping in pfSense, you will find it necessary to use a third-party package such as Snort.

See also

- The *Configuring traffic shaping using floating rules* recipe
- The *Configuring traffic shaping using Snort* recipe

Configuring traffic shaping using floating rules

In this recipe, we will use floating rules to prioritize EchoLink traffic.

The previous recipe used the pfSense traffic-shaping wizard to prioritize Skype traffic and deprioritize BitTorrent traffic. Running the wizard essentially created the traffic-shaping queues as well as the floating rules. Once we have run the wizard, we have a second option for traffic-shaping: manually adding floating rules.

Getting ready

Completing this recipe requires having completed the previous recipe, *Configuring traffic shaping using the traffic-shaping wizard recipe,* or having run the wizard previously. Doing so will ensure the traffic shaping queues have been created.

EchoLink is a program that allows amateur radio operators to communicate over a VoIP connection. It uses UDP on ports 5198 and 5199, and uses TCP on port 6000. In order to prioritize EchoLink traffic, we will create two rules (one for UDP traffic and the other for TCP traffic).

How to do it...

1. Navigate to **Firewall | Rules**.
2. Click on the **Floating** tab.
3. Click on the second **Add** button to add a rule to the end of the list.
4. When the **Edit** page loads, select **Match** in the **Action** drop-down menu:

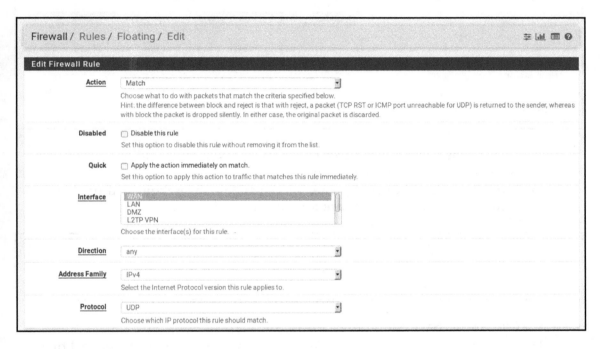

5. Select **WAN** in the **Interface** list.
6. Keep **Direction** set to **any**.
7. In the **Protocol** drop-down menu, select **UDP**.
8. Set **Destination Port Range** to 5198 to 5199.

9. You may enter a brief description in the **Description** text field:

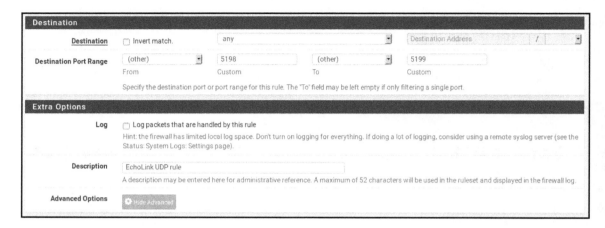

10. Click on the **Display Advanced** button, which will reveal additional settings, some of which we must configure.
11. Scroll down to **Ackqueue/Queue**. Select **qACK** in the **Ackqueue** drop-down menu, and **qVoIP** in the **Queue** drop-down menu.

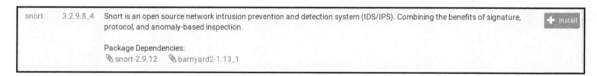

12. Click on the **Save** button when done.
13. To save time, we will create a rule for TCP traffic by copying the original rule. Click on the **Copy** icon for the newly created rule.
14. Change the **Protocol** to **TCP**.
15. Change the **Destination Port Range** to **6000**.
16. Modify the **Description**, if desired.
17. Change the **Queue** to **qOthersDefault**.
18. When done, click on the **Save** button.
19. Click on the **Apply Changes** button to reload the firewall rules.

How it works...

In this recipe, we created a floating rule that matches UDP traffic on ports 5198 and 5199 (the EchoLink ports), and places said traffic into the VoIP queue. We also placed ACK packets into a separate ACK queue (qACK) to try to expedite the sending of ACK packets. We could have placed the UDP packets into the qOthersHigh queue (the high priority queue), but the previous recipe did not create a high priority queue other than the VoIP queue. EchoLink TCP traffic is reserved for non-VoIP purposes (for example, downloading listings of users); therefore, TCP traffic does not need to go into the VoIP queue, so it was placed in the qOthersDefault queue. As with the UDP rule, we diverted ACK packets into a separate queue.

There's more...

In most cases, floating rules we create for traffic shaping will attempt to match traffic based on protocol and/or port. There are, however, other possibilities for matching traffic:

- **Source OS**: If the rule takes effect on TCP packets, you can also try to match the OS of the packets. Several variants of Windows, Linux, and macOS are supported, along with a few less common options, such as BeOS, Dragonfly, and PalmOS, among others.
- **TCP Flags**: You can match packets based on which TCP flags are either set or cleared.
- **VLAN Prio**: If the packets originate on a VLAN, you can match the packets based on the VLAN priority setting.

As mentioned in Chapter 3, *Firewall and NAT*, you can use the scheduler to ensure that the rule only takes effect during certain hours. As a result, you can apply traffic shaping during specific times.

See also

- The *Configuring traffic shaping using the traffic-shaping wizard* recipe
- The *Configuring traffic shaping using Snort* recipe

Configuring traffic shaping using Snort

In this recipe, we will cover using Snort, a third-party network **intrusion detection system** (**IDS**) and **intrusion prevention system** (**IPS**) for traffic shaping. In particular, we will use Snort to block BitTorrent traffic.

Using Snort as a traffic shaping utility is a multi-step process that involves the following:

1. Installing Snort with the pfSense Package Manager
2. Signing up for a Snort account via the Snort website
3. Configuring Snort

How to do it...

1. First, install Snort:
    1. Navigate to **System** | **Package Manager**.
    2. Click on the **Available Packages** tab.
    3. Find Snort in the list and click on the **Install** button:

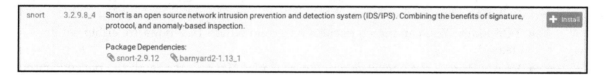

    4. You will be redirected to the **Package Installer** tab. Click on the **Confirm** button on this tab to install Snort and its dependencies.
    5. The **Package Installation** list should keep you informed of the progress in downloading and installing Snort. The process should not take long.
2. If you haven't done so, already, set up a Snort account:
    1. From a web browser, navigate to `https://www.snort.org/subscribe`.
    2. Click on the **Sign up** link. (or navigate to `https://www.snort.org/users/sign_up`).
    3. Enter your email address, password, and password confirmation in the appropriate fields.

4. Check the checkbox for **Agree to Snort License**. There are also several checkboxes for subscribing to Snort mailing lists; check the boxes for whichever lists you wish to receive.
5. Click on the **Sign up** button.
6. Snort will send you a confirmation email. Click on the link in the confirmation email and log into the Snort website again with the credentials you created in the previous steps.
7. Once you are logged in, scroll down to the **Sign Up/Subscribe** button (this should be step 2 on the **Get Started** page).
8. The menu on the left side of the page should have an option that reads **Oinkcode**. Click on this menu item to retrieve your Oinkcode. You will need to enter this code when you begin Snort configuration.

3. Now we can begin Snort configuration:
   1. Navigate to **Services | Snort**.
   2. Click on the **Global Settings** tab.
   3. Check the **Enable Snort VRT checkbox**:

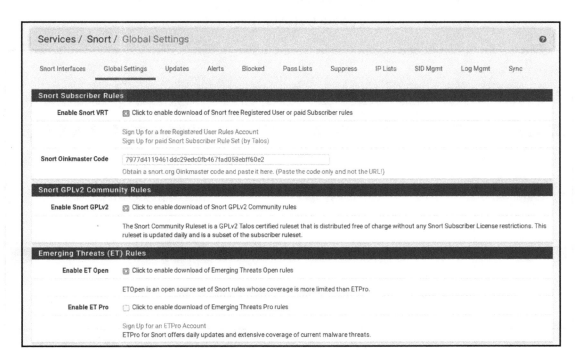

4. Copy your Oinkcode into the **Snort Oinkmaster Code** edit box.
5. Check the **Enable Snort GPLv2** checkbox.
6. Check the **Enable ET Open** checkbox to enable download of **Emerging Threats Open** rules.
7. For the **Update Interval**, select **1 DAY**:

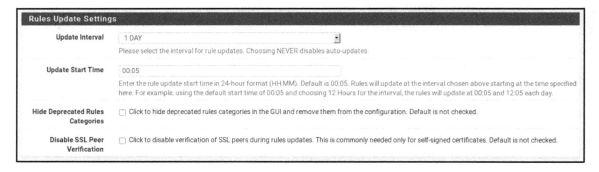

8. Click on the **Updates** tab.
9. Click on the **Update Rules** button:

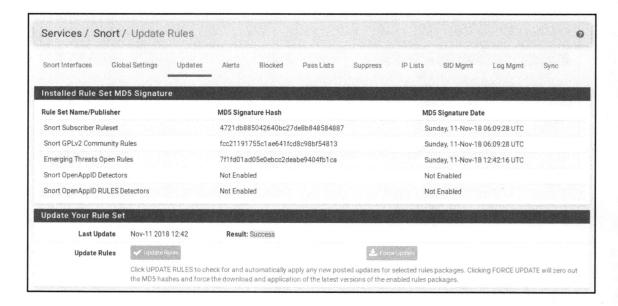

10. We still have to enable Snort on one or more interfaces. Click on the **Snort Interfaces** tab.
11. Click on the **Add** button to add an interface.
12. Check the **Enable interface** checkbox:

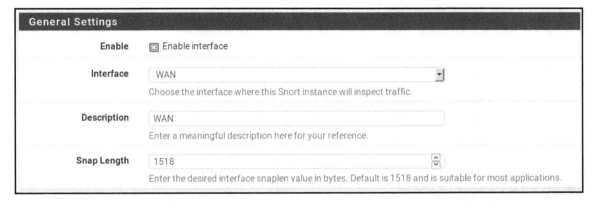

13. Set **Interface** to **WAN**; in most cases, you only need to run Snort on one interface.
14. In the **Alert Settings** section, be sure to check the **Send Alerts to System Log** checkbox.
15. You also should check the **Block Offenders** checkbox (automatically block hosts that generate a Snort alert) and the **Kill States** checkbox (kill firewall states for the blocked IP).
16. Leave the **Which IP to Block** drop-down set to **BOTH** to block both the source and destination IP:

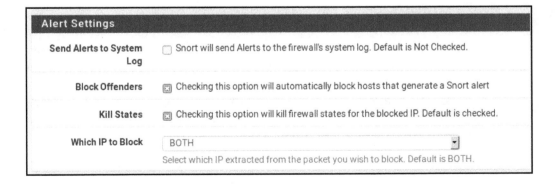

17. When you are done making changes, click on the **Save** button.
18. We still have to select rulesets for Snort, so when the page reloads, click on the **Edit** icon for the **WAN** interface (the pencil).
19. When the page reloads, click on the **WAN** categories tab.
20. In the **ET Open Rules** column, check the **emerging-p2p.rules** ruleset:

☐ emerging-netbios.rules	☐ snort_file-image.rules	☐ snort_protocol-snmp.so.rules
☒ emerging-p2p.rules	☐ snort_file-java.rules	☐ snort_protocol-tftp.so.rules
☐ emerging-policy.rules	☐ snort_file-multimedia.rules	☐ snort_protocol-voip.so.rules

21. When you are done selecting any other rulesets you wish to enable, click on the **Save** button.

How it works...

By installing and configuring Snort and enabling it on the WAN interface with the `emerging-p2p.rules` ruleset, BitTorrent traffic should now be blocked. All IP addresses that attempt to use BitTorrent will be added to Snort's blacklist.

There's more...

In this recipe, we have barely scratched the surface with respect to Snort's capabilities. In reality, **Snort** is a fully-fledged network intrusion prevention system and intrusion detection system. It is capable of being run in the following modes:

- **Packet-sniffing mode**: In this mode, Snort simply intercepts packets in a manner similar to any readily available packet sniffer (for example, Wireshark).
- **Packet-logging mode**: In this mode, Snort takes the process one step further and logs packets to the disk. This mode is useful if you are trying to debug network issues.
- **Network intrusion prevention mode**: In this mode, Snort monitors network traffic, analyses it against a user-defined ruleset, and performs certain actions based on the rule that has been matched.

In this recipe, we ran Snort in network intrusion prevention mode to block peer-to-peer traffic, including BitTorrent traffic. We can do much more with Snort, including using it to block certain websites.

This recipe used the Snort GPLv2 Community rules. However, you can also pay for a Snort Subscriber Rule Set. The current rates for such rules can be found at `https://www.snort.org/products`. A personal subscription is currently $29.99 (USD) a month.

You may also want to use the Open AppID plugin. This plugin enables Snort to detect, monitor, and manage application usage. To use Open AppID, you will find it necessary to download the Sourcefire Open AppID detectors. To do so, check the **Enable OpenAppID** checkbox on the **Global Settings** tab of Snort. You may also want to check the **Enable RULES OpenAppID** checkbox to enable download of OpenAppID rules.

The official Snort website provides copious amounts of documentation, which you will want to read if you want to become adept at leveraging the power of Snort on your networks. You can find this documentation at `https://www.snort.org/documents#OfficialDocumentation`.

See also

- The *Configuring traffic shaping using the traffic shaping wizard* recipe
- The *Configuring traffic shaping using floating rules* recipe
- The official Snort users manual: `https://snort-org-site.s3.amazonaws.com/production/document_files/files/000/000/142/original/snort_manual.pdf`

7
Redundancy, Load Balancing, and Failover

In this chapter, we will cover the following:

- Adding multiple WAN interfaces
- Configuring server load balancing
- Configuring a CARP failover group

Introduction

One of the main selling points of incorporating pfSense into our networks is that it facilitates reliability. This is often expressed in terms of two components: redundancy and high availability. **Redundancy** is defined as the duplication of critical components. This can mean either passive or active redundancy—with passive redundancy, we incorporate excess capacity into a network, so that when a component fails, resources are still available. Active redundancy involves monitoring components and performing an automatic reconfiguration if a component fails. **High availability** means ensuring a specified level of operational performance over a period of time, for example, 99.9% uptime.

pfSense incorporates redundancy and high availability via multi-WAN setups, server load balancing, and **Common Address Redundancy Protocol (CARP)**. Multi-WAN configurations allow you to have more than one outbound interface, either to aggregate multiple internet connections, or to guarantee that if one internet connection goes down, you still have internet access. Server load balancing allows us to set up a server pool, thus distributing the workload across multiple, redundant servers, and ensuring that as long as one of the servers in the pool is still online, the resource will be available. **CARP** is a way of ensuring that the firewall itself remains online even in the event of a catastrophic hardware failure. Such a configuration involves having two (or more) firewalls. The secondary firewall is inactive, but is ready to take over as soon as the primary firewall goes offline. We will consider all of these forms of redundancy and high availability in this chapter.

Adding multiple WAN interfaces

In this recipe, we will add a multi-WAN setup to our pfSense firewall. This recipe will generate a gateway group with two WAN interfaces, although it could easily be altered to cover gateway groups with more than two WAN interfaces.

Getting ready

Adding multiple WAN interfaces makes the most sense when we have more than one internet connection. If you are completing this recipe in order to understand the process of configuring multiple WANs, and you have both a broadband and mobile internet connection, you can use these as your two connections. Otherwise, you will want to acquire two internet connections, preferably from two separate ISPs (otherwise, if you acquire two connections from the same ISP, then both connections to the internet will likely go down if your ISP experiences problems—hardly the redundancy and high availability we seek). If you have no choice but to use a single ISP, it might be helpful to obtain connections with different types of cabling; for example, a broadband and a DSL connection, to minimize the chances that both will go down at the same time.

Configuring a multi-WAN setup involves several steps:

1. Adding WAN interfaces to the firewall and configuring them
2. Configuring DNS servers for each of the WAN interfaces
3. Forming gateway groups and adding the new WAN interfaces to them
4. Adding firewall rules for each new gateway group

We will assume that the additional WAN interfaces have already been physically added to the firewall. We will also assume that our ISP assigns IP addresses via DHCP.

How to do it...

1. First, add a second WAN interface to the firewall:
    1. Navigate to **Interfaces | (assign) | Interface Assignments**.
    2. On the **Interface Assignments** tab, the **Available network ports** drop-down menu lists the unassigned network interfaces.
    3. Click on the **Add** button.
    4. The new interface will initially be assigned a generic name (for example, OPT1, OPT2). Click on the interface's name in the table (or navigate to the configuration page via the interfaces menu).
    5. On the interface configuration page, check the **Enable interface** checkbox.
    6. Enter a brief description in the **Description** text field (for example, OPT_WAN).
    7. In the **IPv4 Configuration Type** dropdown, select **DHCP**. pfSense will automatically configure this interface as a gateway.
    8. Enter a brief, non-parsed description in the **Description** text field.
    9. Check the **Block private addresses and loopback addresses** checkbox.
    10. Check the **Block bogon networks** checkbox.
    11. When you are done making changes, click on the **Save** button.
    12. Click on the **Apply Changes** button.

2. Now we must configure DNS servers for each of the newly added WAN-type interfaces:

   1. Navigate to **System** | **General Setup**.
   2. In the **DNS Server Settings** section, enter a DNS server for the new gateway. Enter the DNS server IP address in the text field on the left side, and select the gateway in the adjacent drop-down menu:

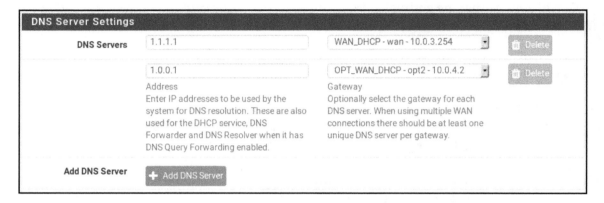

3. Make sure there is at least one unique DNS server per gateway.
4. When you are done, click on the **Save** button.

3. Now, we can begin gateway configuration:

   1. Navigate to **System** | **Routing** | **Gateways**.
   2. Click on the edit icon (the pencil) for the default gateway.
   3. Scroll down to the **Monitor IP** text field and enter the IP address of the gateway's DNS server:

4. Click on the **Save** button.
5. Click on the edit icon (the pencil) for the newly created gateway.
6. Scroll down to the **Monitor IP** edit box and enter the IP address of the gateway's DNS server.
7. Click on the **Save** button.
8. Click on the **Gateway Groups** tab.

9. Click on the **Add** button.
10. Enter the gateway group name in the **Group Name** text field:

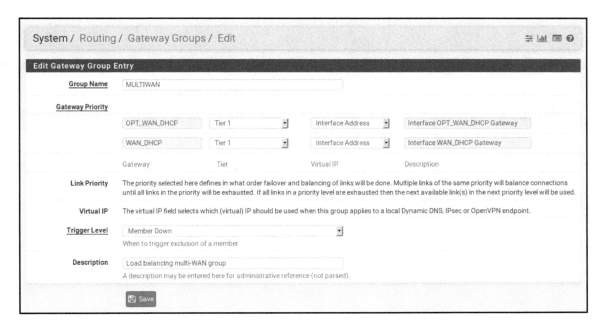

11. Under **Gateway Priority**, select **Tier 1** for all gateways in the gateway group.
12. Leave **Trigger Level** set to **Member Down**.
13. Enter a brief description in the **Description** text field.
14. When you are done, click on the **Save** button.
15. Click on the **Apply Changes** button:

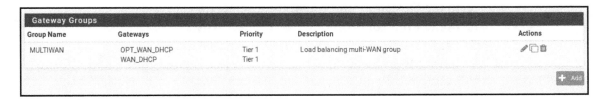

4. Finally, we must create a firewall rule to ensure outbound traffic utilizes the new gateway group:

1. Navigate to **Firewall** | **Rules** | **Floating**.
2. From the **Floating** tab, click on the first **Add** button.
3. Leave the **Action** set to **Pass**:

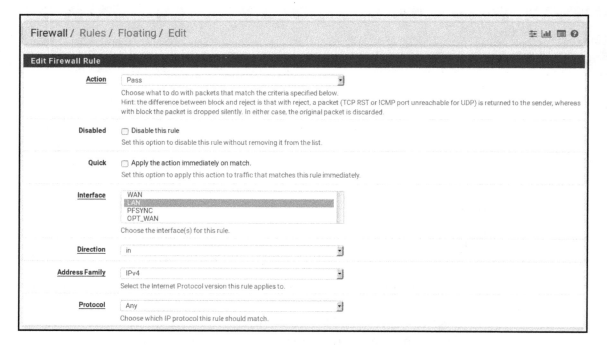

4. In the **Interface** drop-down menu, select every non-WAN interface you want to utilize the gateway group (at a minimum, you probably want to select **LAN**, but there may be others).
5. In the **Direction** drop-down box, select **in**.
6. In the **Protocol** drop-down box, select **Any**.
7. Leave the **Source** and **Destination** set to **Any**.
8. Enter a brief, non-parsed description in the **Description** edit box (for example, `Multi-WAN rule`).
9. In the **Extra Options** section, click on the **Show Advanced** button.

10. In the **Advanced Options** section, scroll down to the **Gateway** drop-down box and select the newly created gateway group:

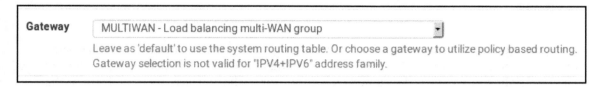

11. When you are done making changes, click on the **Save** button.

 Make sure the new rule is at the top of the list of floating rules.

How it works...

In this recipe, we configured a gateway group for load balancing. Gateway groups may be configured for failover or load balancing. With failover, some gateways have priority over other gateways, and only when all higher priority gateways fail, do the lower priority gateways come online. With load balancing, all gateways handle a share of the total WAN traffic. Load balancing would thus seem to be a good way to implement bandwidth aggregation, as the total bandwidth from all gateways will be available.

There is a significant limitation, however, on bandwidth aggregation using gateway groups. A single connection can only pass through a single gateway; therefore, the connection can at most utilize the bandwidth of the gateway through which it passes—not the total bandwidth of the gateway group. In practice, many file sharing technologies (such as BitTorrent) will use multiple connections when transferring files. Therefore, by making connections through all available gateways in the group, they will be able to utilize the total gateway group bandwidth.

Even after we add WAN-type interfaces, designate them as gateways, and place them in a gateway group, the new gateway group won't affect the default routing. The original WAN interface will still be the default gateway, and all outbound traffic will pass through it unless we change the firewall rules. Therefore, we have to create one or more rules to make sure at least one internal interface utilizes the new gateway group.

You can change the default gateway by navigating to **System | Routing | Gateways** and selecting a gateway from the **Default gateway IPv4** and **Default gateway IPv6** drop-down boxes. Click on the **Save** button when done.

After configuring the additional WAN interfaces, one of the first things we do is assign a DNS server to each of the WAN interfaces. Having a separate DNS server for each interface is a good policy; if we used the same DNS server for each interface, then a failure of that DNS server will cause DNS resolution to fail for the entire gateway group.

There is, however, an issue with using alternate DNS servers. pfSense uses its internal routing tables to find routes to DNS servers. Policy-based routing does not apply to traffic generated by pfSense. Therefore, we have to configure static routes if we want pfSense to use the right OPT WAN interface for a DNS query. Otherwise, all DNS queries will go through the primary WAN interface, and, as a result, DNS queries will fail if the primary WAN interface goes down.

If we don't want to configure a static route for each gateway's DNS server, one possible solution is to set the monitor IP for each gateway to the DNS server IP address. The monitor IP is an IP address (preferably outside of our network) that pfSense pings to determine whether a gateway is still up. If the ping attempts are getting an adequate number of responses, the gateway is considered up; otherwise, it is considered to be down. Very conveniently, pfSense creates an internal static route for monitor IPs. Therefore, if we make the DNS server the monitor IP, we won't have to create a static route for the DNS server. The only drawback to this approach is that unless the DNS server is a server that we control, the administrators running the DNS server may look upon our constant pings as suspicious activity and block them. When our ping attempts fail, pfSense will deem the gateway to be down, resulting in a false positive. This is why the monitor IP is ideally a node outside of our network but still under our control. Nevertheless, setting the monitor IP to the DNS server should work in most cases.

There's more...

When we added the new gateway, all we changed was the monitor IP. We skipped over a number of settings that could be helpful:

- **Disable Gateway Monitoring**: If this box is checked, pfSense will consider the gateway to always be up.
- **Disable Gateway Monitoring Action**: If this box is checked, pfSense will take no action when a gateway monitoring event is triggered.
- **Mark Gateway as Down**: If this box is checked, pfSense will consider the gateway to be down.
- **Weight**: This determines the weight of a gateway within a gateway group. For example, if we set this parameter to 2 while the other gateway's weight is set to 1, then the gateway will have twice as many connections going through it.
- **Data Payload**: This allows us to set the -s parameter of the ping command, which in turn lets us control how many bytes are sent when a ping is sent. The default is 1.
- **Latency Thresholds**: These text fields allow us to enter the low and high latency thresholds (in milliseconds) in cases where latency is one of the criteria for determining if a gateway is down. When the low latency threshold is reached, an alarm is triggered; when the high latency threshold is reached, the gateway goes down. The default is 200 ms/500 ms.
- **Packet Loss**: These text fields allow us to enter the low and high packet loss thresholds (in percentage) in cases where packet loss is one of the criteria for determining if a gateway is down. As with latency, the low threshold triggers an alarm, and the high threshold causes the gateway to go down. The default is 10/20.
- **Probe Interval**: This parameter determines how often an ICMP ping is sent out (default is 500 ms).
- **Loss Interval**: This parameter determines the amount of time that must elapse before a ping is considered lost (the default is 2000 ms).
- **Time Period**: This parameter determines the amount of time over which results are averaged (the default is 60000 ms).
- **Alert Interval**: This parameter determines the time interval before checking for an alert condition (the default is 1000 ms).
- **Use non-local gateway through interface specific route**: This option, if enabled, allows the use of a gateway outside of the interface's subnet.

Moving on to gateway groups, there are also a number of useful settings:

- **Gateway Priority**: This is where we determine which tier a gateway resides on. Gateways on lower-number tiers take priority over higher-numbered tiers (for example, Tier 1 has priority over Tier 2). To set up a load balancing group, we set gateways to the same tier. To create a failover group, we set some gateways with lower tiers than others—a Tier 2 gateway, for example, will only go online if all Tier 1 gateways fail. As a result, it is extremely easy to convert a load balancing gateway group into a failover gateway group, and the other way arounda; all we need to do is change the gateway priority. Note that we can also assign a virtual IP to each gateway in the group, assuming we have created virtual IPs for these gateways previously.

- **Trigger Level**: This determines when a gateway is considered to be down. The following options are available:
    - **Member Down**: A gateway is excluded from the group when it fails to respond to a ping, or fails to ping the monitor IP.
    - **Packet Loss**: A gateway is excluded from the group when packet loss reaches a certain threshold (we can configure the packet loss threshold for each gateway when configuring the gateway).
    - **High Latency**: A gateway is excluded when latency reaches a certain threshold (again, we can configure the latency thresholds for each gateway when configuring the gateway).
    - **Packet Loss or High Latency**: A gateway is excluded either when packet loss or latency reaches a certain threshold.

To see the current status of a gateway or gateway group, navigate to **Status** | **Gateways**. The **Gateways** tab will show statistics for each gateway, including whether the gateway is offline or online, the **round-trip time (RTT)**, and the **round-trip time standard deviation (RTTsd)**:

Gateways	Gateway Groups						
Gateways							
Name	**Gateway**	**Monitor**	**RTT**	**RTTsd**	**Loss**	**Status**	**Description**
OPT_WAN_DHCP	10.0.4.2	1.0.0.1	16.777ms	9.293ms	0.0%	Online	Interface OPT_WAN_DHCP Gateway
WAN_DHCP	10.0.3.254	10.0.3.254	0.771ms	0.7ms	0.0%	Online	Interface WAN_DHCP Gateway
WAN_DHCP6			Pending	Pending	Pending	Pending	Interface WAN_DHCP6 Gateway

The **Gateway Groups** tab will show information about each gateway group:

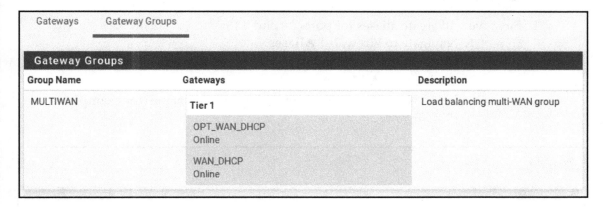

Configuring server load balancing

In this recipe, we will demonstrate how to set up a server load balancing pool for a group of web servers. It is possible to set up such a load balancing pool with third party plugins, but this recipe will demonstrate how to set up load balancing using pfSense's built-in load balancing capabilities.

The web servers in our configuration have IP addresses of 192.168.2.11, 192.168.2.12, and 192.168.2.13.

Getting ready

To effectively use this recipe, you should have a resource on your network, such as an FTP or a web server that has multiple redundant internal servers, and which you want to use in either a load balancing or failover configuration.

How to do it...

1. First, we will create aliases for ports 80 and 443:
    1. Navigate to **Firewall** | **Aliases**.
    2. Click on the **Ports** tab.
    3. Click on the **Add** button.
    4. In the **Name** text field, enter an appropriate name (for example, WEB_SERVER_PORTS):

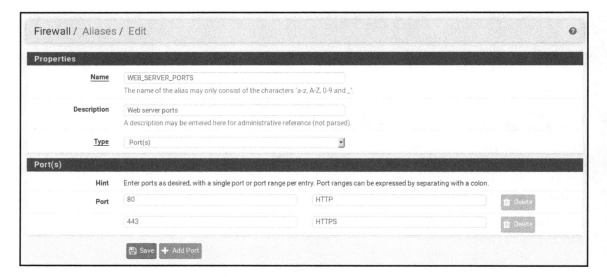

5. In the **Description** edit box, enter a brief, non-parsed description.
6. Enter **80** in the **Port** text field and a description in the adjacent text field (for example, HTTP).
7. Click on the **Add Port** button.
8. A new set of boxes should appear. Enter 443 in the **Port** text field and a brief description (for example, HTTPS).
9. Click on the **Save** button.
10. Click on the **Apply Changes** button.

2. Next, we want to create an alias for the web servers:
    1. Navigate to **Firewall** | **Aliases** | **IP**.
    2. From the IP tab, click on the **Add** button.
    3. In the **Name** edit box, enter an appropriate name (for example, WEB_SERVER_IPS):

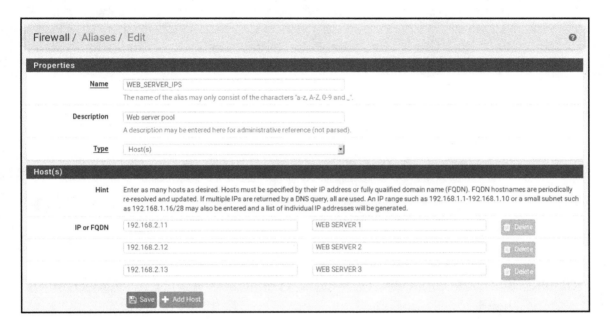

    4. In the **Description** text field, enter a brief, non-parsed description.
    5. Enter 192.168.2.11 in the **IP or FQDN** edit box. Enter a brief description in the adjacent text field (for example, WEB SERVER 1).
    6. Click the **Add Host** button.
    7. Repeat this process for the remaining two web servers.
    8. Click on the **Save** button.
    9. Click on the **Apply Changes** button.

3. Now, we can configure the load balancer:
    1. Navigate to **Services** | **Load Balancer** | **Pools**.
    2. From the **Pools** tab, click on the **Add** button.
    3. In the **Name** text field, enter a name for the pool.

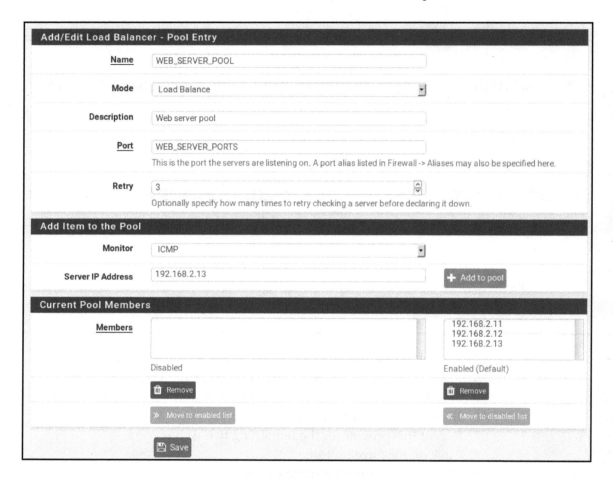

4. In the **Description** text field, enter a brief description.
5. In the **Port** text field, enter the alias we created in step 1.
6. In the **Retry** text field, enter the number of times pfSense will retry a server before declaring it to be down.
7. In the **Add Item to the Pool** section, enter the first web server IP (192.168.2.11) in the **Server IP Address** edit box.

8. Click on the **Add to pool** button.
9. Repeat this process for the second and third web server IPs (`192.168.2.12` and `192.168.2.13`).
10. When you are done, click on the **Save** button.
11. Click on the **Apply Changes** button:

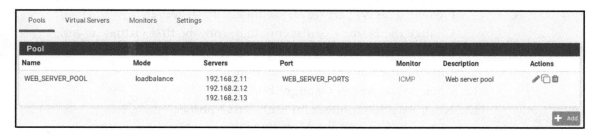

4. Next, we add the virtual servers:
   1. Click on the **Virtual Servers** tab.
   2. Click on the **Add** button.
   3. In the **Name** text field, enter a name:

4. In the **Description** text field, enter a non-parsed description.

5. In the **IP Address** text field, enter the IP address for the web server to listen on (usually the WAN IP address).
6. The **Port** text field should support aliases, but it does not. Thus, enter 80 into this text field.
7. Click on the **Save** button when done.
8. When the page loads, click on the **Copy** icon for the virtual server just created. This will create an identical virtual server.
9. Change the **Name** to differentiate it from the first virtual server.
10. Change the **Port** to 443.
11. Click on the **Save** button when done.
12. Click on the **Apply Changes** button.
13. Next, we add monitors for both active ports:
    1. Click on the **Monitors** tab.
    2. Click on the **Add** button.
    3. In the **Name** text field, enter a name:

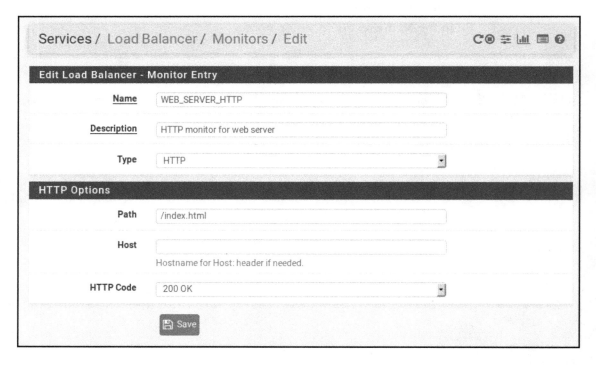

4. In the **Description** text field, enter a non-parsed description.

5. In the **Type** drop-down menu, select **HTTP**.

6. In the **Path** text field, enter a web page path for a page that will return a **200 OK** code (for example, `/index.html`).

7. Click on the **Save** button when done.

8. Click on the **Add** button again.

9. Enter a **Name** and **Description**.

10. In the **Type** drop-down menu, select **HTTPS**.

11. In the **Path** edit box, enter a web page path for a page that will return a **200 OK** code (for example, `/index.php`).

12. Click on the **Save** button when done.

13. Finally, we must add a firewall rule for the web server pool:

    1. Navigate to **Firewall | Rules**.

    2. Click on the **WAN** tab.

    3. Click on the **Add** button.

    4. For **Destination**, select **Single host or alias**:

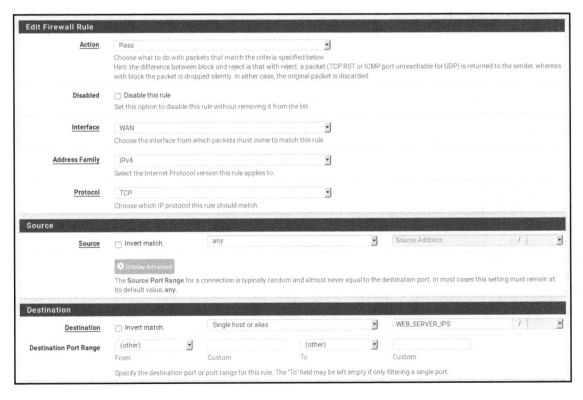

5. Enter the web server pool alias we created in step 2.
6. Set **Destination Port Range** to the port alias we created in step 1.
7. In the **Description** field, enter an appropriate description.
8. Click on the **Save** button.
9. Click on the **Apply Changes** button:

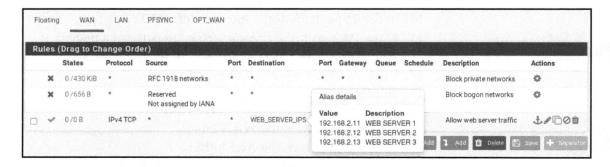

How it works...

In this recipe, we created aliases for the web server ports and the web server IP addresses. We then set up a load balancing pool with all three web servers, and set up pfSense to listen on the WAN IP address. We added monitors to help pfSense keep track of when servers within the pool are still online. Finally, since traffic won't pass to the web server ports unless a firewall rule exists to permit it, we created a firewall rule to allow traffic to pass to the server pool.

There's more...

This recipe created a web server pool that operates in load balancing mode. We could just as easily have put the pool in manual failover mode. To do so, navigate to **Services | Load Balancer** and click on the edit icon for the server pool we created earlier. On the **Edit** page, change the **Mode** to **Manual failover**. Note that the current pool members will change so only one server remains enabled; the other two will be disabled until the first server goes down.

If the pfSense load balancer proves to be inadequate, you might want to consider installing HAProxy, a third-party package that incorporates the following improvements over the built-in load balancer:

- Support for **Access Control Lists (ACLs)**
- Logging options
- Support for different load balancing algorithms
- Support for different methods of informing admins that a server is down (for example, email)

See also

- The *Adding multiple WAN interfaces* recipe
- The *Configuring a CARP failover group* recipe

Configuring a CARP failover group

In this recipe, we will configure a CARP failover group with two firewalls; one firewall will be online, and the other will be offline, ready to take over as soon as the primary firewall fails.

Getting ready

Implementing a CARP failover group requires an additional investment in hardware. Namely, you must have access to the following hardware to complete this recipe, in addition to your primary firewall:

- A secondary firewall that is an exact copy of the first.
- A router for the WAN side of the network, one that will provide a way of connecting both the primary and secondary firewall to the ISP.
- A crossover cable, to provide a way of connecting the pfsync interfaces on the primary and secondary firewalls.

How to do it...

The following recipe is the most involved recipe in this book; nonetheless, if you follow these steps painstakingly, setting up a CARP failover group should prove to be fairly easy.

The following diagram illustrates the new network topology. The **fxp0** represents the WAN interface, **fxp2** the LAN interface, and **fxp1** the pfsync network:

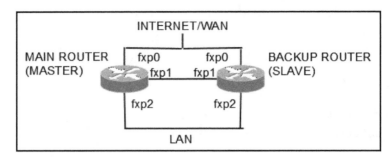

As a preliminary step, the WAN interfaces of both firewalls should be connected to the router mentioned in the previous section. The upstream gateway of the new router should be your ISP:

1. We will begin by configuring the virtual IP addresses we need for a CARP group:
    1. Navigate to **Firewall | Virtual IPs**.
    2. Click on the **Add** button.
    3. Set **Type** to **CARP:**

Firewall / Virtual IPs / Edit

Edit Virtual IP

Type	○ IP Alias ● CARP ○ Proxy ARP ○ Other
Interface	WAN
Address type	Single address
Address(es)	10.0.3.240 / 8

The mask must be the network's subnet mask. It does not specify a CIDR range.

Virtual IP Password	●●●●●●●● ●●●●●●●●

Enter the VHID group password.   Confirm

VHID Group	1

Enter the VHID group that the machines will share.

Advertising frequency	1 0

Base   Skew

The frequency that this machine will advertise. 0 means usually master. Otherwise the lowest combination of both values in the cluster determines the master.

Description	WAN virtual IP for CARP

A description may be entered here for administrative reference (not parsed).

💾 Save

4. In the **Interface** drop-down menu, select **WAN**.
5. In the **Address(es)** text field, enter the virtual IP for the WAN interface. Enter the subnet mask in the adjacent drop-down menu.
6. In the **Virtual ID Password** edit boxes, enter the **Virtual Host ID** (**VHID**) password (in the second text field, re-enter it for confirmation).
7. In the **VHID Group** drop-down menu, select the VHID Group for this interface (or just leave it set to its default value).
8. In **Advertising** frequency, leave **Base** set to 1 and **Skew** set to 0. The lowest combination of Base and Skew determines who is the master, and since we are setting up the virtual IPs on the primary firewall now, we want this to be the master.
9. Enter a brief description in the **Description** text field (for example, WAN virtual IP for CARP).
10. Click on the **Save** button.

11. Click on the **Add** button again.
12. Set **Type** to **CARP**.
13. In the **Interface** drop-down menu, select **LAN**.
14. Enter the virtual IP and subnet mask for the **LAN** interface.
15. Enter the password in the **Virtual ID Password** edit boxes. Since this is a different VHID group from the one for the WAN interface, it can be a different password from the one entered for the WAN VHID.
16. Select the VHID Group, or just leave it set it its default value—pfSense should automatically increment the VHID Group number.
17. In **Advertising** frequency, leave **Base** set to 1 and **Skew** set to 0.
18. Enter a brief **Description**, (for example, LAN virtual IP for CARP).
19. Click on the **Save** button.
20. Repeat the process for as many interfaces you want to add virtual IP addresses.
21. Click on the **Apply Changes** button:

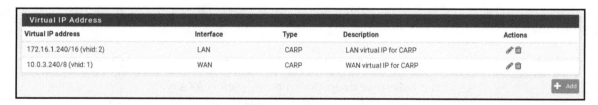

Virtual IP address	Interface	Type	Description	Actions
172.16.1.240/16 (vhid: 2)	LAN	CARP	LAN virtual IP for CARP	✎ 🗑
10.0.3.240/8 (vhid: 1)	WAN	CARP	WAN virtual IP for CARP	✎ 🗑

+ Add

2. In the next step, we will add a dedicated pfsync interface:
    1. Navigate to **Interfaces | Assignments**.
    2. In the **Available network ports:** drop-down box, select an unused interface.
    3. Click on the **Add** button.
    4. Click on the newly created interface's name.
    5. Check the **Enable interface** checkbox:

6. Enter a name in the **Description** text field.
7. Select **Static IPv4** in the **IPv4 Configuration Type** drop-down menu.
8. If desired, select **Static IPv6** in the **IPv6 Configuration Type** drop-down menu.
9. In the **IPv4 Address** text field, enter an IPv4 address (and CIDR in the adjacent drop-down box).
10. If necessary, enter an IPv6 address in the **IPv6 Address** text field.
11. When you are done making changes, click on the **Save** button.
12. Click on the **Apply Changes** button.

3. Next, we need to add a firewall rule for the pfsync interface:
    1. Navigate to **Firewall** | **Rules**.
    2. Click on the **PFSYNC** tab.
    3. Click on the **Add** button.
    4. Set the protocol in the **Protocol** drop-down menu to **PFSYNC**.
    5. In the **Source** drop-down menu, select **PFSYNC net**.

6. Enter a brief description in the **Description** text field (for example, `Allow PFSYNC to any rule`).

7. When you are done, click on the **Save** button.

8. Click on the **Apply Changes** button.

4. The next step is to enable pfsync and XML-RPC:

1. Navigate to **System | High Availability Sync**.

2. Check the **Synchronize States** checkbox:

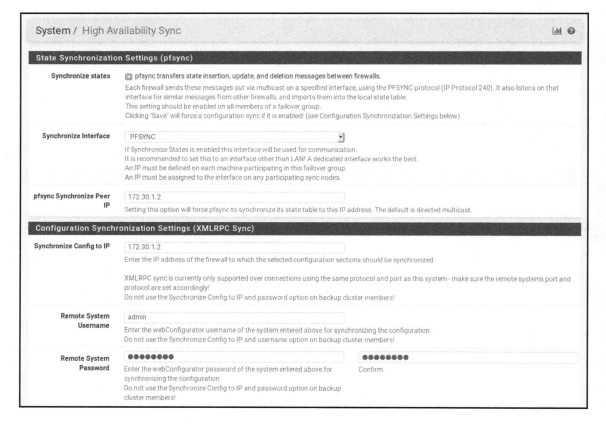

3. In the **Synchronize Interface** drop-down menu, select **PFSYNC**.

4. In the **pfsync Synchronize Peer IP** text field, enter the IP address of the pfsync interface on the secondary firewall.

5. In the **Synchronize Config to IP** text field, enter the IP address entered into **Synchronize Peer IP**.
6. In the **Remote System Username** text field, enter **admin**.
7. In the **Remote System Password** text field, enter the password for admin (you must enter this twice).
8. In the **Select options to sync section**, check off everything that should be synced.

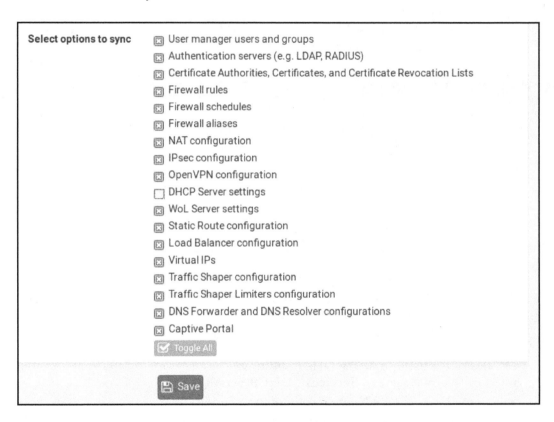

9. When you are done, click on the **Save** button.

5. Now we must perform manual outbound NAT configuration:
    1. Navigate to **Firewall | NAT**.
    2. Click on the **Outbound** tab.
    3. Select either **Hybrid Outbound NAT** rule generation or **Manual Outbound NAT** rule generation.
    4. Click on the **Save** button.
    5. Find the **auto-created LAN to WAN** rule and click on the edit icon (a pencil) for it.
    6. In the **Translation** section, set **Address** to the WAN virtual IP we created in step 1:

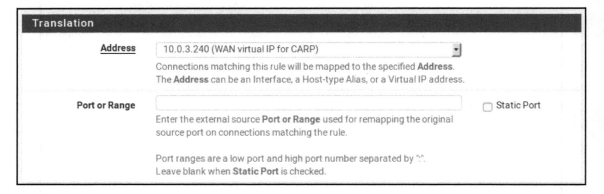

7. Click on the **Save** button when done.
8. Repeat the process for all non-WAN interfaces that will be replicated across firewalls (for example, DMZ).
9. Click on the **Apply Changes** button.

6. Next, we must update the DHCP settings:
    1. Navigate to **Services | DHCP Server | LAN**.
    2. On the **LAN** tab, scroll down to **Servers**.
    3. In the **Servers** section, set the first DNS server to the LAN virtual IP created in step 1.
    4. In the **Other Options** section, set **Gateway** to the LAN virtual IP:

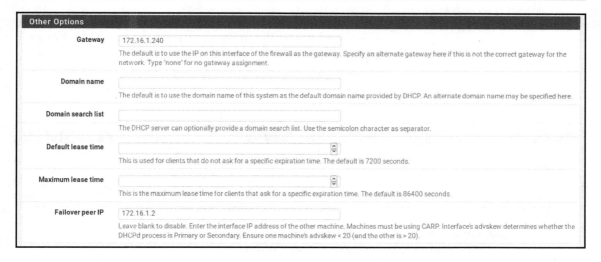

5. Click on the **Save** button.
6. Repeat the process for all interfaces on which DHCP is running, and which have virtual IPs.
7. Click on the **Save** button.

7. We have now completed CARP configuration on the primary firewall. The next step is to move to the secondary firewall and ensure that the settings are correct. Log into the secondary firewall, while keeping it offline for now:
    1. Make sure the virtual IPs we created in step 1 are duplicated on the secondary firewall:
        1. Navigate to **Firewall** | **Virtual IPs**.
        2. Duplicate the CARP virtual IPs we created in step 1 for the WAN and LAN interfaces, with one exception: the advertising frequency (Base + Skew) should be higher than the advertising frequency on the primary firewall.
        3. Save each virtual IP when done, and then click on the **Apply Changes** button.
    2. Add a firewall rule for the pfsync interface:
        1. This rule will have two purposes. First, it will allow the initial pfsync data to pass through the firewall. Second, it will (hopefully) be overwritten during the synchronization process, thus helping us to confirm that the synchronization process was a success.

2. Add a firewall rule similar to the rule we created in step 3 on the primary firewall, but find a way to differentiate it from the primary firewall's rule, so we will know it is overwritten (for example, change the **Description** to `PFSYNC rule to be overwritten`):

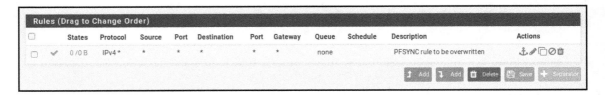

8. Now, we can activate CARP from the secondary firewall:
    1. Bring the secondary firewall online.
    2. Make sure the crossover cable provides connectivity between the pfsync interfaces of the primary and secondary firewalls.
    3. Navigate to **System | High Availablity Sync** on the secondary firewall.
    4. Check the **Synchronize States** checkbox.
    5. In the **Synchronize Interface** drop-down menu, select **PFSYNC**.
    6. In the **Synchronize Peer IP** text field, enter the IP address of the **PFSYNC** interface of the primary firewall.

 In order for the username/password combination to work, the admin password must be identical on both the primary and secondary firewalls.

    7. Click on the **Save** button.

9. Verify functionality of the failover group. Navigate to **Status | CARP (failover)** on both the primary and secondary firewall. If there is a button labeled **Enable CARP** on either side, click on it. Once you do, one side should be designated as **MASTER** and the other should be designated as **BACKUP**. To further test your failover group, disable the primary firewall and see how long it takes for the secondary firewall's designation to change from **BACKUP** to **MASTER**:

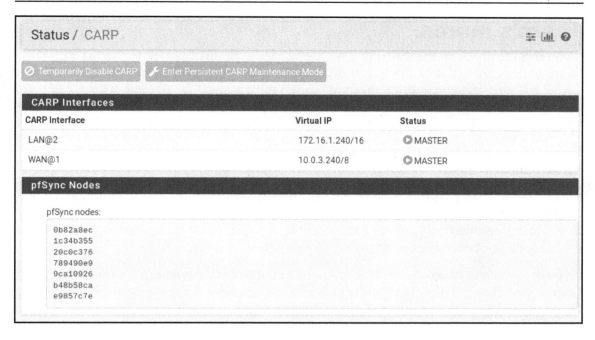

How it works...

CARP allows multiple hosts to share a set of IP addresses. These IP addresses are known as virtual IPs, and they provide a layer of abstraction above the actual hardware. Thus, if the primary firewall goes down, the secondary firewall takes over and the virtual IPs will now refer to the interfaces on the secondary firewall. Computers on either side of the firewall are unaware of what has happened, and operation continues as normal.

Adding the virtual IPs is critical, as it provides a means of interacting with the firewall's interfaces that will remain constant even in the event of a hardware failure. It is also critically important that we have a means of synchronizing data between the firewalls. The PFSYNC interface provides such a means.

There's more...

If you need to check on the status of CARP, navigate to **Status | CARP (failover)**. You will notice that there are two buttons on this page that can prove useful. **Temporarily Disable CARP** will, as the name implies, disables CARP on the firewall by removing the CARP virtual IPs. If the firewall was designated as MASTER before this function was invoked, then temporarily disabling CARP should cause the secondary firewall to become MASTER. This function, however, will not survive a reboot, and if you reboot the primary firewall, it will revert to being MASTER. CARP will also become re-enabled if you press the **Enable CARP** button.

If you need to keep CARP disabled through a reboot, you can click on the **Enter Persistent CARP Maintenance Mode** button. Invoking this functionality will disable CARP, and CARP being disabled will survive a reboot. In fact, CARP won't become re-enabled until you click on the **Leave Persistent CARP Maintenance Mode** button.

If you are trying to diagnose a CARP issue, you may want to navigate to **Status | System Logs**, especially right after attempting synchronization. Recent log activity will document the attempted synchronization and might provide a clue as to what went wrong.

See also

- The *Adding multiple WAN interfaces* recipe
- The *Configuring server load balancing* recipe
- The Wikipedia CARP page: `https://en.wikipedia.org/wiki/Common_Address_Redundancy_Protocol`

Routing and Bridging

8

In this chapter, we will cover the following:

- Bridging interfaces
- Adding a static route
- Configuring RIP using routed
- Configuring BGP using FRR
- Configuring OSPF using FRR

Introduction

Routing and bridging are often employed for similar reasons, but there are significant differences between the two. **Routing** refers to the process of moving packets between two or more networks, while **bridging** refers to connecting two or more network segments together. Thus, routing involves inter-network traffic, while bridging can involve intra-network traffic.

Routing

Most routing in pfSense is handled transparently, and, as a result, we tend to take it for granted. A pfSense router will know where to send traffic between two networks if both networks are connected to pfSense. If it doesn't know where to send a packet, pfSense will send it, by default, to the gateway, which in most cases is the WAN interface. Thus, if we request Google's home page, pfSense's routing daemon will realize that Google's IP address is not on any of the local networks and send the request through the default gateway.

There are cases, however, where the destination network is a local network not directly connected to pfSense, and not reachable though pfSense's default gateway. If there are only a few such cases in our network topology, then we may be able to define static routes to cover them. Otherwise, we might have to consider using a dynamic routing protocol to enable our routers to learn the network topology.

Dynamic routing

Dynamic routing is not supported natively by pfSense, but there are several third-party packages available that make dynamic routing possible. Both **distance vector** and **link state protocols** are available. Distance vector protocols use a distance calculation plus an outgoing network interface to find the shortest path to another network. Such a protocol only queries neighboring routers, and works best when all links in a network are of the same speed. Examples of distance vector protocols include **RIPv1** and **RIPv2**. Link state protocols track the status and connection type of each link, and perform a calculated metric. An example of a link state protocol is **Open Shortest Path First (OSPF)**.

Bridging

Before switched ports were commonplace, **bridging**, which takes place at layer 2 (the Data Link layer) of the seven layer OSI model, was an effective way of connecting multiple network segments into a single broadcast domain, while limiting the amount of traffic that spans more than one segment. For example, consider a network with two network segments; Nodes A and B are on the first segment, and node C is on the second segment.

If we connect the two segments with a repeater, then a packet from A whose destination is B will flood both sides of the repeater, even though B is on the same side of the repeater as A. But consider the case in which we place a bridge between the two segments. At first, the bridge does not know which nodes are on which side of the bridge. Gradually, however, a bridge will learn which side of the bridge a node is on, and packets from A to B will be confined to a single segment. This potentially reduces the amount of traffic on a network.

You can bridge two interfaces in pfSense and form a single broadcast domain. In such cases, two nodes on bridged interfaces act as if they are on the same switch. The main difference is that firewall rules for the bridged interfaces must allow traffic between the interfaces, or traffic will be blocked.

Bridging interfaces

This recipe will demonstrate how to bridge two interfaces on a pfSense firewall—the LAN and DMZ interfaces.

How to do it...

1. Navigate to **Interfaces | Assignments**.
2. Click on the **Bridges** tab.
3. Click on the **Add** button.
4. In the **Member Interfaces** list box, select **LAN** and **DMZ**:

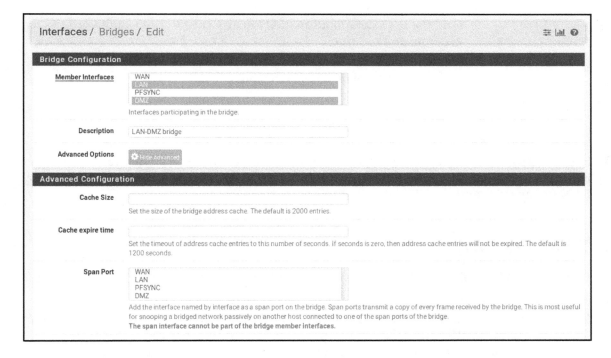

5. Enter a brief description in the **Description** text field (for example, LAN-DMZ bridge).
6. Click on the **Save** button.

7. We now have bridged the two interfaces, but unless the firewall rules allow traffic to flow between them, traffic will be blocked. Therefore, we will add firewall rules to allow traffic to flow between LAN and DMZ:

   1. Navigate to **Firewall | Rules**.
   2. Click on the **LAN** tab.
   3. Find the IPv4 default **allow LAN to any** rule and click on the **Copy** icon for this rule.
   4. Change **Interface** to **DMZ**.
   5. Change **Source** to **DMZ net**.
   6. Change the description in the **Description** text field (for example, `Allow DMZ to any rule`).
   7. Click on the **Save** button.
   8. Click on the **LAN** tab again.
   9. Find the IPv6 default **allow LAN to any rule** and repeat the process to generate an IPv6 rule.
   10. When you are done making changes, click on the **Save** button.
   11. Click on the **Apply Changes** button.

How it works...

In this recipe, we bridged two interfaces on our network to create a single layer 2 network. In order to ensure that traffic would flow between the interfaces, we took the default **allow LAN to any** rules and modified them.

There's more...

When adding a bridge, click the **Show Advanced** button to configure any of the following:

- **STP/RSTP**: You can choose which spanning tree protocol to use. pfSense currently supports the **Spanning Tree Protocol (STP)** and **Rapid Spanning Tree Protocol (RSTP)**. STP creates a spanning tree within a network of layer 2 spanning tree bridges and disables links that are not part of the spanning tree, leaving a single path between any two nodes on the spanning tree. Every port on a spanning tree is either a root port (the port from which we begin the algorithm), designated (active), or disabled (inactive). RSTP decreases the convergence time for responding to a topology change to a matter of seconds, but at a cost of added complexity.

- **Cache size**: The size of the bridge address cache (default is 2000 entries).
- **Cache entry expire time**: The timeout of address cache entries (default is 1200 seconds).
- **Span port**: An interface set as a span port will transmit a copy of each frame received by a bridge. This can be useful for monitoring network traffic. A span interface cannot be one of the bridge members.
- **Edge ports**: An edge port is a port that is only connected to one bridge. Thus it cannot create bridging loops in the network and can transition directly to a forwarding state. The **Auto Edge Ports** listbox allows us to select which ports will automatically detect edge status.
- **PTP ports**: Interfaces selected in the PTP ports listbox are designated at point-to-point links, which can make a direct transition to forwarding. **Auto PTP ports** are ports for which pfSense can automatically detect the point-to-point status by checking the full duplex link status.
- **Sticky ports**: This listbox allows you to designate ports as sticky ports, which means that dynamically-learned addresses are converted to static entries and are never aged out of the cache or replaced.
- **Private ports**: This listbox allows you to designate ports as private ports, which will not forward traffic to any other port that is also a private interface.

Adding a static route

In this recipe, we will demonstrate how to add a static route to a network not directly connected to pfSense. Assume that the LAN network uses the subnet 192.168.1.0/24, and there is an external router on the LAN network. The WAN interface of the external router has an IP address of 192.168.1.2, and the external router's LAN network uses the subnet 192.168.2.0/24. The following diagram illustrates our network (the DMZ router is our external Cisco router):

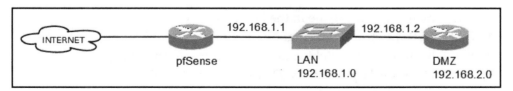

How to do it...

1. Navigate to **System | Routing | Gateways**.
2. On the **Gateways** tab, click on **Add**.
3. Set **Interface** to **LAN**:

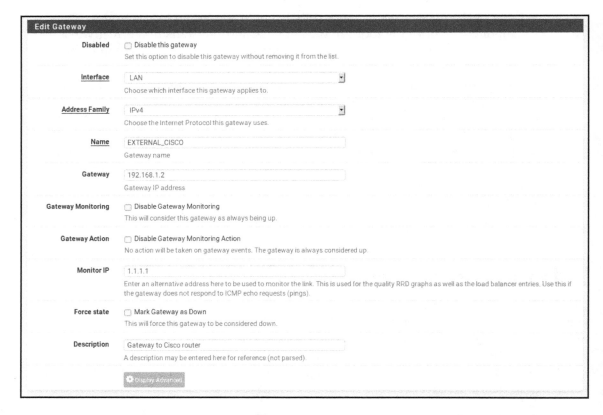

4. Enter an appropriate name in the **Name** edit box.
5. In the **Gateway** text field, enter **192.168.1.2**.
6. In the **Monitor IP** text field, enter an IP for monitoring the gateway.
7. Enter a brief description in the **Description** text field.
8. When done, click on the **Save** button.
9. Click on the **Apply Changes** button.
10. Click on the **Static Routes** tab.
11. Click on the **Add** button.

12. In the **Destination network** text field, enter `192.168.2.0`. In the adjacent CIDR drop-down box, select **24**:

13. In the **Gateway** drop-down menu, select the gateway created in steps 1-9.
14. Enter a brief description in the **Description** text field.
15. Click on the **Save** button.

How it works...

In this recipe, we created a static route to a node on the LAN side of an external router. In order to do so, we first had to add a gateway to the router. Once we did, we were able to add a static route that utilized this gateway.

There's more...

Although this recipe demonstrated how to configure a basic static route, we glossed over a rather important detail involving asymmetric traffic. Suppose there is a node on the LAN network with an IP address of `192.168.1.3`.

Assume this node wants to establish a session with a node on the DMZ network with an IP address of `192.168.2.3`. So far, so good: the LAN default gateway is `192.168.1.1`, and pfSense uses our newly created static route to send the packet to the gateway at `192.168.1.2`, ensuring that the packet reaches its destination on the `192.168.2.0/24` network. An entry is added to the state table.

The return traffic is a different story. Return traffic will ultimately pass through the DMZ's gateway at `192.168.1.2`, and from there to `192.168.1.3`, which will be recognized as a LAN net address. Thus, while the original packet was inter-network traffic (LAN to DMZ), the return traffic is seen as intra-network traffic by pfSense (LAN to LAN). The return traffic is thus never filtered by pfSense, since pfSense only filters traffic between networks. As far as pfSense is concerned, the packet never received a response; the connection was never completed, the entry is dropped from the state table, and the connection between `192.168.1.3` and `192.168.2.3` is dropped.

There are two ways to deal with this scenario. One is to ensure that traffic that enters and leaves through the same interface is not checked by pfSense. In our case, all traffic between the two nodes enters and leaves via the LAN interface, so it would work. We can do this by following these steps:

1. Navigate to **System | Advanced**.
2. Click on the **Firewall & NAT** tab.
3. Check the **Static route filtering** checkbox.
4. Click on the **Save** button.

Another possibility is to create firewall rules to cover both the sending of packets to the DMZ node and the return traffic. We won't discuss this solution in detail, but any attempt to solve the problem in this way would include the following elements:

1. A LAN network rule to cover traffic from the LAN to the DMZ, specifying as the destination the DMZ gateway (`192.168.1.2`).
2. A floating rule to cover return traffic, specifying as the source the DMZ gateway.
3. Both rules should use the **Sloppy** option for **State type**, which will cause pfSense to perform a less strict state match on return traffic.

At a minimum, you should consider using the **Static route filtering** option in situations such as this. While adding static routes is often unavoidable, hopefully this digression illustrates why we try to avoid static routes when possible.

Configuring RIP using routed

In this recipe, we will install and configure routed, the Routing Information Protocol daemon.

How to do it...

1. Navigate to **System | Package Manager**.
2. Click on the **Available Packages** tab.
3. Find **routed** on the list of available packages and click on the **Install** button for **routed**.
4. Click on the **Confirm** button. Installation should take less than 2 minutes.
5. Once the **Package Installer** indicates that installation is complete, navigate to **Services | RIP**.
6. Check the **Enable RIP** checkbox to enable the routed daemon:

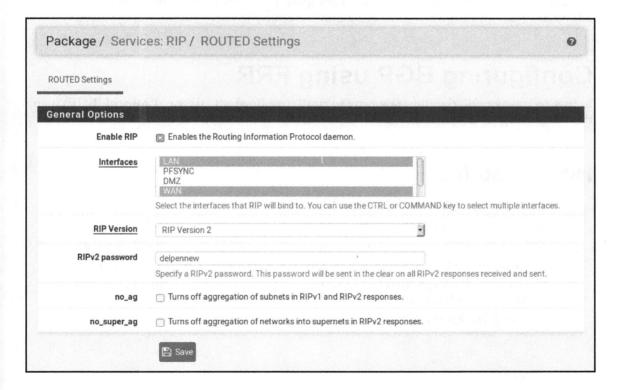

7. In the **Interfaces** list box, select the interfaces which RIP will bind to.
8. Select the appropriate RIP version in the **RIP Version** drop-down menu (**1** or **2**).
9. If you selected RIP Version 2, enter a password in the **RIPv2 password** text field.
10. Check the **no_ag** checkbox to turn off aggregation of subnets in RIPv1 and RIPv2 responses.
11. Check the **no_super_ag** checkbox to turn off aggregation of networks into supernets in RIPv2 responses.
12. When you are done making changes, click on the **Save** button.

How it works...

RIP is a relatively simple routing protocol. A RIP-enabled router receives routing information from RIP-enabled neighboring routers, and builds a routing table with the reachable IP address, hop count, and next hop. The main limitation of RIPv1 was a hop count limit of 15. RIPv2 was introduced a few years later; the hop count limit of 15 remained in order to maintain backward compatibility with RIPv1, but other features were added, such as support for multicasting and the ability to carry subnet information.

Configuring BGP using FRR

In this recipe, we will demonstrate how to configure **Border Gateway Protocol** (**BGP**) using the **FRRouting** (**FRR**) package.

How to do it...

1. Navigate to **System | Package Manager**.
2. Click on the **Available Packages** tab.
3. Find `frr` on the list of available packages and click on the **Install** button for `frr`.
4. Click on the **Confirm** button. Installation should take less than 2 minutes.
5. Once the **Package Installer** indicates that installation is complete, navigate to **Services | FRR BGP**.
6. Check the **Enable** checkbox to enable BGP routing:

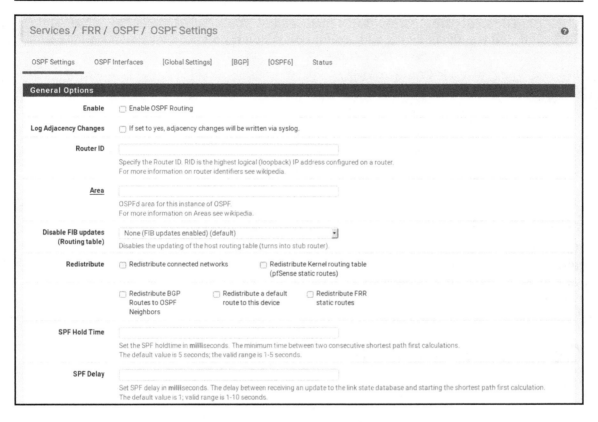

Services / FRR / OSPF / OSPF Settings

OSPF Settings   OSPF Interfaces   [Global Settings]   [BGP]   [OSPF6]   Status

General Options

Enable	☐ Enable OSPF Routing
Log Adjacency Changes	☐ If set to yes, adjacency changes will be written via syslog.
Router ID	
	Specify the Router ID. RID is the highest logical (loopback) IP address configured on a router. For more information on router identifiers see wikipedia.
Area	
	OSPFd area for this instance of OSPF. For more information on Areas see wikipedia.
Disable FIB updates (Routing table)	None (FIB updates enabled) (default)
	Disables the updating of the host routing table (turns into stub router).
Redistribute	☐ Redistribute connected networks ☐ Redistribute Kernel routing table (pfSense static routes)
	☐ Redistribute BGP Routes to OSPF Neighbors ☐ Redistribute a default route to this device ☐ Redistribute FRR static routes
SPF Hold Time	
	Set the SPF holdtime in **milli**seconds. The minimum time between two consecutive shortest path first calculations. The default value is 5 seconds; the valid range is 1-5 seconds.
SPF Delay	
	Set SPF delay in **milli**seconds. The delay between receiving an update to the link state database and starting the shortest path first calculation. The default value is 1; valid range is 1-10 seconds.

7. In the **Local AS** text field, enter the **Autonomous System** router number (a 32-bit unsigned integer).
8. In the **Router ID** text field, enter a router ID, or keep it blank to use the default.
9. In the **Timers** section, you may adjust a series of timers:
    - The **Keep alive interval** determines how long BGP will maintain routes from a peer without getting a response. If a BGP peer misses three keepalives, its route information is suppressed.
    - **Hold time** determines how long a peer should wait to hear a keep alive message before assuming the node is down.
    - **Update delay** is the maximum initial delay period that starts running when the first peer is detected.
    - **Peer wait** is the amount of time a peer is given for a peer to reset itself without danger of being blocked.

10. The **Redistribute** drop-down menus allow you to select either **No** or **Yes**, and give you the ability to redistribute the following:
    - Connected networks
    - FRR static routes
    - Kernel routing table/pfSense static routes
    - OSPF routes
11. You may also specify one or more **Networks to Distribute**, along with a corresponding **Route Map**, if available.
12. When done, click on the **Save** button.

How it works...

Border Gateway Protocol (**BGP**) is a path vector protocol, which means that path information is updated dynamically. It exchanges routing information between nodes known as **Autonomous Systems** (**AS**), and can make routing decisions based on paths, network policies, or administrative rulesets.

Configuring OSPF using FRR

In this recipe, we will configure OSPF using the FRRouting package.

Getting ready

This recipe assumes you have already **installed FRRouting** (**FRR**), per the instructions outlined at the beginning of the previous recipe. If not, you should navigate to **System | Package Manager | Available Packages**, and install FRRouting first.

How to do it...

1. Navigate to **Services | FRR OSPF**.
2. Check the **Enable** checkbox to enable OSPF routing.
3. In the **Router ID** text field, specify the Router ID (RID).
4. In the **Area** text field, enter the OSPFd area for this instance of OSPF.

5. In the Disable FIB updates (Routing table) drop-down menu, you may select any of several stub options to bring the router online without immediately routing any traffic:
    - **None**: The routing table is updated.
    - **Stub area**: Router is shielded from external routes, but receives information about networks that belong to other areas of the same OSPF domain.
    - **Totally stub**: Only the default summary route is allowed.
    - **Not so Stub Area**: Type 7 **Link-State Advertisements** (**LSAs**) are allowed.
6. You may choose one or more **Redistribute** options:

    - Connected networks
    - pfSense static routes
    - BGP routes
    - Static routes
    - FRR routes
7. You may set the **SPF Hold Time**, which is the minimum hold time between SPF calculations (anywhere between 1-5 seconds).
8. You may set the **SPF Delay**, which is the minimum time between updates to the link state database and SPF calculations.
9. You may check the **RFC 1583 compatible** checkbox if you want to ensure AS-external routes are evaluated according to RFC 1583.
10. You may add one or more subnets to routes to distribute, or disable route distribution entirely.
11. Click on the **Save** button when done.

How it works...

Open Shortest Path First (**OSPF**) is a link state protocol, which means it will try to calculate the shortest path to a destination based on changing network parameters, such as data transfer rates. A cost is calculated, based on account bandwidth, delay, and load. It thus differentiates itself from distance vector protocols, such as RIP, which take into account dynamic routing and changing network topologies, but do not take into account network conditions.

Services and Maintenance

9

In this chapter, we will cover the following:

- Enabling Wake-on-LAN
- Configuring PPPoE
- Configuring external logging with a syslog server
- Using ping
- Using traceroute
- Using netstat
- Using pfTop
- Using tcpdump
- Using tcpflow

Introduction

This chapter begins by covering services that are useful, and in some cases necessary, and moves on very quickly to utilities used primarily for diagnostics and troubleshooting.

If you are involved with configuring and maintaining computer networks, it is a virtual certainty that, at some point, a network will not function as intended. Fortunately, pfSense provides us with a number of services and applications to help us troubleshoot networking issues. This chapter focuses on those services and applications.

A structured approach to problem solving

As our networks become more complex, it becomes more difficult to find the cause or causes of a problem, and even more difficult to implement solutions while minimizing the impact on users. Against such a background, it becomes advantageous to follow a more structured approach to troubleshooting. Namely, we advocate the following multi-step approach:

1. **Identify the problem**: This step involves gathering information, identifying symptoms, and, in some cases, interrogating users. Such an approach should help you to isolate the cause.

2. **Formulate a theory of probable cause**: Although a problem can have multiple causes, as long as you have exercised due diligence, you should be able to eliminate at least some of the causes and emerge with a theory of probable cause.

3. **Test the theory**: Now that you have a theory of probable cause, you can test this theory. If you are able to confirm the theory, then you can move on to the next step. Otherwise, you will have to move back to step 2, and consider other possible causes.

4. **Establish a plan**: Although we have a theory of probable cause that seems to be valid, we still need to formulate a plan for restoring the network to full functionality. This may be a simple procedure if we only have a few users on the network. As we move toward more enterprise-level networks, our plan may well involve scheduling downtime for the network and making sure we abide by whatever formal or informal procedures have been established.

5. **Implement the solution**: Make the corrective changes, but also test the solution several times, and take into account the fact that early results may be deceptive.

6. **Verify system functionality**: Keep in mind that the solution might create another problem, and you will need to verify full system functionality before moving on to the next step.

7. **Document the problem and solution**: Keeping a record of all steps taken when solving the problem, and documenting both successes and failures, will potentially save you time in the long run. In large organizations, knowing who implemented the solution can be important, especially if other technicians have follow-up questions later on.

While you may have encountered the problem yourself, the more people there are using your network, the less likely that this will be the case. If a regular user reports the problem, you may want to provide feedback to the user after asking them questions. It could provide them with an incentive to report problems in the future.

Enabling Wake-on-LAN

pfSense can send a wake-on packet (also known as a magic packet) to compatible computers to *wake* the device out of sleep or standby mode. This can sometimes be useful in performing network diagnostics. This recipe describes how to send a wake-on packet using pfSense.

How to do it...

1. Navigate to **Services | Wake-on-LAN**.

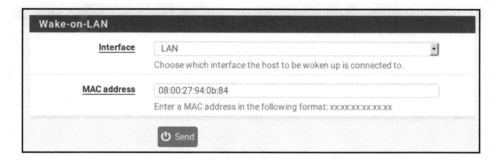

2. In the **Interface** drop-down menu, select the pfSense interface to which the host to be woken up is connected. For example, if the node we need to wake is on the LAN network, select **LAN**.
3. In the **MAC address** text field, enter the MAC address of the network interface on the node to be woken.
4. Click on the **Send** button.

How it works...

The Wake-on-LAN feature involves sending *magic packets* to properly-configured devices that support Wake-on-LAN. When such a device receives such a packet, it will *wake* the device out of its sleep or standby mode.

Note that, on older hardware, *properly configuring* a **network interface card** (**NIC**) can involve attaching a special Wake-on-LAN cable to the motherboard, and then enabling Wake-on-LAN in that machine's BIOS.

There's more...

You can also add a MAC address to a list of nodes that you can wake up later:

1. In the **Wake-on-LAN Devices** section of the page, click on the **Add** button:

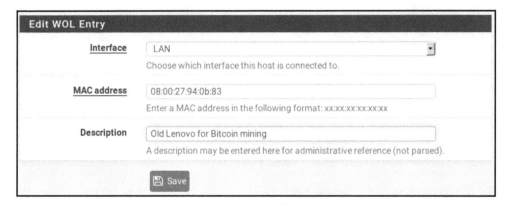

2. Select the **Interface** and enter the device's MAC address in the **MAC address** text field.
3. You may also enter a brief description in the **Description** field.
4. Click on the **Save** button.
5. You will now be able to wake the device by clicking on its MAC address in the **Wake-on-LAN** section of the page (or click on **Wake All Devices** to try take wake all the listed devices):

See also

- pfSense Wake-on-LAN documentation: `https://www.netgate.com/docs/pfsense/services/wake-on-lan.html`
- Wikipedia Wake-on-LAN page: `https://en.wikipedia.org/wiki/Wake-on-LAN`

Configuring PPPoE

PPPoE stands for **Point-to-Point Protocol over Ethernet**, a network protocol that allows and encapsulates Point-to-Point frames over Ethernet frames. PPPoE allows two clients to connect to pfSense using PPPoE and to conveniently pass data between each other.

This recipe describes how to enable a PPPoE server on pfSense.

How to do it...

1. Navigate to **Services** | **PPPoE server**, as shown in the following screenshot:

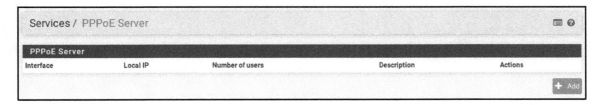

2. Click on the **Add** button.

3. Check the **Enable PPPoE Server** checkbox:

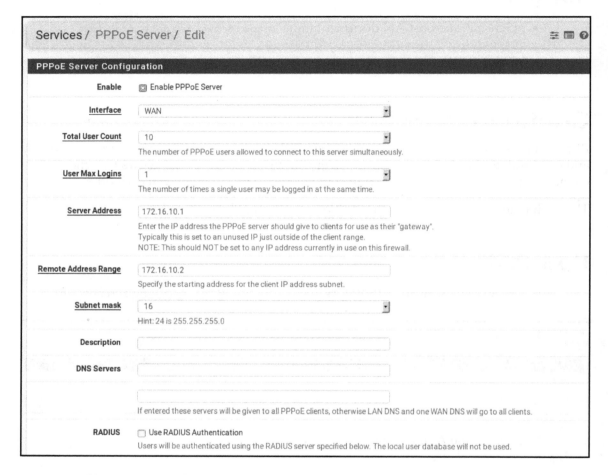

4. Choose an interface in the **Interface** drop-down menu (probably WAN).
5. Set **Total User Count** to the maximum number of users you want to be able to use the PPPoE server at the same time.
6. In the **Subnet mask** drop-down box, select the CIDR corresponding to your subnet mask (for example, **24** is **255.255.255.0**).
7. In **Remote Address Range** text field, specify the starting address of the client IP address subnet. The total range will be the starting address, plus the number specified in **Total User Count**.
8. In the **Server Address** text field, enter a currently unused IP address the PPPoE server should give to clients for use as their gateway.

9. In the **Description** text field, enter a brief non-parsed description.

10. In the **DNS Servers** text fields, enter custom DNS servers, or leave them blank to use the default DNS servers.

11. Scroll to the bottom of the page to add users. You need to specify a **Name**, **Password**, and **IP Address** in the appropriate text fields, and click on the **Add User** button each time you add a user:

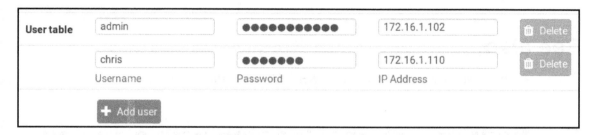

12. Click on the **Save** button when done making changes.

13. Click on the **Apply Changes** button.

14. You still need to add a firewall rule to allow PPPoE traffic to pass. Navigate to **Firewall | Rules**.

15. Click on the **PPPoE Server** tab.

16. Click on one of the **Add** buttons to add a rule.

17. Leave the **Action** set to **Pass**.

18. Change the **Proctocol** to **Any**.

19. Enter a brief, non-parsed description in the **Description** text field.

20. When you are done making changes, click on the **Save** button.

21. Click on the **Apply Changes** button.

How it works...

The PPPoE service is generally used to fill the gap between PPP connections (dial-up) and Ethernet connections (broadband). Internet service providers often want to enable their customers to use their existing dial-up authentication systems over broadband lines, and PPPoE allows ISPs to do just that, with a simple shim at the line-encoding stage enabling them to convert from PPP to PPPoE. Setting up PPPoE with pfSense requires us to add a firewall rule as well, and we did that.

There's more...

As is the case with a captive portal, the PPPoE server supports authentication through a RADIUS server. If you want to use a RADIUS server instead of the local user database, navigate to **System** | **Package Manager** and install the freeradius package. Consult the *Creating a captive portal with RADIUS authentication* recipe for more detailed information on how to configure the RADIUS server and how to get it to work with a service.

See also

- The *Creating a captive portal with RADIUS authentication* recipe

Configuring external logging with a syslog server

Syslog is a standardized system for logging all types of information. Syslog client and server implementations exist for all major operating systems.

If you primarily use Linux to run servers, then setting up syslog should be easy. Most Linux distributions already run the syslog service, so setting up a centralized server is only a matter of deciding which machine to use, configuring that machine to listen for syslog data on the network, and then configuring all other machines to direct syslog messages to that server.

This recipe describes how to configure pfSense to write logs to an external syslog server.

Getting ready

To turn a Windows machine into a centralized syslog server, take a look at the Kiwi Syslog Server and Log Viewer.

How to do it...

1. Navigate to **Status** | **System Logs**.
2. Click on the **Settings** tab.

3. Check the **Enable Remote Logging** checkbox:

4. In the **Remote Log Servers** text fields, specify the IP addresses of up to three remote syslog servers.
5. Check the **Everything** checkbox in the **Remote Syslog Contents** section to record all messages or select specific events.
6. Click on the **Save** button when done.

Using ping

Ping is a command-line utility developed in the early 1980s, which has been included in every major OS since then. Ping tests the reachability of hosts on an Internet Protocol network. It measures the round-trip time for packets sent from a source node to a destination node to be echoed back to the source.

This recipe describes how to use the Ping utility in pfSense.

How to do it...

1. Navigate to **Diagnostics** | **Ping**:

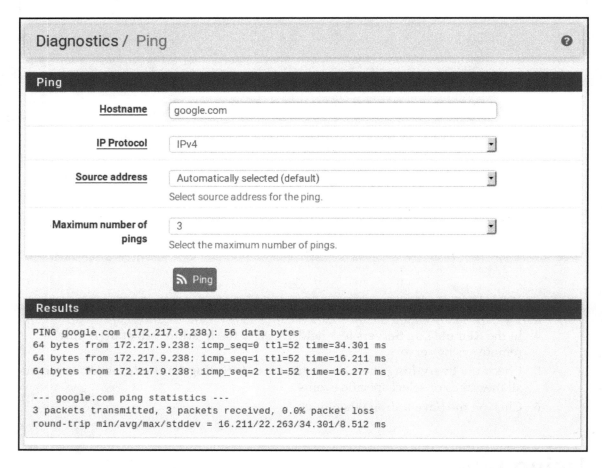

2. In the **Hostname** text field, enter the hostname or IP address of the destination.
3. In the **IP Protocol** drop-down menu, select **IPv4** or **IPv6** as required.
4. In the **Source address** drop-down menu, select an interface to use as the source address, or leave it set to **Automatically selected (default)**.

5. In the **Maximum number of pings** drop-down menu, select the maximum number of ping attempts (1-10).
6. Click on the **Ping** button.

How it works...

The Ping utility allows administrators to ping any machine on any interface, *from* any interface. Ping is indispensable, and having it built into the firewall's web interface makes it a great tool for administrators.

See also

- pfSense Ping documentation: https://www.netgate.com/docs/pfsense/monitoring/ping-host.html

Using traceroute

Traceroute is a network diagnostic tool for displaying the route and measuring transit delays of packets across an IP network. The round-trip times of packets received from each host on the route is recorded. Each step in the route is called a hop, and the sum of the mean times of each hop is a measure of the total time taken to establish the connection. Thus, traceroute provides more detailed information than Ping, which only computes the final route-trip times from the destination.

This recipe describes how to use the traceroute utility in pfSense.

How to do it...

1. Navigate to **Diagnostics | Traceroute**.

2. In the **Hostname** text field, enter the hostname or IP address of the destination:

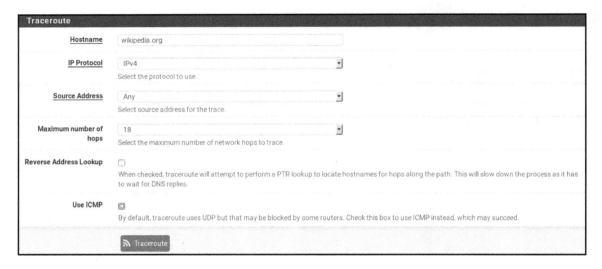

3. In the **IP Protocol** drop-down menu, select **IPv4** or **IPv6**.
4. In the **Source Address** drop-down menu, select the interface that will be the source IP address of the traceroute operation (or leave it set to **Any**).
5. In the **Maximum number of hops** drop-down menu, select the maximum number of hops to trace (**1** to **64**).
6. Check the **Reverse Address Lookup** checkbox if you want traceroute to perform a reverse DNS lookup on each hop (this will slow down the process considerably).
7. Check the **Use ICMP** checkbox to make traceroute use ICMP as the protocol, instead of UDP.
8. Click on the **Traceroute** button.
9. The output should be displayed as follows:

```
 Results

  1  10.0.3.254   0.562 ms   0.423 ms   0.256 ms
  2  10.0.2.2   0.696 ms   0.665 ms   0.650 ms
  3  192.168.2.1   1.654 ms   1.589 ms   2.157 ms
  4  10.240.163.109   10.614 ms   9.896 ms   9.338 ms
  5  67.59.242.66   14.477 ms   10.564 ms   10.221 ms
  6  67.83.248.146   13.399 ms   14.763 ms   13.144 ms
  7  67.59.239.235   21.236 ms   16.151 ms   14.660 ms
  8  64.15.3.250   15.000 ms   16.222 ms   15.283 ms
  9  * 4.35.80.5   16.646 ms   15.210 ms
 10  * * 4.69.150.206   21.985 ms
 11  64.125.13.29   25.790 ms   23.843 ms   16.512 ms
 12  64.125.27.196   27.209 ms   23.200 ms   25.348 ms
 13  64.125.29.31   25.487 ms   25.791 ms   31.508 ms
 14  64.125.30.249   23.098 ms   23.110 ms   23.083 ms
 15  64.125.29.123   22.862 ms   22.781 ms   22.277 ms
 16  64.125.192.142   22.797 ms   23.880 ms   21.847 ms
 17  208.80.154.224   21.663 ms   20.242 ms   21.867 ms
```

How it works...

The traceroute utility allows administrators to perform an ad hoc trace directly from the pfSense web interface.

> Traceroute can sometimes take a long time to complete. Click the browser's Stop button at any time to cancel the traceroute process and display the results.

See also

- pfSense Traceroute documentation: https://www.netgate.com/docs/pfsense/monitoring/traceroute.html

Using netstat

Netstat is a command-line utility that displays network connections for the TCP routing tables, and a number of network interface and network protocol statistics.

This recipe describes how to use netstat in pfSense.

How to do it...

1. Navigate to **Diagnostics | Command Prompt**.
2. In the **Execute Shell Command** text field, enter `netstat`, along with any parameters you wish to pass to the program. For example, `netstat -a` displays all network connections, for both TCP and UDP.
3. Click on the **Execute** button.
4. The output should resemble the following:

```
Diagnostics / Command Prompt                                    ❷

Shell Output - netstat -a

Active Internet connections (including servers)
Proto Recv-Q Send-Q Local Address          Foreign Address        (state)
tcp4       0      0 pfSense.https          172.16.1.102.48426     ESTABLISHED
tcp4       0      0 pfSense.utime          172.16.1.2.50256       ESTABLISHED
tcp4       0      0 pfSense.utime          *.*                    LISTEN
tcp6       0      0 *.http                 *.*                    LISTEN
tcp4       0      0 *.http                 *.*                    LISTEN
tcp6       0      0 *.https                *.*                    LISTEN
tcp4       0      0 *.https                *.*                    LISTEN
tcp4       0      0 localhost.rndc         *.*                    LISTEN
tcp4       0      0 *.domain               *.*                    LISTEN
tcp6       0      0 *.domain               *.*                    LISTEN
```

Using pfTop

pfTop is available in both the web GUI (via **Diagnostics | pfTop**) and from the console/SSH (where pfTop is 9 on the console menu). **pfTop** is extremely useful because it provides a live view of the state table, as well as the total amount of bandwidth utilized by each state.

pfTop contains several column headings; here, we will enumerate each of the default headings. **PR** stands for protocol; **D** stands for direction (this can be in or out); **SRC** stands for source; and **DEST** stands for destination. **AGE** is how long since the entry was generated. **EXP** is when the entry expires; **PKTS** is the number of packets that have been handled by the rule; and **BYTES** is the number of bytes handled by the rule.

The **STATE** column provides a little less clarity. This column indicates the state of both sides of the connection, using the format client:server. The states will not fit into an 80-column computer display, so pfTop uses integers (for example, 1:0). This is what the numbers in the following table signify:

Number	State
0	TCP_CLOSED
1	TCP LISTEN
2	TCP_SYN_STATE
3	TCP_SYN_RECEIVED
4	4 TCP_ESTABLISHED
5	TCP_CLOSE_WAIT
6	TCP_FIN_WAIT1
7	TCP_CLOSING
8	TCP_LAST_ACK
9	TCP_FIN_WAIT2
10	TCP_TIME_WAIT

As an example, an entry of 4:4 would indicate the state on either side of the connection is TCP_ESTABLISHED. An entry of 1:3 would indicate the state on the client side is TCP_LISTEN and the state on the server side is TCP_SYN_RECEIVED.

This recipe describes how to use pfTop in pfSense.

How to do it...

1. Navigate to **Diagnostics | pfTop**.

2. In the **View** drop-down menu, select the criteria that will determine which entries will appear (for example, selecting **size** will display the connections that have been responsible for most of the traffic), or just leave it set to default to display the top of the pf table:

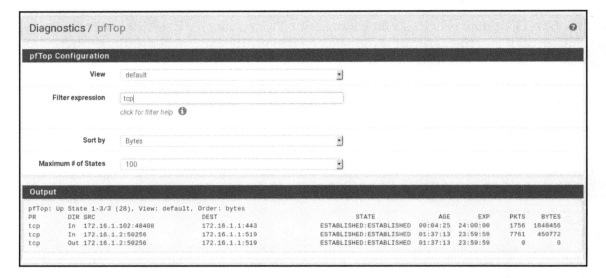

3. In the **Filter expression** text field, enter an optional expression to narrow down which entries are shown. For example, entering `tcp` will result in only TCP connections being shown.
4. In the **Sort By** drop-down menu, enter the criteria by which pfTop entries should be sorted (for example, selecting **Bytes** will display connections that have processed the greatest number of bytes first), or leave it set to **None**.
5. In the **Maximum # of States** drop-down menu, select the number of state table entries to display.

See also

- The pfSense documentation on monitoring bandwidth usage: `https://www.netgate.com/docs/pfsense/monitoring/monitoring-bandwidth-usage.html`

Using tcpdump

When you are troubleshooting network problems, you may find it necessary to use packet capturing, which is also known as packet sniffing. One way you can perform packet capturing is by using **tcpdump**, which is a command-line tool.

This recipe describes how to use tcpdump in pfSense.

How to do it...

1. Navigate to **Diagnostics | Command Prompt**.
2. In the **Execute Shell Command** text field, enter `tcpdump`, along with any parameters you wish to pass to the program. For example, `tcpdump -w output_file` will save tcpdump's output to a file.
3. Click on the **Execute** button.
4. The output should be displayed as follows:

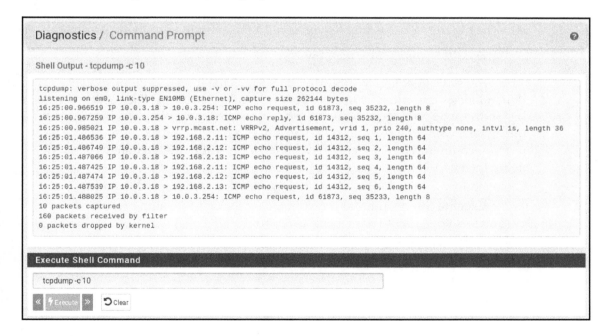

Using tcpflow

Like tcpdump, tcpflow gives you the ability to view the text contents of network packets in real time. Tcpdump, however, is more suited to capturing packets and protocol information. Tcpflow is more suited toward viewing the actual data flow between two hosts. While tcpdump displays output to the console by default, tcpflow writes output to a file by default, and you must use the −c option if you want to see the tcpflow output on the console.

This recipe describes how to use tcpflow in pfSense.

How to do it...

1. Tcpflow is not part of the default pfSense installation. Perhaps the easiest way to install tcpflow is to use the Linux/Unix repositories at https://pkgs.org: the 64-bit binaries for tcpflow v. 1.5.0 can be found at https://freebsd.pkgs.org/12/freebsd-ports-latest-amd64/tcpflow-1.5.0.txz.html. Install these into a suitable location on your pfSense system, such as /usr/sbin/tcpflow. Make sure the binaries are executable; you can do this with the following command:

   ```
   chmod 755 /usr/sbin/tcpflow
   ```

2. After you have installed tcpflow, the package is likely to have uninstalled dependencies that must be installed before tcpflow will run. The easiest way to install those dependencies is to consult a list of dependencies, and install them one by one using the pkg utility. For example, entering the pkg install pixman command into the command line will result in the pixman dependency being installed, if it hasn't already been installed.
3. Once tcpflow is installed, navigate to **Diagnostics | Command Prompt**.
4. In the **Execute Shell Command** text field, enter tcpflow, along with any parameters you wish to pass to the program.
5. Click on the **Execute** button.

Backing Up and Restoring pfSense

In this chapter, we will cover the following recipes:

- Backing up pfSense
- Restoring pfSense
- Updating pfSense

Introduction

If you are running pfSense in an enterprise-level environment, and even if you aren't, backing up your pfSense system on a regular basis is a sound decision, for a variety of reasons:

- A catastrophic hardware failure could bring your pfSense system down. While we can try to minimize the effect of such failures by using such redundancy methods such as CARP, by backing up our system we can reduce the amount of time needed to restore our firewall setup.
- We are constantly making changes to our configuration, and occasionally, these changes have unintended consequences. Often, the easiest way of resolving such a problem is to roll back our configuration to a previous version, which we can do easily if we previously backed up pfSense.

Backing up and restoring pfSense are two sides of the same coin, but updating pfSense is also an integral part of maintaining a robust system. Updates often incorporate bug fixes, security patches, and new features. Since we will want to take advantage of all of these, we will want to keep our pfSense systems relatively up-to-date. We will not always have the luxury of being able to update pfSense right away—such activities may have to be reserved for scheduled maintenance windows—but neither will we want to allow our systems to get out-of-date.

Backing up pfSense

Backing up our pfSense system is an important part of minimizing downtime and maintenance time. In this recipe, we will demonstrate how to back up pfSense.

How to do it...

1. Navigate to **Diagnostics** | **Backup & Restore**.
2. Click on the **Backup & Restore** tab:

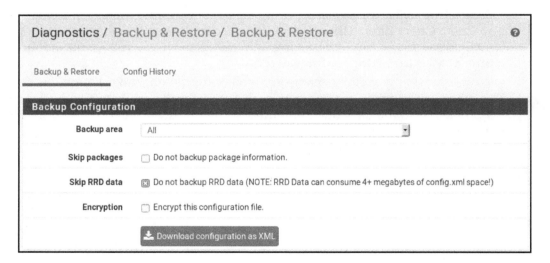

3. Leave the **Backup area** drop-down menu set to **All**.
4. Leave the **Skip packages** checkbox unchecked.
5. Leave **Skip RRD data** checked.
6. Check the **Encryption** checkbox.
7. Enter a password in the **Password** text field.
8. Click on the **Download configuration as XML** button and save the configuration file to a secure location.

How it works...

The **Backup & Restore** configuration section allows us to save the system settings as an XML file. With this XML file, we can restore pfSense to these settings in two different ways:

- After a hardware or software failure, we can reinstall pfSense, and then restore the previous configuration using the previously-saved back up XML file.
- In the absence of a hardware or software failure; say, we just want to rollback pfSense to a previous restore point, then we can use the previously-saved back up file to do so.

There's more...

In the recipe, we backed up all configuration areas, but we can select only a subset of the configuration using the Backup area drop-down menu. This is useful if we only need to backup a specific portion of the configuration. Note that we can select **All** and still exclude package and **Round Robin Database** (**RRD**) data. While it is generally good practice to save package information, you probably do not need to save RRD data; although it might prove useful later as a diagnostic tool, it can consume four megabytes or more of `config.xml` space.

If you need to review the recent config changes, click on the **Config History** tab. This tab provides functionality similar to the Restore recent configuration command available from the console/SSH. In addition to viewing all recent config changes, you can perform the following operations:

1. View the difference between two configurations by selecting the older configuration in the right column of radio buttons, selecting the newer configuration in the left column, and clicking on the **Diff** button:

⇄ Diff		Date	Version	Size	Configuration Change	Actions
	○	11/24/18 11:13:01	18.9	28 KiB	(system): Upgraded config version level from 18.5 to 18.9	Current configuration
○	○	11/24/18 11:03:04	18.5	28 KiB	admin@172.16.1.102: Saved system update settings.	↺ ⬇ 🗑
○	○	11/24/18 10:25:59	18.5	28 KiB	(system): Overwrote previous installation of FRR.	↺ ⬇ 🗑
○	○	11/24/18 10:25:58	18.5	25 KiB	(system): Intermediate config write during package install for FRR.	↺ ⬇ 🗑
○	○	11/24/18 10:25:55	18.5	26 KiB	(system): Intermediate config write during package removal for frr.	↺ ⬇ 🗑
○	○	11/24/18 10:25:45	18.5	28 KiB	(system): Overwrote previous installation of routed.	↺ ⬇ 🗑
○	○	11/24/18 10:25:44	18.5	27 KiB	(system): Intermediate config write during package install for routed.	↺ ⬇ 🗑
○	○	11/24/18 10:25:42	18.5	27 KiB	(system): Intermediate config write during package removal for routed.	↺ ⬇ 🗑
○	○	11/24/18 10:25:11	18.5	28 KiB	(system): Configured default pkg repo after restore	↺ ⬇ 🗑
○	○	11/18/18 18:07:12	18.5	27 KiB	admin@172.16.1.102: /interfaces.php made unknown change	↺ ⬇ 🗑
○	○	11/18/18 18:05:44	18.5	28 KiB	admin@172.16.1.102: Gateways: removed gateway 0	↺ ⬇ 🗑
○	○	11/18/18 18:05:17	18.5	29 KiB	admin@172.16.1.102: Gateway Groups: removed gateway group 0	↺ ⬇ 🗑
○	○	11/18/18 18:00:18	18.5	29 KiB	admin@172.16.1.102: Enter CARP maintenance mode	↺ ⬇ 🗑
○	○	11/18/18 17:59:57	18.5	29 KiB	admin@172.16.1.102: Leave CARP maintenance mode	↺ ⬇ 🗑

2. The XML file contents will appear at the top of the page, showing what has been added (text with a green background), what has been removed (text with a red background), and what is unchanged (body text with a gray or white background; unchanged headers take gray backgrounds). An example of this is shown in the following screenshot:

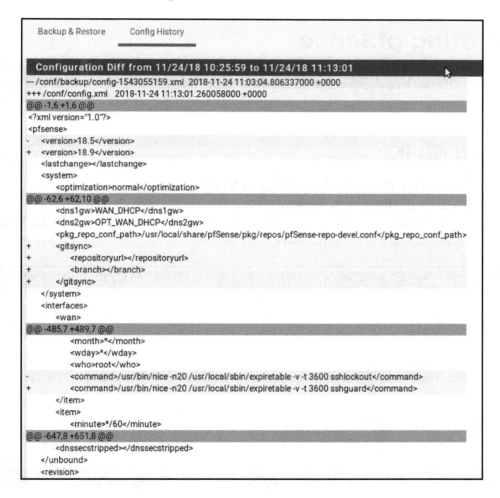

3. Revert to a previous configuration (the reverse arrow symbol).
4. Save a previous configuration as a backup XML file (the downward arrow).
5. Delete a previous configuration (the trashcan).

See also

- pfSense Backup and Restore documentation: `https://www.netgate.com/docs/pfsense/backup/configuration-backup-and-restore.html`

Restoring pfSense

Often, we need to restore pfSense, either to recover from a hardware or software failure or to roll back pfSense to a previous point. In this recipe, we will demonstrate how to restore pfSense.

How to do it...

1. Navigate to **Diagnostics | Backup & Restore**.
2. Click on the **Backup & Restore** tab.
3. In the **Restore Backup** section, select the subset of data to restore in the **Restore area** drop-down menu (or leave it set to **All**):

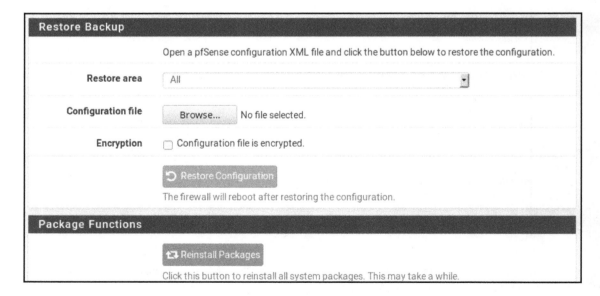

4. Next to **Configuration file**, click on the **Browse** button and use the dialog box to navigate to an XML backup file that you previously saved.
5. If the backup file is encrypted, check the **Encryption** checkbox and enter the password in the **Password** text field.
6. Click on the **Restore Configuration** button. A dialog box will appear, asking you to confirm that you want to restore the configuration. The firewall will reboot after restoration is complete.
7. If there are packages to restore, click on the **Reinstall Packages** button.

How it works...

In this recipe, we used the backup XML file generated in the previous recipe, and used it to restore pfSense.

There's more...

There is another way of restoring pfSense, without even having to save an XML file. From the console/SSH, menu item 15 is Restore recent configuration. The options for the command are as follows:

- **List backups**: Lists the last 30 backups, with backup #30 being the most recent
- **Restore backup**: Restores one of these 30 backups
- **Quit**: Returns to the main menu

This can be useful if you need a quick and dirty way to roll back a system. If you need to restore a system to factory defaults, you can select menu item 4.

Updating pfSense

Odds are that, at some point, you are going to want to update pfSense, whther it's to take advantage of bug fixes, security patches, or new features. In this recipe, we will demonstrate how to update pfSense.

How to do it...

1. Navigate to **System** | **Update**.
2. Click on the **Update Settings** tab.
3. In the **Branch** drop-down menu, select the correct branch (choices are **Latest development snapshots** and **Latest stable version**):

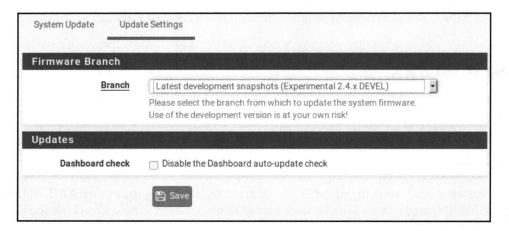

You can select the branch from either the **System Update** or the **Update Settings** tab.

4. If you want to disable the dashboard auto-check, uncheck the **Dashboard check** checkbox.
5. Click on the **Save** button when you are done making changes.
6. Click on the **System Update** tab.
7. Take note of the current base system and the latest base system, as shown in the following screenshot, and then click on the **Confirm** button to update the system:

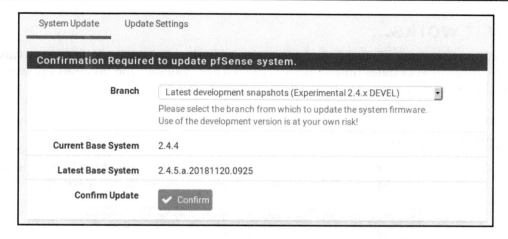

8. The output will resemble the following, informing you of the updates being made to the system:

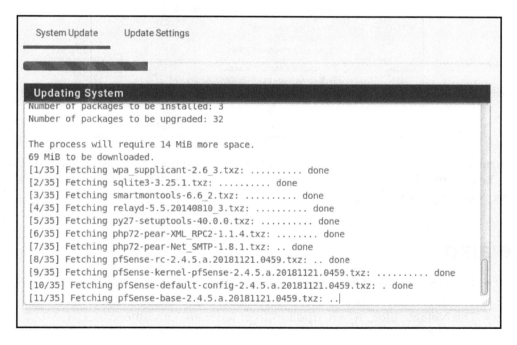

9. When the update is complete, pfSense will reboot.

How it works...

An internet-connected pfSense system is capable of finding out when updates are available. Once we determine updates for our current branch are available, the process of updating pfSense is relatively easy.

There's more...

By default, the pfSense dashboard provides us with information about the latest updates. This is presented in the **System Information** widget, in a section called **Version**:

As it turns out, we can begin the installation from the dashboard. To do so, click on the update link on the dashboard (look for a cloud with a down arrow inside it). This will redirect you to **System | Update**.

See also

- The pfSense Upgrade Guide: https://www.netgate.com/docs/pfsense/install/upgrade-guide.html
- The Netgate blog, where updates to pfSense are announced: https://www.netgate.com/blog/

Determining Hardware Requirements

One of the keys to getting the most out of pfSense at a reasonable cost is to spend some time on hardware sizing and selection. It is entirely possible that you may already have hardware, such as an old desktop computer, that you can repurpose for use with pfSense. But even in these cases, it is beneficial to start by determining exactly what you need from your pfSense firewall.

With pfSense, we are presented with a wide array of configuration choices that can make a determination of minimum requirements somewhat difficult. It will run well on state-of-the-art hardware, but often this is not the most cost-effective option. In this chapter, we will discuss some of the factors we consider when deciding which hardware to use. By presenting these factors as a series of recipes, we can follow a step-by-step approach, an approach that tends to ensure the hardware we use is capable of getting the job done at a reasonable cost.

In this chapter, we will cover the following topics:

- Determining our deployment scenario
- Determining our throughput requirements
- Determining our interface requirements
- Choosing a standard or embedded image
- Choosing a form factor

Determining our deployment scenario

This section will determine which pfSense deployment scenarios is most applicable by analysing our network diagram.

In this section, we will make use of our network diagram to understand how and where pfSense will fit into our environment. As an example, we will use a relatively typical small Office/Home Office setup. We begin by looking at our network diagram:

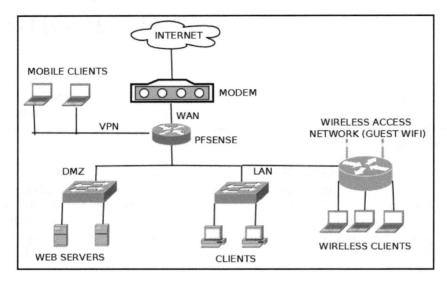

In this small office scenario, the firewall that we have diagrammed clearly meets the definition of a perimeter firewall, which is the most common of pfSense deployments.

A perimeter firewall becomes the gatekeeper of all traffic flowing between interfaces. We will define firewall rules based on how we want that traffic to flow. A few common rules that most networks enforce are:

- **Allow all from LAN to WAN**: The LAN should have outbound access to the WAN so its users can access the internet.
- **Allow some from LAN to WAN**: The practice known as egress filtering involves limiting the types of traffic allowed to leave a network to ensure unauthorized or malicious traffic never leaves it.
- **Block all from WAN to LAN**: Do not allow external users to get into our own private network.
- **Allow HTTP from LAN to DMZ**: Allow our internal users to access our company's web server.

- **Allow HTTP from WAN to DMZ**: Allow external users to access our company's web server.
- **Block all from DMZ to LAN**: Our DMZ is insecure since we are allowing external users to come and access the web server. We want to protect ourselves by blocking any traffic that attempts to access our LAN from the DMZ.

pfSense also employs many advanced firewall features to accommodate the needs of more complex networks. pfSense is capable of the following:

- Supporting dozens of interfaces.
- Handling multiple internet connections, in case the primary internet connection fails (multi-WAN).
- Failover protection, in case the primary firewall dies (CARP).
- Load balancing, to optimize network traffic by balancing demanding loads.

pfSense is highly flexible and can also be configured as any of the following devices. It's important to note that these roles are simply services that we will use within our perimeter firewall deployment, but larger environments may want to build these roles as separate machines to improve performance:

- **Router**: This is the second most common deployment of pfSense. A router determines a packet's destination and then sends it on its way, without applying any firewall rules. A router is not necessarily deployed at the perimeter of a network.
- **VPN appliance**: A VPN server provides encrypted remote network connections. pfSense supports all the major virtual private networking protocols, such as IPsec, OpenVPN, and L2TP.
- **DHCP appliance**: A DHCP server assigns IP addresses to clients that request them.
- **DNS appliance**: A DNS server associates names with IP addresses. It's much easier to remember `google.com` than its IP address.
- **VoIP appliance**: **Voice over IP** (**VoIP**) is digital telephony, possible with pfSense.
- **Sniffer appliance**: Sniffers analyse packets for patterns. This is often to detect and prevent traffic that attempts to exploit known vulnerabilities. pfSense utilizes the most widely deployed sniffer package in existence, Snort.
- **Wireless Access Point**: pfSense can be deployed strictly as a wireless access point, through it rarely is.
- **Switch**: It is possible to disable all filtering in pfSense and use it as a switch. That makes for one expensive switch (by way of comparison, a simple 5-port GBEthernet switch can be obtained for less than $20 USD), but it is an option.

pfSense can be configured with many more devices—pfSense being deployed as a special purpose appliance is only limited by the number of packages supported by the platform.

 For more information on pfSense deployment scenarios, read through the Common Deployments section of the documentation `https://www.netgate.com/docs/pfsense/book/intro/common-deployments.html`

Determining our throughput requirements

In this section, we will understand the throughput requirements, and subsequently the processing and memory requirements needed for our environment.

We'll want to prepare for determining our requirements by gathering the following information:

- Our internet connection speed
- Our network hardware speed (10/100/1000 Mbps)
- The connection speeds different users will be expecting

Let's begin by considering the throughput guidelines provided on the official pfSense website:

Firewall throughput	Processing power required	Hardware (PCI-X/PCI-e NICs)
21-50 Mbps	500 MHz CPU	No
51-200 Mbps	1 GHz CPU	Recommended (for 100 Mbps and faster)
201-500 Mbps	2 GHz CPU	Recommended
501+ Mbps	3 GHz CPU	Recommended

The following table defines any additional system requirements that would be necessary if deploying optional features.

Feature	Additional requirements
VPN	A CPU's encrypted throughput is roughly 20 percent of its unencrypted throughput. If you have a 500 MHz processor (50 Mbps unencrypted) and you need more than 10 Mbps encrypted throughput, you need a faster processor, or a separate encryption card.
Captive portal	Environments with a larger number of captive portal users (100+) may need to bump their processing power up slightly to achieve the same throughput.
Large state tables	The default state table size of 10,000 entries takes up 10 MB of RAM. Large environments with hundreds of thousands of entries will want to make sure they have the necessary memory available. It may require you to have at least 2 GB of RAM.
Squid package	This is a package used for caching web content, and this requires extensive use of a hard disk with a large amount of storage. It is not for use with an embedded installation where writes to the compact flash card are kept to a minimum.
Snort package	This is a packet sniffer/intrusion prevention and detection system (**IPS/IDS**). A minimum of 512 MB RAM is required.
NTop package	This is a network traffic reporting tool. A minimum of 512 MB of RAM is required.

Now, we need to determine our requirements:

- Our small business rarely has more than a dozen users on the LAN, but all the PCs in the department have GB Ethernet NICs, and the switches are all Gigabit or faster. The internet connection is only about 100 Mbps, so our network hardware is actually much faster than what we need for using the internet. Nevertheless, Gigabit Ethernet ensures that we get fast, reliable transfer times when accessing resources over the local network.
- We want to provide VPN access for remote employees, but we do not anticipate more than a few VPN users at any given time.
- We have also decided that we want to install Ntop to diagnose network traffic problems.
- Finally, since we are saving money by using pfSense, we have decided to reinvest some of the savings into added redundancy. To this end, we will implement a CARP failover group on our network.

At this point, we have identified our minimum requirements as:

- 1 Gbps network hardware (cables and switches)
- Unencrypted throughput of 100 Mbps (bound by speed of Internet connection)
- Encrypted throughput (VPN) of 20 Mbps
- 1 GHz CPU, 1 GB RAM
- A second, identical machine to be used as a failover.

Throughput is the amount of data that can be processed at any given time. For example, we might have a 100 Mbps broadband connection, but if the WAN interface on our firewall can only handle 10 Mbps, that's all we're going to get. Conversely, if we have a Gigabit Ethernet adapter for the WAN interface, but we still only have a 100 Mbps broadband connection, now our internet connection has become the bottleneck.

Firewall throughput is only a factor for traffic passing through the firewall. Internet traffic meets this requirement (LAN <| WAN), as would any traffic between our own networks (LAN <| DMZ). However, traffic between two computers on the same network (for example, the LAN) will not be processed by the firewall and, therefore, the firewall will not be a bottleneck in that scenario.

 You should remember that certain firewall features have their own hardware requirements. For example, VPN connections require additional processing power and the Squid web caching package is not suitable for an embedded compact flash disk installation.

With the release of pfSense 2.4, many obsolete packages have been removed from the **Package Manager** and many new packages are now available. To view available packages, navigate to **System | Package Manager | Available Packages**.

Read more about the minimum hardware requirements here: `https://www.netgate.com/docs/pfsense/book/hardware/minimum-hardware-requirements.html`.

Determining our interface requirements

This section will help us determine our interface requirements by analyzing our network design. We will make use of our network diagram to understand how many interfaces our network will require.

Let's begin by analyzing our network design:

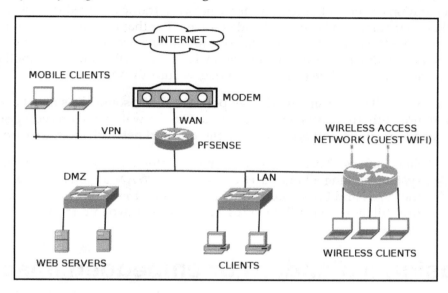

We can see that our environment consists of four separate interfaces:

- **Wide Area Network** (**WAN**): Directly connects to our cable modem, which in turn provides access to the internet.
- **Local Area Network** (**LAN**): Our primary internal network.
- **Demilitarized Zone** (**DMZ**): Our internal network, on which we allow external access. Our web servers belong to this interface.
- **Wireless guest network** (**GUEST WIFI**): We've created this network for the convenience of guests. They can all connect with an easy-to-remember password (or perhaps no password at all) and surf the web. We consider this interface insecure and treat it as such. We will define rules so it has no access to other networks—not even the also insecure DMZ.

It is apparent that our network requires four **Network Interface Cards** (**NICs**).

We could have also accomplished this result with two NICs (WAN and LAN). and two VLANs (DMZ and GUEST WIFI).

A firewall requires a separate NIC for every interface it hopes to support. This ensures a physical separation of network traffic. All inter-network traffic is forced to pass through the firewall where our rules will be applied and enforced. For that reason, a firewall requires a minimum of two NICs to function properly, one for internal traffic and one for external traffic (LAN and WAN). Each subsequent optional interface will require yet another NIC, which can be added at any time (unless, of course, we use VLANs).

Typically, an NIC will have a single Ethernet port. However, some NICs may have two, four, or even more Ethernet ports on a single card. Our firewall in the preceding scenario could have had four single-port NICs, or a single four-port network interface card.

 Since pfSense 2.0, only a single physical interface is required to install the system, making all interfaces except for the WAN optional. Theoretically, the WAN and LAN could both be VLANs on the same interface. A proper firewall, however, still requires a minimum of two interfaces.

Choosing a standard or embedded image

In this section, we will understand when to use the standard or embedded version of pfSense.

Every standard feature of pfSense is supported on both the standard and embedded platforms, but certain packages are not. The Squid web caching package, for example, required extensive writing to disk and should not be run on a compact flash drive.

There is a third type of image called Netgate ADI, which is designed and optimized for Netgate embedded appliances that run pfSense. If you are installing onto one of these appliances (for example, the SG-2440), you should use the Netgate ADI.

First, we should review the package we've chosen to install:

NTop package: This is a traffic analysis tool. It requires a minimum of 512 KB RAM, but has no restrictions on the storage type.

Based on this and the overall convenience of compact flash cards, we're going to install the embedded version of pfSense.

The standard image is meant to be installed on a hard drive. The embedded version is meant to be installed on a compact flash drive. Compact flash drives only have a limited number of writes during their lifespan, and the embedded version of pfSense is designed to limit writes to the disk for that very reason. That being said, each platform has advantages and disadvantages:

Platform	Pros	Cons
Standard	All packages and features supported	Entire drive must be overwritten Requires larger power supply
Embedded	Fast access times Cards can be easily swapped (backups, upgrades, and so on) Requires little power Silent	CF cards have a limited number of writes Not all packages supported
Netgate ADI	Designed to work optimally with Netgate pfSense appliances	Not designed to work with non-Netgate hardware

Refer to the pfSense online documentation: Versions of pfSense and FreeBSD: `https://www.netgate.com/docs/pfsense/releases/versions-of-pfsense-and-freebsd.html`

Choosing a form factor

This section describes how to choose the best hardware configuration based on our firewall requirements.

It's easiest to choose a form factor if we've already decided on the rest of our prerequisites:

- Deployment scenario
- Throughput requirements
- Interface requirements
- Image platform

Before choosing a form factor, we first need to evaluate the different types of form factors:

- **Small form**: Energy-efficient, quiet (often silent), small footprint form factor.
- **Desktop**: Standard desktop hardware. Easily upgradable and most people will have an older machine lying around that's perfectly suited for running pfSense.
- **Server**: Larger or more complex environment may require server-class hardware.

Consider whether any of our requirements require special hardware. In our case, we need moderate throughput and aren't using any packages that require special hardware. Low power consumption and silent operation are important to our small office/home office, so we're opting for small form factor.

The choice of a form factor has more to do with our environment than our pfSense installation. Every environment will vary and form factors will differ. Thanks to the vast variety of computer hardware on the market, any deployment of pfSense is possible on any type of form factor, with the exception of Netgate ADI. While most standard platforms are installed on desktops, and most embedded platforms on appliances, there's no reason they can't be swapped if we've equipped our hardware properly.

There's no reason we can't use a laptop. If we have an old laptop lying around, it would probably make a great, albeit unusual, pfSense machine. The biggest obstacle we'd likely face is adding NICs. Typical laptop NICs that fit into laptop expansion slots (such as ExpressCard) might not be compatible with pfSense, and USB Ethernet adapters are often unreliable. One possibility is an all-VLAN setup with both WAN and LAN and any other network on the same interface as a VLAN, but this would mean having WAN and LAN traffic on the same physical interface, which clearly is a security concern.

 As with all open source projects, it's best to refer to the project's hardware compatibility list before adding new hardware.

Installing the embedded platform on a desktop/server/laptop

Some people really enjoy the convenience of running a system from a compact flash card. Testing a new version of pfSense, or reverting back to a backup, is as easy as swapping CF cards. Most desktops don't come with a CF card reader installed, but there are plenty of adapters to choose from.

Installing the standard platform on an appliance

Of all the different installation scenarios, installing the standard version on an appliance equipped with a hard drive can be the most challenging. Appliances are meant to be small, so if they've already fitted a hard drive in there, you can be fairly certain there won't be an optical drive. Secondly, most appliances don't have built-in video-out, which means other means of connection (usually serial or USB) is required. We'll have to refer to our manufacturer's documentation if we find ourselves in this situation.

 Read more about pfSense Appliances and Security Gateways here: https://www.pfsense.org/products/.

Summary

While pfSense will run on pretty much any hardware that will run the underlying operating system (FreeBSD), allowing you the opportunity to re-purpose old hardware, the process of hardware sizing and selection is still a useful exercise, especially if you embark on a career in **Information Technology** (**IT**), where the ability to choose the optimal hardware setup can be a valuable skill. If so, and even if you only have a passing interest in hardware sizing and selection, you may want to review this chapter before installing and configuring pfSense. A short-term investment in learning the fundamentals of hardware sizing and selection can yield long-term savings on equipment.

Other Books You May Enjoy

If you enjoyed this book, you may be interested in these other books by Packt:

Learn pfSense 2.4
David Zientara

ISBN: 978-1-78934-311-3

- Install pfSense
- Configure additional interfaces, and enable and configure DHCP
- Understand Captive portal
- Understand firewalls and NAT, and traffic shaping
- Learn in detail about VPNs
- Understand Multi-WAN
- Learn about routing and bridging in detail
- Understand the basics of diagnostics and troubleshooting networks

Mastering pfSense - Second Edition
David Zientara

ISBN: 978-1-78899-317-3

- Configure pfSense services such as DHCP, Dynamic DNS, captive portal, DNS, NTP and SNMP
- Set up a managed switch to work with VLANs
- Use pfSense to allow, block and deny traffic, and to implement Network Address Translation (NAT)
- Make use of the traffic shaper to lower and raise the priority of certain types of traffic
- Set up and connect to a VPN tunnel with pfSense
- Incorporate redundancy and high availability by utilizing load balancing and the Common Address Redundancy Protocol (CARP)
- Explore diagnostic tools in pfSense to solve network problems

Leave a review - let other readers know what you think

Please share your thoughts on this book with others by leaving a review on the site that you bought it from. If you purchased the book from Amazon, please leave us an honest review on this book's Amazon page. This is vital so that other potential readers can see and use your unbiased opinion to make purchasing decisions, we can understand what our customers think about our products, and our authors can see your feedback on the title that they have worked with Packt to create. It will only take a few minutes of your time, but is valuable to other potential customers, our authors, and Packt. Thank you!

Index

A

Access Control Lists (ACLs) 207
Advanced RISC Machines (ARM) 8
aliases
  creating 72
  deleting 74
  editing 74
  host(s) 73
  multiple IP addresses, importing 75
  network(s) 73
  port(s) 73
  reference 75
  URL (IPs) 73
  URL Table (IPs) 73
  URL Table (Ports) 73
  using 72, 74
alternate DNS servers
  DNS resolver, using 58
  specifying 57, 58
  WAN DNS servers, using 59
Authentication Header (AH) 140
Authentication, Authorization, and Accounting
  (AAA) 119
authorized RSA keys
  generating 22, 24
Autonomous Systems (AS) 230

B

bandwidth usage
  reference 248
Border Gateway Protocol (BGP)
  about 228, 230
  configuring, with FRRouting (FRR) 228, 229,
  230
bridge
  Show Advanced button 222

bridging 219, 220

C

captive portal
  creating, with RADIUS authentication 119, 120,
  121, 122, 123, 124, 125, 126
  creating, with User Manager authentication 114,
  115, 116, 117, 118
  creating, with voucher authentication 109, 110,
  111, 112
  creating, without authentication 106, 107, 108
  pages, customizing 109
  Vouchers tab 113, 114
CARP failover group
  configuring 207, 208, 209, 210, 211, 212, 214,
  215, 216, 217
  status, checking 218
Certificate Authority (CA) 139
Class-Based Queuing (CBQ) 177
Common Address Redundancy Protocol (CARP)
  190
console menu
  used, for assigning interfaces 32, 34
  used, for configuring LAN interface 36, 38
  used, for configuring optional interfaces 39, 40
  used, for configuring WAN interface 34

D

dedicated links 176
deep packet inspection 170
DeMilitarized Zone (DMZ) 18
deployment scenario
  determining 261, 263, 264
DHCP relay
  configuring 55, 57
DHCP server
  additional BOOTP/DHCP options 50

configuring 46, 47
default lease time 49
Deny unknown clients checkbox, clicking 48
DNS servers 48
domain name 49
dynamic DNS 50
failover peer IP 49
Gateway edit box 49
maximum lease time 49
static ARP 50
DHCP6 server
configuring 50, 52
prefix delegation 52
Direct Client-to-Client (DCC) 93
distance vector protocol 220
DNS resolver
configuring 59, 61, 62
DNS Servers 9
dynamic DNS
alternative service. specifying with RFC 2136 66
configuring 64, 66
reference 66
dynamic routing 220

E

EchoLink 178
embedded image
selecting 268
embedded platform
installing, on desktop/server/laptop 271
pros and cons 269
Encapsulating Security Payload (ESP) 140
End User Licence Agreement (EULA) 106
external logging
configuring, with syslog server 240, 241

F

firewall rule
advanced features 80
creating 76, 78
duplicating 80
options 78
ordering 80
schedule, setting 81, 83, 84
source port 79

week dates or days, selecting 84
first-in, first-out (FIFO) 169
floating rule
creating 84, 85, 87, 89, 91, 92, 93
port redirection 94
port redirection example 94
possibilities, for matching traffic 181
used, for configuring traffic shaping 178, 181
form factor, types
desktop 270
server 270
small form 270
form factor
embedded platform, installing on
desktop/server/laptop 271
selecting 269, 270
standard platform, installing on appliance 271
FreeBSD
reference 269
FRRouting (FRR)
about 228
Border Gateway Protocol (BGP), configuring
228, 229, 230
Open Shortest Path First (OSPF), configuring
230, 231

H

hardware requirements
reference 266
Hierarchical Fair Service Curve (HFSC) 177
high availability 189
hop 243

I

interface requirements
Demilitarized Zone (DMZ) 267
determining 266, 267
Local Area Network (LAN) 267
Wide Area Network (WAN) 267
wireless guest network (GUEST WIFI) 267
interfaces
assigning, console menu used 32, 34
bridging 221, 222
Internet Control Message Protocol (ICMP) 160
Internet Key Exchange (IKE) 95

Internet Relay Chat (IRC) 93
Internet Service Provider (ISP) 12, 119
interoperability 132
intrusion detection system (IDS) 182
intrusion prevention system (IPS) 182
IPsec connections
   configurations 139, 140
IPsec mobile client configuration
   options 146
IPsec OpenVPN server (peer-to-peer)
   configuring 133, 137, 138, 140
IPsec settings page
   Advanced Settings 147
   Pre-Shared Keys 147
IPsec VPN service (client/server)
   configuring 141, 144, 146
IPsec VPN service
   connecting to 147, 150

L

L2TP VPN service
   configuring 166, 168
LAN interface
   configuring 15, 17
   configuring, from console menu 36, 38
link state protocol 220
Link-State Advertisements (LSAs) 231
Local Area Network (LAN) 15

M

management information bases (MIBs) 128
multiple WAN interfaces
   adding 190, 191, 192, 193, 194, 195, 196
   gateway groups, settings 198, 199
   gateway, settings 197

N

NAT-PnP
   enabling 102
   reference 103
net neutrality 170
Netgate ADI 268
netstat
   about 245
   using 246

Network Address Translation (NAT) 71
Network Address Translation (NAT) rules
   about 89
   Network Prefix Translation (NPt) 89
   one-to-one NAT entry 89
   outbound NAT 88
network configuration
   interfaces, identifying 11
network interface card (NIC) 235
Network Interface Cards (NICs) 267
network management station (NMS) 128
Network Prefix Translation (NPt) entry
   creating 100, 101
Network Time Protocol (NTP)
   about 126
   configuring 126, 127
   hostnames 128
   IP addresses 128
NTop package 268

O

one-to-one NAT entry
   creating 98, 100
Open Shortest Path First (OSPF)
   about 220, 231
   configuring, with FRRouting (FRR) 230, 231
OpenVPN service
   configuring 151, 154, 158, 160
   connecting to 160, 165, 166
optional interfaces
   configuring 18, 20
   configuring, from console menu 39, 40
outbound NAT entry
   creating 95, 97, 98

P

PFS (Perfect Forward Security) 140
pfSense Appliances
   reference 271
pfSense
   about 7
   backing up 252, 253, 255
   backup and restore documentation, reference
      256
   interfaces, assigning 11

reference 269
restoring 256, 257
settings 8, 10
updating 257, 260
Upgrade Guide, reference 260
pfTop
about 246
using 247, 248
ping
about 241
reference 243
using 242, 243
Point-to-Point Protocol over Ethernet (PPPoE)
configuring 237, 238, 239
RADIUS server, using 240
Point-to-Point Tunneling Protocol (PPTP) 8, 132
port redirection
example 94
security through obscurity 94
single public IP address 94
Priority Queuing (PRIQ) 177
problem solving
structured approach 234

R

Rapid Spanning Tree Protocol (RSTP) 222
redundancy 189
Remote Authentication Dial-In User Service
    (RADIUS)
about 119
reference 126
Remote Desktop Protocol (RDP) 94
RIP
configuring, with routed 227, 228
Round Robin Database (RRD) 253
routing
about 219
dynamic routing 220

S

Security Gateways
reference 271
server load balancing
configuring 199, 200, 201, 203, 204, 205, 206
manual failover mode, enabling 206

Shrew
reference 147
Simple Network Management Protocol (SNMP)
configuring 128, 129
reference 130
trap server, specifying 130
Small Office/Home Office (SOHO) 15
Snort
documentation, reference 187
network intrusion prevention mode 186
packet logging mode 186
packet sniffing mode 186
used, for configuring traffic shaping 182, 186
Spanning Tree Protocol (STP) 222
SSH access
enabling 21, 22
SSH RSA key authentication
enabling 24, 25
SSH
accessing 26, 28
stand-alone DHCP/DNS server
configuring 62, 64
Register DHCP Leases in DNS Resolver option
    64
standard platform
installing, on appliance 271
pros and cons 269
static DHCP mappings
configuring 53, 55
static route
adding 223, 224, 225
asymmetric traffic, handling 225, 226
syslog server
external logging, configuring 240, 241

T

tcpdump
about 249
using 249
tcpflow
about 250
reference 250
using 250
throughput requirements
determining 264, 265, 266

traceroute
  about 243
  reference 245
  using 243, 244, 245
traffic shaping wizard
  used, for configuring traffic shaping 171, 173,
    176, 178
traffic shaping
  configuring, Snort used 182, 185, 187
  configuring, traffic shaping wizard used 171,
    175, 178
  configuring, with floating rules 178, 181

U

Unified Extensible Firmware Interface (UEFI) 8
UPnP
  enabling 102, 103
  reference 103
User Datagram Protocol (UDP) 170

V

Virtual LAN (VLAN)
  about 29
  configuring 29, 31
  configuring, at console menu 40, 42
Virtual Private Networks (VPNs)
  about 131
  server, selecting 132
Voice over IP (VoIP) 169, 263

W

Wake-on-LAN
  enabling 235
  MAC address, adding 236
  reference 237
WAN interface
  configuring 12
  configuring, from console menu 34, 36
Wide Area Network (WAN) 12
wireless access point
  adding 67, 70
Wireless Encryption Protocol (WEP) 8

CPSIA information can be obtained
at www.ICGtesting.com
Printed in the USA
FFHW010753110819
54162963-59867FF